Critical
Educational Psychology

BPS Textbooks in Psychology

BPS Blackwell presents a comprehensive and authoritative series covering everything a student needs to complete an undergraduate degree in psychology. Refreshingly written to consider more than North American research, this series is the first to give a truly international perspective. Written by the very best names in the field, the series offers an extensive range of titles from introductory level through to final year optional modules, and every text fully complies with the BPS syllabus in that topic. No other series bears the BPS seal of approval!

Each book is supported by a companion website, featuring additional resource materials for both instructors and students, designed to encourage critical thinking and providing for all your course lecturing and testing needs.

For other titles in the series, please go to http://psychsource.bps.org.uk

Critical Educational Psychology

EDITED BY

ANTONY WILLIAMS
University of Sheffield, UK

TOM BILLINGTON
University of Sheffield, UK

DAN GOODLEY
University of Sheffield, UK

TIM CORCORAN
Deakin University, Australia

WILEY Blackwell

This edition first published 2017
© 2017 John Wiley & Sons Ltd

Registered Office
John Wiley & Sons Ltd, The Atrium, Southern Gate, Chichester, West Sussex, PO19 8SQ, UK

Editorial Offices
350 Main Street, Malden, MA 02148-5020, USA
9600 Garsington Road, Oxford, OX4 2DQ, UK
The Atrium, Southern Gate, Chichester, West Sussex, PO19 8SQ, UK

For details of our global editorial offices, for customer services, and for information about how to apply for permission to reuse the copyright material in this book please see our website at www.wiley.com/wiley-blackwell.

The right of Antony Williams, Tom Billington, Dan Goodley and Tim Corcoran to be identified as the authors of this work and of the editorial material in this work has been asserted in accordance with the UK Copyright, Designs and Patents Act 1988.

Wiley also publishes its books in a variety of electronic formats. Some content that appears in print may not be available in electronic books.

Designations used by companies to distinguish their products are often claimed as trademarks. All brand names and product names used in this book are trade names, service marks, trademarks or registered trademarks of their respective owners. The publisher is not associated with any product or vendor mentioned in this book.

Limit of Liability/Disclaimer of Warranty: While the publisher and authors have used their best efforts in preparing this book, they make no representations or warranties with respect to the accuracy or completeness of the contents of this book and specifically disclaim any implied warranties of merchantability or fitness for a particular purpose. It is sold on the understanding that the publisher is not engaged in rendering professional services and neither the publisher nor the author shall be liable for damages arising herefrom. If professional advice or other expert assistance is required, the services of a competent professional should be sought.

Library of Congress Cataloging-in-Publication Data applied for

Paperback ISBN: 9781118975947

A catalogue record for this book is available from the British Library.

Cover image: al_1033 / Gettyimages

Set in 11/12.5 pt Dante MT Std by Aptara

Printed in Singapore by C.O.S. Printers Pte Ltd

1   2017

Contents

Contributors

Ansgar Allen is a Lecturer of Education at the University of Sheffield and author of *Benign Violence: Education in and beyond the Age of Reason* (2014, Palgrave).

Catherine Beal currently works as an educational psychologist (Complex Needs Service, East North East Leeds, and Youth Offending Sector). She has experience within mainstream and specialist settings with young people described as complex/vulnerable and those who demonstrate challenging behaviour or have specialist therapeutic needs. Catherine works directly with young people, provision and systems development. Her qualifications include a Doctorate in Educational and Child Psychology, University of Sheffield, National Programme for Specialist Leaders in Behaviour and Attendance (NPSL-BA) and she is currently completing a Diploma in Narrative Therapy.

Pat Bennett worked previously as an Associate Tutor, and is now an Honorary Lecturer at the University of Sheffield. She is a Chartered Educational Psychologist working in both local authority and private practice.

Tom Billington is Professor of Educational and Child Psychology at the University of Sheffield and Director of the existing research Critical Educational Psychology Centre for the Human.

Dawn Bradley is a Chartered Educational Psychologist with the British Psychological Society. Before training to be an educational psychologist, Dawn taught in a young offenders institute for young men and has also taught in mainstream schools at secondary level. Dawn trained to be an educational psychologist in 2005 at the University of Sheffield, where she completed her Doctorate in Educational Psychology in 2012. Dawn is a member of the Divisions of Child and Educational Psychology and Counselling Psychology as well as being registered as a practitioner psychologist with the Health and Care Professions Council. As an applied psychologist, Dawn is particularly interested in working with vulnerable, marginalised and excluded children and young people. From a methodological perspective she is particularly interested in qualitative, feminist and relational research with her interests sitting more generally within the wider frame of social justice.

Harriet Cameron is Academic Director for the Specialist SpLD Tutorial Service within the English Language Teaching Centre at the University of Sheffield. She has worked with students with specific learning difficulties within higher education for over 10 years. Prior to this, Harriet worked as a school teacher and as a teacher of academic English to overseas students studying at university. She has a master's degree in Applied Psychology and a doctorate in Critical Educational Psychology with a focus on dyslexia. Her particular interest is in how dyslexia and other learning differences are discursively and ideologically constructed, and how a better understanding here may assist students to reflect critically on their learning identities.

Tim Corcoran is Associate Professor and Academic Director for Professional Learning at the School of Education, Deakin University, Melbourne, Australia. He has extensive experience in educational psychology as a school psychologist and researcher/academic. His work has involved teaching, research and professional practice in Australia, the UK, Singapore and Iraq. He edited *Psychology in Education: Critical Theory Practice* (2014, Sense Publishers), an international collection of contributions examining critical approaches to educational psychology. More recently he co-edited *Disability Studies: Educating for Inclusion* (2015, Sense Publishers) and *Joint Action: Essays in Honour of John Shotter* (2016, Routledge).

Sahaja Davis is a mindfulness practitioner and teacher. He lectures at the University of Sheffield and is Honorary Lecturer at Manchester University. In addition, Sahaja is a senior practitioner educational psychologist at Leeds City Council.

Niall Devlin is a Senior Educational Psychologist, Wakefield Metropolitan District Council. He gained his Doctorate in Educational Psychology at University of Newcastle following an MSc. Niall has a wide range of experience as a practising educational psychologist, having worked in numerous local authorities in the north of England.

Penny Fogg is an Educational Psychologist for Bradford EPS and also a Lecturer in Educational Psychology at the University of Sheffield. Her substantive experience is as a generic educational psychologist working with families and schools. Penny's areas of specialism relate to the social and emotional well-being of children who have experienced relationship trauma, and working with parents to improve their relationships with their children. Penny qualified as an educational psychologist at Manchester University in 2004 and has also been a teacher, both in mainstream and special schools.

Dan Goodley is Professor of Disability Studies and Education at the University of Sheffield.

Nick Hammond is Senior Educational and Child Psychologist at Norfolk County Council, a trained social theatre practitioner and film maker. He is a Fellow of the Royal Society of Arts and Associate Fellow of the British Psychological Society. Nick is Honorary Lecturer at the University of Manchester and delivers regular workshops to universities and at conferences.

Victoria Harold has worked as an educational psychologist since qualifying in 2006 from the University of Manchester, prior to which she worked as a primary teacher. Victoria gained a BSc in Psychology (University of Leeds), a PGCE (Manchester Metropolitan University), an MSc in Educational Psychology (University of Manchester) and most recently an EdD in Educational Psychology (University of Sheffield).

Martin Hughes has taught on the Doctor of Educational and Child Psychology course since 2008 and is currently the Professional Practice Programme Director. Previously, he taught in a secondary school for five years and since training in 1988, has been recognised as a Chartered Psychologist, gaining experience in Essex, Nottinghamshire and in Singapore, working for the Ministry of Education. Martin currently works part-time for Sheffield City Council as one of the Principal Educational Psychologists where he has been responsible for a large multidisciplinary service as well as managing a multidisciplinary team.

Majid Khoshkhoo is a senior practitioner, educational psychologist, early years. He also works as a Lecturer and Senior Associate Lecturer for the Open University. He gained his Doctorate in Educational Psychology at University of Sheffield following an MSc and prior to that a BSc Hons Psychology. Majid has a wide range of experience, including working in electronics, computing and data analysis, teaching and training.

Daniela Mercieca is a practising educational psychologist and Senior Lecturer within the Department of Education Studies at the University of Malta. Her research interests are in problematising the assumptions that underpin educational practice with children and deconstructing situations in which decisions are made concerning children's well-being in schools.

Duncan P. Mercieca is Senior Lecturer of Philosophy of Education in the Department of Education Studies at the University of Malta. His research draws on French post-structuralist philosophers to think through educational issues.

China Mills is a Lecturer in Critical Educational Psychology at the School of Education, University of Sheffield. China carries out research into global mental health and the intersections of mental health and poverty, using post-colonial and psycho-political methodologies.

Helen Monkman works in Wakefield as an educational psychologist. She gained her Doctorate in Educational Psychology (University of Sheffield) following an MSc (University of Sheffield) and prior to that a BSc Hons Psychology (University of Nottingham). Helen previously taught in numerous schools and has a long-standing professional interest in the nuances of language and discourse.

Kathryn Pomerantz is Deputy Principal Educational Psychologist working for Derbyshire County Council. She is the former Academic Director of the Doctor of Educational and Child Psychology initial training course for educational psychologists at the University of Sheffield. Kathryn is a qualified practitioner in video interaction guidance (VIG); she actively uses this technique in her work with parents/carers and with staff in schools. She also provides supervision to professionals training to become VIG practitioners.

Samana Saxton currently works as Senior Educational Psychologist with Kirklees LEA, having first worked as an educational psychologist at Leeds Psychology Service after qualifying. Prior to this, Samana worked as a religious education teacher in a mainstream secondary school in Leeds. Samana gained a BSc in Psychology (University of Leicester), a PGCE (Leeds University) and DEdCPsy (University of Sheffield). Samana is particularly interested in working with multicultural communities.

Antony Williams is Lecturer in Educational and Child Psychology at the University of Sheffield where he is Academic Director of the professional training programme in Educational and Child Psychology.

AND TIM CORCORAN

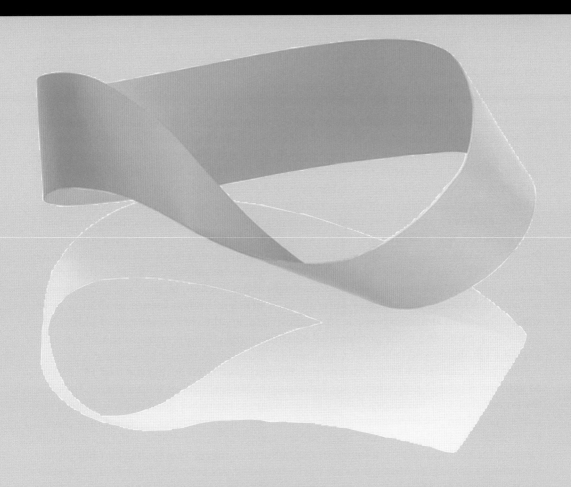

EDUCATIONAL PSYCHOLOGY: TOWARDS A HUMAN SCIENCE

Many of us have committed our working lives ostensibly to help young persons who are experiencing difficulties of one kind or another. For many who work as educational psychologists, it can be more than a job, it can be our life's work, not only a professional commitment but a highly principled activity underpinned by a seemingly solid foundation in psychological knowledge.[1]

What a cruel twist then when we can find the humanity of our concerns constantly challenged, not merely by the difficult social, economic and political circumstances in which as practitioners we ply our trade but by the very psychological discourses upon which are we are supposed to base our work. For those sociocultural arenas in which we operate are dominated by discursive repertoires of quantification and ableism in which young people can be subjected to batteries of tests, schools ranked in terms of a host of performance indicators and curricula are narrowed in ways that reduce educational success to individual achievement. Meanwhile, as we know from studies of ableism and disablism, young people find themselves faced with ever more pressurising assessment procedures that demand student autonomy and make it easier to mark out those students who disrupt these educational practices (Goodley, 2014). As a profession we have too often been required only to contribute to particular processes in which individual young people are singled out for special attention in ways which are not so straightforward as might at first seem to be the case, and as targets of psychological models which position them as deficient human beings, a position from which it becomes almost impossible to escape. These are the root conditions of a disabling educational psychology: one in which we become complicit in the constitution of the individualised problems and failings of education.

This book is the product of (mainly) practitioners associated during the past 15 years or so with the School of Education at the University of Sheffield, all of whom share a belief in the potential of educational psychology to contribute to the public good but who believe too that some of the practices historically associated with its performance are not only flawed but potentially damaging. In this book we are searching for alternative ways in which we can support educational psychologists in their efforts to engage more ethically, critically yet scientifically with those people who are the recipients of our practice. The familiar vision of the therapeutic dyad invokes a scene set in a school office where the practitioner intervenes with a student. But as we envisage it, critical educational psychology takes place in a variety of settings and includes all stakeholders in education – from headteachers and their staff, to students and their families – as well as policies and regulations that seek to define our work's agenda.

The book clearly does not come from nowhere: it has a history; and that history has local, national and international antecedents. The origins of educational psychology in the United States can be found in the works of William James, G.S. Hall, Edward Thorndike and John Dewey while the history of educational psychology in the UK is inexorably linked to the appointment in 1913 by the City of London of Cyril Burt as the country's first educational psychologist. All these men [sic] and others too (e.g., Binet in France) were confronted by a problem which we still share today, what should be done with those young people who, for one reason or another, struggle to thrive in schools? A century ago, the mass schooling systems, then only recently created by the newly industrialised societies, were themselves struggling to accommodate many young people and it seemed only natural that the new science of psychology be enlisted to help with the new social phenomena. We are now at a vantage point from which we can survey the hundred years of subsequent practice and can reflect on the successes and failures of educational psychology during that time and its contributions to the social (and political) problem bestowed on us.

Certainly, many of us would like to think that through our work we have been contributing to improved circumstances for many individual young people, their families and their teachers but, while this will undoubtedly often be the case, as authors in this book we share some concerns. We do not intend to side-step a suspicion long held in critiques of educational psychology that arguably its most notable achievement during the 20th century was its development of the technical means, systems and individual practices by which selected individuals could be positioned as defective, deviant or as a member of a transgressive category; for example, as a disability or in special need. This would clearly be a challenging critique for us and indeed such an analysis is itself reductionist as well as an affront to the commitments of the many practitioners and scholars who have dedicated themselves to the needs of the disadvantaged or those in distress. Unfortunately, the focus of our work, however well intentioned, has ushered in practices which function politically in respect of the kinds of gendered, racialised, dis/abled populations being targeted for scrutiny.

It is thus important to state from the outset that as authors in this book we are challenged by the epistemological roots of our discipline, and unite in unequivocal opposition against much of what Burt (1913) chose to focus on in his work: that is, his insistence on the concept of a fixed and innate intelligence; the straightforward biological hereditability of that intelligence; the consequent need for human selection; and the ableist, class-, gendered- and race-based explanations for human difference. Burt was a eugenicist and while this begs more detailed and sensitive historical and contextual analysis, we are opposed to all those practices which uncritically align with such ideological positions. Indeed we have explored elsewhere the non-science of Burt which, in our view, owes more to a technological entrepreneurship than to a science of the human (Billington & Williams, 2015).

While we do not claim in this book to be the only educational psychologists who recoil at images of the person constructed by a Burtian dystopia, our motivations are to be found directly in the research and practice of many other educational psychologists associated with the University of Sheffield during the past 15 years, and likewise with a longer tradition in the School of Education, of scholars who have shared our concerns for social justice in education, especially within the field of inclusive education and disability studies (Armstrong, Armstrong & Barton, 2000; Barton, 2001; Barton & Clough, 1998; Barton & Oliver, 1997; Carr, 1995; Moore, Beazley & Maelzer, 1998). Educational psychology at Sheffield also has a context within the wider university. William Henry Hadow (vice chancellor at Sheffield between 1919 and 1930) was the principal author of six highly influential reports for the British government on a range of educational matters and from 1923 onwards he was chair of consultative committees whose reports were to influence British educational policy for a large part of the 20th century.

Specifically in respect of this book, Hadow was the author of the very first UK government '*Report…on psychological tests of educable capacity*' (Hadow, 1924). This document set the agenda to this day, not only for the performance of educational psychology in British schools but actually for the whole system of selection in British schools which has haunted, in particular, the secondary mass schooling system ever since. Cyril Burt was allowed to write some of the appendices and in some instances his name presents as joint author for the whole report. However, it is not only the subsequent disrepute which he brought upon our profession for the fraudulent use of test results that leads us to distance ourselves from his work here (Hearnshaw, 1979; Mackintosh, 2013) but also the wish to overcome the reluctance of our profession to sustain an effective critique in respect of the scientific bases of such work. Psychological 'tests' were Burt's way of invoking the power of scientific discourse, relying on a culture of measurement of young people which has underpinned many professional practices, and purporting to be (erroneously in our view) a science of the human. It is important to state at the outset our belief that, while undoubtedly there are many circumstances when psychological tests can be used genuinely to identify levels of need, misconceptions have arisen that the tests are scientific in the same sense that a natural scientist would use the word. Indeed, it is our position that psychological tests are not scientific in that sense but the product of technological endeavours, subject to economic and political forces, which construct human subjects according to their own ideological image and likeness, for example, as either 'normal' or deficient.

First, therefore, psychological ideas or indeed tests cannot be anything other than a product of the social conditions in which they were constructed. Any devices such as tests are technologies, infused with social and cultural bias (typically constructed in the past by white males from a particular Western cultural and political caste) and continue to propagate restricted and reductionist psychological discourses in relation to specific aspects of human functioning (Corcoran, 2016). These ableist discourses became established in the early years of our discipline, manifest in such concepts as mental deficiency, hereditability and in attempts to fix intelligence as something static. As critical educational psychologists, however, we maintain:

1. that the (mis)use of such concepts continues to misrepresent and undermine the potentialities of human subjects;
2. that the aetiology of human functioning is a complete reversal from that popularly circulated – rather, as human organisms our development is defined by the 'conditions' (James, 1890) of our environment (i.e., we are *a priori* 'relational beings' (Gergen, 2009));
3. that psychology's tendency to individualise invites a reduction of the complexities of being-in-the-world to simplistic psychological categories.

Psychological tests do not reveal the nature of the person but a view of the person from a particular vantage point, sometimes providing descriptions which the persons themselves might not recognise, either now or perhaps even in the future.

Second, many of the ideas and practices generated under the banner of educational psychology, while seemingly based on the kinds of methods derived from the natural sciences, bear a likeness to science only insofar as they use numbers, statistics and mathematical formulae. Our claims to science are flawed since, in our efforts to attain the status accorded to the natural sciences, we have sought as psychologists initially to mimic only the research methods used and in the process created our own discrete world of non-human methodologies which are unable to capture the phenomena of persons. We are thus concerned about the dangers of a 'logical positivism [which has] elevated discussions about the scientific method above empirical science itself' (Costa & Shimp, 2011, p. 26). It is our contention that the experimental natural sciences appear to be more successful in remaining focused on the phenomena to be considered while educational psychologists have often been encouraged in research or practice which:

1. prioritises methodology over the phenomena to be studied (a practice known as methodolatry, expanded on with wit and verve by C. Wright Mills (1970));
2. adopts methods that are ill-suited to recognise the phenomena under scrutiny (i.e., the study of the human);
3. investigates and reinvestigates versions of persons it has itself constructed (e.g., as evidenced in the development of the psychological industry around the label of autism: Runswick-Cole, Mallett & Timimi, in press).

PSYCHOLOGY IN EDUCATION: BUILDING BLOCKS FOR RECONSTRUCTION

Since William James first began to delineate the boundaries of a positivistic psychology (1890), there have been many psychologists who have been alert to the theoretical omissions of educational psychology. Initially Dewey (1916), later Vygotsky (1978), then Bruner (1991), for example, each in their own way, envisaged a psychology of the person which was impossible to contain within discourses of isolated individuals. Dewey was convinced of the importance of the social environment on human mind and behaviour and Vygotsky too focused on explanations more obviously rooted in the social world while Bruner arguably emphasised the more expressly human. Deweyan ideas about school and social reform, neo-Vygotskian ideas about learning and language as well as Brunerian narrative approaches have encouraged many psychologists and social scientists to aspire to less disabling forms of practice by demanding that analyses become more sensitive to the dynamic, intrinsically social possibilities within human beings and their situations (White & Epston, 1990; Berliner, 1992; Reissman, 2002; Daniels et al., 2009).

In 1974, Bruner joined with Martin Richards, Ryan, Shotter, Harré, Ingleby and the Newsons to produce *The Integration of the Child into the Social World*, which, along with *Reconstructing Social Psychology*, published the same year, sought to articulate the fundamentally social (and hence also political) nature of human development. In the UK the emergence of these publications alongside a growing interest in the recently translated works of Vygotsky led to critical stirrings within UK educational psychology, most clearly articulated by *Reconstructing Educational Psychology* (Gillham, 1978). *Changing the Subject* (Henriques et al., 1984) and *Children of Social Worlds* (Bruner, 1986), the follow-up to *The Integration of the Child into the Social World*, reflected the growing interest in, and understanding of, the fundamental importance of the social world when contemplating children, childhood and the gaze we bring to bear on them. The mid-1980s was also a time when we heard the term 'psy-complex' (Ingleby, 1985; Rose 1985), which had been coined to develop critiques of the influence of psychological knowledge and which were informed by Foucault's introduction of the genealogical method. Critical thinkers drew upon strands of psychology, psychoanalysis, linguistics and semiotics to examine the structuring influence of language. Two seminal works published in 1987, Potter and Wetherell's *Discourse and Social Psychology* and Billig's *Arguing and Thinking*, signalled an increasing appreciation of the power and influence of language in structuring what we accept as reality (see also Hollway, 1989; Parker, 1992). It is upon the work of these critical thinkers, their colleagues and the resources they have provided that we seek to build this book.

Critical psychology can help us to recognise the ways in which educational and other authorities not only regulate – which is not necessarily a problem – but also effectively exclude – which is a problem, especially given a growing unease as to the quality of the 'science' on which (politicised) decisions are being justified. There are many resources now that psychologists and their services can use when constructing professional practices which are not only sensitive to social, cultural and political variables but also provide the means of achieving a more scientific discipline. Erica Burman's (2008) utilisation of deconstruction as a tool for critiquing development narratives together with her exploration of a feminist agenda reaffirm the potentially debilitating nature of many current theoretical preferences and practices in childcare and educational arenas. Isaac Prilleltensky emphasises critical approaches and the possibility of community solutions (Fox, Prilleltensky & Austin 2009; Nelson & Prilleltensky 2005) while Ben Bradley (2005) similarly employs critiques of psychological paradigms to provide alternatives in respect of professional training. There are increasing numbers of psychologists working in education globally who are developing a more critical psychological research and practice – for instance, Newman and Holzman (1993); Bird (1999); Neilsen & Kvale (1999); Billington (2000); Sloan (2000); Gallagher (2003); Kincheloe (2006, 2008); Corcoran (2007); Goodman (2010); Goodley (2011, 2014); Mercieca (2011); Martin and McLellan (2013); Vassallo (2013); Williams (2013); Sugarman (2014); and Todd (2014).

This renaissance of enthusiasm for the potential in our discipline is in marked contrast with an unjustifiably complacent neo-Burtian educational psychology, which rested on an intellectually limited personal agenda, 'It is my personal conviction that the main outlines of our human nature are now approximately known, and that the whole territory of individual psychology has, by one worker or another, been completely covered in the main' (Burt, in Hearnshaw 1979, p. 49). It is to Hadow's credit that he was clearly suspicious of such grandiose claims and there are several examples where, in 1924, he provides more cautious analysis relating to the narrowness of the psychological landscape being envisaged. As co-authors of this book we want to find ways of re-engaging with the hopeful possibilities for educational psychology first realised by both James and Dewey in order to construct a canvas upon which we can create new forms of social activity, re-envisage its scientific credentials and find ways of speaking ethically to an emerging globalisation of the process of psychologisation. Indeed, as scholars at the University of Sheffield, we have found ourselves pushed into (not unwillingly we might add) transdisciplinary contexts in which we seek to talk of the human in ever more complex ways. The establishment of a new research centre – The Institute for the Study of the Human (iHuman) – came from a number of conversations and collaborations with colleagues across faculties of science, medicine, the humanities and social sciences about the kinds of intellectual projects that can be made to respond to not only rapid expansions in technology, but also an epidemic of psychological knowledge about what it means to be a valued or marked human being.[2] This book, then, is timely not least in reminding educational psychology to think carefully about the ways in which it marks, values, pathologises or expands humanity.

STRUCTURE OF THE BOOK

This book is delivered in three parts. The first part focuses on introducing the theoretical resources that we suggest can be drawn upon in situating a critical psychological practice. These theoretical starting points are diverse, but have in common the fact that they are all in differing ways reflexive foundations on which to build a psychological practice. They envision both ourselves as practitioners and those with whom we work as thinking, speaking subjects with agency, who thus offer the potential to appreciate a complex subjectivity 'in which a sense of agency is tangled up in cultural forms' (Parker, 1997, p. 12), which is a starting point for a potentially emancipatory practice. It would be naive to suggest that practice with emancipatory potential is limited to the theoretical resources we offer or that a practice grounded in these approaches will necessarily offer such potential. However we do suggest that the theoretical approaches in Part I may be drawn upon and, indeed, produce in their application a more complex subjectivity than has often been offered. A vision of the human, as Parker (1997) recognises, is one that takes seriously both the intentions and desires of the individual and the operation of social structures and discourse which structure the spaces in which we all live and work. As such Part I begins with Allen's questioning of the assumptions that permeate both education and psychology. In exploring how psychology and education define and thereby limit our freedom, Allen asks whether or not they are 'good' or 'bad'. Chapters 2 to 5 introduce constructionist (Corcoran), narrative (Fogg), post-conventionalist (Goodley) and psychoanalytic (Williams) theoretical resources for the construction of a critical educational psychology practice.

Part II focuses on ethics and values in practice. In this part, Goodley and Billington explore connections between critical educational psychology and critical disability studies. The ethics of practice are then interrogated in three chapters which examine in differing ways how ethical concerns are inherent in everyday practice (Bennett; Devlin; Mercieca & Mercieca). Chapter 10 (Beal) explores the notion of expertise in practice, calling for a recognition of the multiple and diverse forms of expertise that are required for psychologists and clients to produce empowering working alliances. Martin Hughes then introduces Q methodology, presenting the approach from an ethical and practical perspective. Part II concludes with a chapter that asks: Are we all psychologists now? In posing the question, Williams introduces the concept of psychologisation and its ongoing shaping of modern Western culture, suggesting that in the age of the psychologised subject the role of the critical educational psychologist may be that of the psychologist willing and able to critique the ideological function of psychological knowledge in any particular situation.

Part III contains a series of chapters that put the critical theoretical resources to work in practice. These chapters are written in the main by practitioners who focus on specific arenas of practice, including mental health (Mills; Monkman), school behaviour policies (Harold), faith and educational psychology (Saxton) and the role of gender in school-based exclusion practices (Bradley). Further chapters critically explore mindfulness (Davis), the use of stories in practice (Khoshkhoo), video interactive guidance (Pomerantz), social theatre (Hammond), dyslexia diagnosis (Cameron) and the growing influence of neuroscience (Billington).

GETTING ON WITH IT

In the groundbreaking text *Changing the Subject*, Couse Venn (1989) posed the following question: What is the subject of psychology? His answer, and one with which we agree, is the living human subject. Educational psychology has for a hundred years understood its subject as a young person who will require some kind of intervention. In practice, this subject has quickly become known in terms of available psychological discourses of the isolated and static individual, assessed and probed according to practices which, ultimately, demand the improvement of the subject in relation to a narrow understanding of their deficiency.

What could be the subject of educational psychology? Critical psychology intervenes to advise: 'Rather than "telling it like it is", the challenge for the [critical educational] psychologist is to "tell it as it may become"' (Gergen, 1992, p. 27). This affirmative, forward looking and inherently reflexive statement demands that as educational psychologists we look for opportunities to construct practices which potentially empower children and young people, not as individuals disconnected with the (social) world but as social living beings, and look for occasions when we could work as allies with them, their families and the educational professionals that seek to support them.

Yet such potential alliances require us to remain mindful of the potential dangers of psychology; a discipline that has been historically built on the construction of a model of human subjects who are inherently flawed, lacking or deficient. Whether researchers or practitioners we aspire to a criticality which involves:

1. identifying the ontological, epistemological and methodological assumptions which populate the landscape of educational psychology;
2. exposing the kinds of human subject constituted and restricted through these discursive knowledges;
3. identifying ideas, practices and support mechanisms which enable children and young people to successfully resist and move beyond any such oppressive regimes and navigate more successfully their educational lives.

Our work at Sheffield and in this book is intended to develop and support communities dedicated to resisting the psychopathologisation of human difference, wherever in the world educational practice exists.

NOTES

1. As this is a BPS textbook, reference throughout is made to educational psychology, inferring inclusion of both educational and school psychology.
2. See the following link: http://www.sheffield.ac.uk/faculty/social-sciences/ihuman

REFERENCES

Armstrong, F., Armstrong, D. & Barton, L. (Eds.) (2000). *Inclusive education: Policy, contexts and comparative perspectives*. London: David Fulton.

Barton, L. (Ed.) (2001). *Disability, politics and the struggle for change*. London: David Fulton.

Barton, L. & Clough, P. (Ed.) (1998). *Articulating with difficulty: Research voices in special education*. London: Paul Chapman.

Barton, L. & Oliver, M. (Eds.) (1997). *Disability studies: Past, present and future*. Leeds: The Disability Press.

Berliner, D.C. (1992). Telling the stories of educational psychology. *Educational Psychologist, 27*, 143–152.

Billig, M. (1987). *Arguing and thinking: A rhetorical approach to social psychology*. Cambridge: Cambridge University Press.

Billington, T. (2000). *Separating, losing and excluding children: Narratives of difference*. London: Routledge Falmer.

Billington, T. & Williams, A. (2015). Education and psychology: Change at last? In I. Parker (Ed.), *Routledge handbook of critical psychology*. London: Routledge.

Bird, L. (1999). Towards a more critical educational psychology. *Annual Review of Critical Psychology, 1*(1), 21–33.

Bradley, B.S. (2005). *Psychology and experience*. Cambridge: Cambridge University Press.

Bruner, J.S. (1986). *The culture of education*. Cambridge, MA: Harvard University Press.

Bruner, J.S. (1991). The narrative construction of reality. *Critical Inquiry, 18*(1), 1–21.

Burman, E. (2008). *Deconstructing developmental psychology* (2nd edn). Hove: Routledge.

Burt, C. (1913). The inheritance of mental characters. *The Eugenics Review, 4*, 168–200.

Carr, W. (1995). *For education: Towards critical educational inquiry*. Buckingham: Open University Press.

Corcoran, T. (2007). Counselling in a discursive world. *International Journal for the Advancement of Counselling, 29*(2), 111–122.

Corcoran, T. (2016). What results from psychological questionnaires? In P. Towl & S. Hemphill (Eds.), *Locked out: Understanding and tackling school exclusion in Australia and Aotearoa New Zealand* (pp. 71–88). Wellington: NZCER Press.

Costa, R.E. & Shimp, C.P. (2011). Methods course and texts in psychology: 'Textbook science' and 'tourist brochures'. *Journal of Theoretical and Philosophical Psychology, 31*(1), 25–43.

Daniels, H., Edwards, A., Engestrom, Y. & Ludvigsen, S. (Eds.) (2009). *Activity theory in practice: Promoting learning across boundaries and agencies*. London: Routledge.

Dewey, J. (1916). *Democracy and education: An introduction to the philosophy of education*. New York: The Macmillan Company.

Fox, D., Prilleltensky, I. & Austin, S. (Eds.) (2009). *Critical psychology: An introduction*. London: Sage.

Gallagher, S. (2003). *Educational psychology: Disrupting the dominant discourse*. New York: Peter Lang.

Gergen, K.J. (1992). Toward a postmodern psychology. In S. Kvale (Ed.), *Psychology and postmodernism* (pp. 17–30). London: Sage.

Gergen, K.J. (2009). *Relational being*. New York: Oxford University Press.

Gillham, B. (Ed.) (1978). *Reconstructing educational psychology*. London: Croom Helm.

Goodley, D. (2011). *Disability studies: An interdisciplinary introduction*. London: Sage.

Goodley, D. (2014). *Dis/ability studies: Theorising disablism and ableism*. London: Routledge.

Goodman, G.S. (2010). *Educational psychology reader: The art and science of how people learn*. New York: Peter Lang.

Hadow, W.H. (1924). *Report of the consultative committee on psychological tests of educable capacity*. London: HMSO.

Hearnshaw, L. (1979). *Cyril Burt: Psychologist*. London: Hodder & Stoughton.

Henriques, J., Hollway, W., Urwin, C., Venn, C. & Walkerdine, V. (1989). *Changing the subject: Psychology, social regulation and subjectivity*. London: Methuen.

Hollway, W. (1989). *Subjectivity and method in psychology: Gender, meaning and science*. London: Sage.

Ingleby, D. (1985). Professionals as socializers: The 'psy complex'. *Research in Law, Deviance and Social Control*, 7, 79–109.

James, W. (1890). *Principles of psychology*. Vols. 1 & 2. Mineola, NY: Dover Publications.

Kincheloe, J.L. (2006). A critical politics of knowledge: Analyzing the role of educational psychology in educational policy. *Policy Futures in Education*, 4(3), 220–235.

Kincheloe, J.L. (2008). *Critical pedagogy primer*. New York: Peter Lang.

Mackintosh, N.J. (2013). The Burt affair: 40 years on. *Educational & Child Psychology*, 30(3), 13–32.

Martin, J. & McLellan, A.-M. (2013). *The education of selves: How psychology transformed students*. New York: Oxford University Press.

Mercieca, D. (2010). *Beyond conventional boundaries: Uncertainty in research and practice with children*. Rotterdam: Sense.

Mills, C.W. (1970). *The sociological imagination*. Oxford: Oxford University Press.

Moore, M., Beazley, S. & Maelzer, J. (1998). *Researching disability issues*. Buckingham: Open University Press.

Neilsen, K. & Kvale, S. (1999). Current issues in apprenticeship. *Nordisk Pedagogik*, 17(3), 160–169.

Nelson, G. & Prilleltensky, I. (Eds.) (2005). *Community psychology: In pursuit of liberation and well-being*. Basingstoke: Palgrave Macmillan.

Newman, F. & Holzman, L. (1993). *Lev Vygotsky: Revolutionary scientist*. London: Routledge.

Parker, I. (1992). *Discourse dynamics: Critical analysis for social and individual psychology*. London and New York: Routledge.

Parker, I. (1997). Discourse analysis and psycho-analysis. *British Journal of Social Psychology*, 36, 479–495.

Potter, J. & Wetherell, M. (1987). *Discourse and social psychology: Beyond attitudes and behaviour*. London: Sage.

Riessman, C.K. (2002). Doing justice: Positioning the interpreter in narrative work. In W. Patterson (Ed.), *Strategic narrative: New perspectives on the power of personal and cultural storytelling*. Lanham, MA, and Oxford: Lexington Books.

Rose, N. (1985). *The psychological complex: Psychology, politics and society in England 1869–1939*. London: Routledge & Kegan Paul.

Runswick-Cole, K., Mallett, R. & Timimi, S. (Eds.) (in press). *Re-thinking autism: A critique of the autism industry*. London: Jessica Kingsley.

Sloan, T. (Ed.) (2000). *Critical psychology: Voices for change*. London: Palgrave.

Sugarman, G. (2014). Neo-Foucaultian approaches to critical inquiry in the psychology of education. In T. Corcoran (Ed.), *Psychology in education: Critical theory-practice*. Rotterdam: Sense.

Todd, L. (2014). Critical dialogue, critical methodology: Bridging the research gap to young people's participation in evaluating children's services. In G. Porter, J. Townsend & K. Hampshire (Eds.), *Children and young people as knowledge producers*. London: Routledge.

Vassallo, S. (2013). *Self-regulated learning: An application of critical educational psychology.* New York: Peter Lang.

Venn. C. (1989). The subject of psychology. In J. Henriques et al. (Eds.), *Changing the subject: Psychology, social regulation and subjectivity* (pp. 115–147). London: Methuen.

Vygotsky, L. (1978). *Mind in society: The development of higher psychological processes.* Eds. M. Cole, V. John-Steiner, S. Scribner & E. Souberman. Cambridge, MA: Harvard University Press.

White, M. & Epston, D. (1990). *Narrative means to therapeutic ends.* New York: Norton.

Williams, A. (2013). Critical educational psychology: Fostering emancipatory potential within the therapeutic project. *Power and Education, 5*(3), 304–317.

Part I Reflexive Foundationalism: Critical Psychological Resources

In this section of the book, contributors consider the theoretical foundations required to conceptualise the notions of 'education', 'psychology' and 'critical'. The authors recognise the need to continually re-create our foundations, precisely because we find existing ones unsatisfactory. What results is a reflective or creative foundationalism, in which values are lived out and discussions of ethics and values can never be separated from and are inherent to every act.

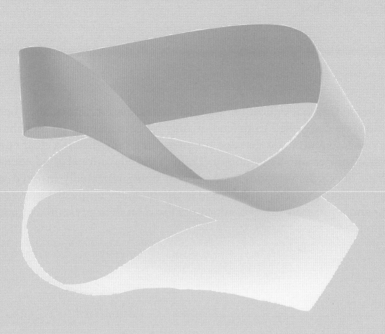

PREFACE

Both psychology and education are defended as if they were unquestionable goods. Psychology is associated with the notion that psychological knowledge itself is intrinsically beneficial. Educational activity is similarly associated with the notion that education itself is basically good. This chapter seeks to unsettle the presumed good of each field. It explores how psychology and education define and thereby delimit our freedom to ask whether or not they are 'good' or 'bad'.

1.

Educators often claim that education is under attack. As educators, they believe this is something they are compelled to defend, if only by complaining on its behalf. The collective response is so automatic that one might assume they shared a clear conception of the object under protection. They do not. Though the educational good educators are so sensitive about does achieve widespread support being repeatedly invoked as an entity worthy of protection, this educational good is also uniquely ungraspable. As defenders of a good they cannot precisely discern, educators focus on their presumed attackers by way of a distraction.

2.

Occasionally education is defended against the popular effects of psychology, or 'psychologisation'. This is the unwelcome (some would say excessive) attribution of psychological ideas to educational problems. But psychologisation is not in itself a problem for education. It is not an imposition, even if it is sometimes imposed. Education willingly adopts psychological understandings or practices or, at least, it does so 'unconsciously' and without hesitation.

3.

'Education' is a vague signifier. Nobody seems to know what it is; they can only tell you what education sometimes does. Since those activities that traditionally coalesce around this signifier have indeed done quite a bit (of damage, some would say), we might well consider the likely 'educationalisation' of psychology. This would accompany the psychologisation of education as its reflection.

4.

Mass schooling – the great educational achievement of the modern state – has been a major contributor to the educationalisation of psychology. This is because psychology emerged in part as a product of 19th-century developments in schooling. From the outset these institutions served as laboratories. They furnished would-be psychologists with captive populations from which to extract data, defining many of the problems psychology set out to answer as well as the purposes those investigations would serve.

5.

While schools served as laboratories, they also functioned like prisons; prisons in turn resembled schools. Both prisons and schools share a heritage and continue to trade techniques. In 1791 Jeremy Bentham published a design for a prison, which could also serve as a school. This circular building was organised around the superintending 'eye' of its central observation tower. Bentham called it 'The Panopticon'.

Many years later, Michel Foucault explored the greater political significance of Bentham's architectural scheme in *Discipline and Punish* (1991 [1975]). The 'panoptic gaze' described in that book captured the imagination of many, eventually becoming a rather tired metaphor overused in critiques of both education and psychology. As Foucault himself soon recognised, 'the principle of visibility' that governed the panopticon was already 'archaic' insofar as it attached so much importance to observation. By contrast, the 'procedures of power resorted to in modern societies are far more numerous and diverse and rich' than those of panoptic surveillance (Foucault, 1996 [1977], pp. 236, 227). Education resorts to far more than panoptic surveillance; it forms us in many other ways too. So if you shake your fist at the unseemly spread of CCTV cameras[1], make sure you also take a critical look at the wider education of the fist that does the shaking.

Still, when approached with caution, the panopticon makes an important point about the educationalisation of psychology. Before psychology existed in any systematic form, an institution was designed whose principles could be applied to 'work-houses, mad-houses, lazarettos, hospitals and schools' as well as to prisons. Bentham recalls a certain 'King of Egypt'[2] who 'thinking to re-discover the lost original of language, contrived to breed up two children in a sequestered spot, secluded from the hour of their birth, from all converse with the rest of humankind'. Suitably inspired, Bentham declares that a panoptic school, run on similar lines, 'might afford experiments enough that would be rather more interesting'. Perhaps a '*foundling-hospital*', at the very least, could be run along these experimental lines, isolating individuals and examining their development under controlled conditions (Bentham, 1843 [1791], p. 64).

Insofar as Bentham's principles were extended to early 19th-century schools, one might say that the experimental school he envisaged was, broadly speaking, in operation and generating data long before experimental psychology was founded. The so-called father of experimental psychology, Wilhelm Wundt (1832–1920), was not yet born.

6.

The typical case of an exchange between education and psychology is located in the early history of mental testing. Mental testing, we discover, was the byproduct of our proudest modern educational commitment, which goes like this:

Education for all **it says.**

The schools that were established to fulfil this beguilingly simple (if not deludedly cheerful) ideal offered much more than instruction. They generated norms of conduct and performance, organising behavioural space in ways that established the implicit standards against which variations between children could be measured. Within these normative confines a new category of child arrived. Though appearing fully functional at first sight, this child did not seem able to benefit from instruction. This was the so-called 'feeble-minded' child who was to be located at the outer limits of the normal.

Alfred Binet was appointed to a commission in 1904 that sought to perfect the distribution of such borderline cases. Many children were now located on these artificial borders of normality. Without an accurate test, it was hard to decide whether or not they would be better off in the so-called 'special' schools that had been established to mop up the problematic remainder of the school population. Following the arrival of universal schooling and the new problem of borderline children, the separation of this school-age population became an urgent necessity. The response was to use criteria of separation that were directly educational and behavioural (see Rose, 1999, pp. 141–142). In effect, here we have a landmark case in the educationalisation of psychology.

7.

We could not object to schools as scientific laboratories if they were not at the same time institutions designed to domesticate their populations through the knowledge they accumulate. Today's schools continue to experiment with the formation and distribution of subjects and subjectivities. In this respect they inform psychology and set its agenda. They also connect psychology to instruments of government.

During the huge expansion of 19th-century schooling, two distinct regimes of power were devised: roughly speaking, these can be divided into the disciplinary supervision of bodies in the early 19th-century monitorial school and the pastoral care of souls in the mid-19th-century moral training school. Initially the techniques these schools developed were aimed at the working poor, the dispossessed and the colonised. These potentially dangerous populations were to be aligned with the newly defined needs of 19th-century industrial societies and their protectorates. Each regime of power borrowed from established religious practices, drawing respectively from medieval monasticism and the Christian pastorate. Developed in partial isolation, these regimes were combined towards the end of the 19th century in the modern classroom. This institutional space was to become a uniquely domesticating site for the formation of individual subjects (see Allen, 2013, 2014).

It should be clear, then, that the manipulation of bodies and the inspection of souls (including self-inspection) was a banal fact of institutional life long before psychology, as a scientific specialism, was established.

8.

This is not a matter of precedence, however. A genealogy of psychology and education reveals that they interpenetrate to such an extent that you cannot be for one, and against the other. The psychologisation of education and the educationalisation of psychology must be set within a broader context.

9.

This context is that of modernity. To take the long view, and at the risk of being overly schematic, one might define this period as one in which religious practices were secularised. These practices set the limits for what it meant to live a good life. When religious practices were borrowed from and extended, they were adapted to the needs of the modern context. Roughly, the good life was redefined as living well within a modern state, which itself was to become acclimatised to the demands of an emergent capitalism.

The so-called masses were to be formed so that they would act appropriately in two domains. They were to be disciplined at the level of production, so that they worked well, diligently and without demur; and they were to be trained at the level of consumption, so that they could consume well (where the formation of good workers preceded the formation of good consumers). In other words, when workers are not at work they cannot be allowed to escape capital. In their spare time they must pay back into the system that has exploited them by buying its products and accepting the needs it defines as their own.[3]

In late modernity, commodification has been taken one step further as individuals are encouraged to turn themselves into articles of commerce. Individuals are expected to modify themselves and market themselves as flexible and adaptable workers in response to the uncertain demands of the marketplace. Psychological discourses and educational practices perform an important role here, conditioning everyday life so that it accords with these demands, educating individuals to live within these confines. Everyday life has been proletarianised in the sense that we are induced to commodify our relations with one another by turning them into strategic opportunities.

10.

Academics are not immune to this. The effects of institutional ranking by research output, impact and environment, and of an increased pressure to secure funds from an ever-diminishing 'pot', separate researchers from an intellectual engagement with their work. Research time is instrumentalised according to its methods, outputs, or what it may lead to in the future, and work commitments are increasingly measured against their likely returns in terms of esteem factors and future prospects (or, at the very worst, in a campaign for retention). One's relationships and links are commodified as potentially lucrative network-building opportunities, to be sold in one's own research bids, or sold to other bidders. High-flying academics are co-opted as key stakeholders in bids they have not written, for no other reason than that they are well established and connected to other stakeholders.

Slavoj Žižek (2009) divides today's proletariat into three mutually antagonistic groupings: (1) intellectual labourers, (2) representatives of the old manual working class, and (3) outcasts. This last category includes the unemployed, those living in slums and those occupying other interstices of public space. In this rough schema, one might expect that intellectual workers in general, and academics in particular, would be best placed to resist. Academics are able to draw from the security their comparative wealth affords as well as a long memory of other forms of life, which have been documented, categorised and preserved with scholarly diligence. Despite their apparent advantage, however, academics are also being proletarianised in a more restricted but nevertheless dangerous sense. Indeed, academics are perhaps most closely, most personally and most willingly invested in their own subjection, in their own alienation from the values that caused them to take up their work in the first place. As an academic discipline located in such an educational environment, psychology has a lot to be fearful of. In this sense alone, the educationalisation of psychology remains a very real, very current danger.

11.

These are just some of the techniques by which a society organised according to a divine purpose was succeeded by a social order with more immediate, secular objectives. These secular objectives may appear comparatively utilitarian. Arguably they diminish human relations, in some cases to a commodity form. They are nevertheless, still orientated towards an abstract good. This orientation is missed when critics bemoan the dangerous instrumentalism that seems everywhere entrenched. High-minded religious objectives are not simply replaced in modernity by lower earthly commitments; they are infused and invested with new higher meaning and purpose.

12.

Early psychologists recognised the continued importance of religion in a secular context. Raymond Cattell (1905–1998) was foremost among them. He appreciated religion not only for its unremitting devotion to some kind of abstract good, but for its ability to combine this orientation with techniques of subjective and intersubjective government. Cattell appreciated how religious practices were able to orient psychologies and thereby coordinate the minutiae of day-to-day life. His work is worthy of close consideration as it demonstrates in microcosm how religious techniques could be transformed for secular purposes. We find clues here for how a connection was maintained between personal and interpersonal techniques, and the pursuit of an unquestionable abstract good.

13.

Raymond Cattell was a celebrated psychologist. In 1992 he received the American Psychological Association's Gold Medal Award for Lifetime Achievement in the Science of Psychology. He was also a committed eugenic thinker.

14.

As a young man Cattell made some rather prescient remarks about the future of psychology. He was also speaking about the future of eugenics.

In his rather oddly titled *Psychology and the Religious Quest*, Cattell considered the eugenic potentiality of religion. Christianity, he argued, 'is impossible without eugenics, or, rather, eugenics is a growth of Christianity' (Cattell, 1938, p. 99). Cattell wished to demonstrate that Christianity and eugenics could become mutually dependent. In his view, eugenics must attach itself to 'positive' religious force because of the necessary limits of conventional 'negative' eugenics. Since 'we can only cut off the tail of stragglers by direct eugenic methods', he argued, 'we must leave to culture the breeding of vanguard qualities' (Cattell, 1937, p. 94). The best hope for eugenics is to embed the eugenic sensibility in the free action of individuals, and rely on compulsory action only in the most extreme cases where extermination or sterilisation was an unavoidable necessity. Eugenic activity, he claimed, must become an intrinsic part of the day-to-day self-regulation of individuals.

What Cattell offers us here is a way of understanding the broader social significance of psychology in an increasingly secular order. Here we see an envisaged handover from religious techniques to secular ones.

15.

Christian love is radicalised and reworked by Cattell for eugenic purposes. It becomes a violent commitment to the future happiness of those yet to be born; a commitment that is driven by the eugenic condition that they 'shall be fit for the world' in which they will live; for happiness and fitness, Cattell (1938, p. 131) claims, are intimately linked. While this reconditioned and upgraded love for the unborn would result in 'the greatest turning-point in the history of the human race' at least since the advent of Christianity, a eugenic religion of this kind would also constitute 'a continuation of Christianity, an extension of its values to the field of the unborn' (Cattell, 1938, p. 130). This bold redeployment of Christian sentiment 'as love of the best in man' (rather than love and propagation to all, feeble and strong alike) would substitute for the 'reckless, cruel and wasteful methods of Nature the humane control of kindness and reason'. Once further propagation was prevented, a 'thoroughly Christian treatment' of any remaining 'defectives' could be pursued, committing to them the best available care and support (Cattell, 1938, p. 69).

Cattell's overall point is this: once the 'admitted ideal of civilization' is recognised as being that project which aims to 'shift regulation entirely to the individual', the eugenic visionary will understand just how crucial the 'maintenance of morality by conscience' will become (Cattell, 1933, pp. 158, 156). Guided by such a conscience, individuals would live ethical eugenic lives. Newly concerned with the quality of their children, they would learn to regulate themselves independently.

16.

It is tempting to react with disgust; we might reject Cattell entirely, or at the very least seek to marginalise his thought. But we should take these proposals seriously, and perhaps bring them back from the periphery. Moral indignation is dangerous to the extent that it denies a line of continuity extending from Cattell to our present.

17.

Eugenics 'should not', he argued, 'throw away the great, slow-built, emotional attitudes, with all their poetry and wealth of human associations, which have grown up through the centuries around the concept of God' (Cattell, 1938, p. 186). Rather, eugenics must adopt from religion an adjusted, pastoral mode of power whereby individuals willingly submit themselves and the details of their lives to a higher authority. Cattell believed that these individual acts of submission could orientate themselves towards an adjusted religious creed. As the 'greatest turning-point in the history of the human race' since the advent of Christianity, this new religion would be accompanied by a new conception of God (Cattell, 1937, p. 130). God would cease to be a divine transcendental being. His symbolic form would find itself relocated in the material realities of our universe. This new entity that we would then come to identify as 'God' would be linked to an age-old accumulation of human effort. It would constitute a 'collective mind' or 'Theopsyche' to which we are all unwittingly linked. As a psychic entity in the most general sense, it would represent the legacy and continuing project of all good human action; where 'Goodness is the human tendency towards progress' (Cattell, 1933, p. 219).

> This [secular] God, which is all that is altruistic, intelligent, wise, powerful, courageous, and unselfish in the group mind of man, is a reality in the fullest sense. We meet it in every kind action, every effort to discover further secrets of the universe, every creation of beauty, and every sacrifice for a super-personal object. It lives in the idealistic organisation of all minds, and each one of us is part of it in proportion to his idealism. (Cattell, 1933, pp. 200–201)

Cattell's Theopsyche is a God that has grown out of our collective labours. It is the accumulated deposit of individual efforts towards progress, and has purportedly developed into a reality that anticipates and outlives all of us. While it may have been formed of human interaction, it is based in nature. 'It perishes in part if mankind perishes, but it is inherent in matter and will emerge again' (Cattell, 1933, p. 200). It 'has its roots in the material cosmos from which it is an emergent', and so we must conclude that the 'worship of nature is one with the worship of God' (Cattell, 1933, p. 183). It is to this deification of the human project that individual conscience is to be wedded. Religious overtures will now prepare individual lives for acts of devotion that are to be coordinated with the overall progress of humanity. With an updated conception of religion, eugenics can draw upon forces far more pervasive than mere techniques of disciplinary compulsion. Individuals will adopt procedures of self-examination and a willingness to confess, all of which is ruled by absolute submission to the eugenic creed.

18.

Cattell claimed that evil deeds are those that are 'opposed to group welfare' and sin is a 'failure to make the best out of the whole race' (Cattell, 1938, pp. 75, 104). All calculations of welfare are to be framed in evolutionary terms. Karl Pearson, another influential psychologist and eugenic thinker, made a similar point years earlier. That which is good is that which promotes overall social welfare, he said. Nevertheless, while Pearson believed only very few are 'capable of being really moral' – for only they would be 'in possession of all that is known of the laws of human development' (Pearson, 1901, p. 107) – Cattell appears to be more optimistic. By adopting religion and reformulating God, we may all come to worship and obey 'a super-individual consciousness with which the individual can maintain a communion' (Cattell, 1938, p. 77). In theory, any individual may contribute in a positive way to the group project, just as any individual may enter the more conventional religious fold. Of course, from the eugenic perspective, relative contribution is dictated by the normal distribution where 'the lower variant' can 'achieve happiness and avoid criminal self-assertion by [direct] submission', while 'the upper variant' is 'rescued from cynicism and despair' by their commitment to the communal project towards which all genius will turn with religious fervour (Cattell, 1938, p. 120). Across the spectrum of human variability we will be governed by our emotional commitment to this religion of human progress. Everyone will seek to contribute according to what is deemed good and beneficial for human development where all troubles and hardships are justified as necessary steps. Reproduced here is the circular logic of biblical discourse:

> And we know that in all things God works for the good of those who love him, who have been called according to his purpose. (Romans 8:28)

19.

So this is my provocation: both psychology and education continue Cattell's work. Insofar as we deny this statement and snub Cattell, rejecting his inhumanity and celebrating our own, we only descend further into the reductive, circular logic that Cattell exemplifies so well and so clearly.

Psychology and education are similarly attached to abstract ungraspable ideals that proclaim their humanity and hence elevate themselves above dispute. Where eugenics was committed to the pursuit of biological health, psychology and education add notions of social, economic and political health. Orientated by the idea that health in this world is calculable in the most general sense, and realisable, education and psychology came to redefine the appropriate limits of everyday conduct. In pursuit of a healthy, which is to say ordered and orderly population, education secularised and adapted practices of moral formation through the newly established mass school, while psychology secularised practices of subjective care by promoting itself as their replacement. Psychology and education took on the role of assisting individuals to live the good life, a life that was increasingly defined 'biopolitically'.[4] This is dangerous since a biopolitical order is one that also hides conflict, contradiction and systematic exploitation behind a commitment to its own, specifically scientist, definition of human flourishing, where overall population health and security become its principal concerns. It is at this point that the totalising moral scheme of religious discourse is replaced by its secular equivalent, combining the attempted realisation of an abstract calculable good with individuated techniques designed to align subjectivity with this effort. The good that is to be worked towards remains, of course, as indisputable as it is ill-defined.

20.

As disciplines, psychology and education take social and individual well-being as their primary object. The problem with this achievement is that in claiming to be its guardians, they actively exclude other rival conceptions of the good life. Indeed, other conceptions of the good life are scarcely possible now that the definition and defence of social and individual well-being has been so comprehensively defined by these agents of government.

21.

In their institutional forms, both psychology and education have managed to firmly embed their moral imperium in everyday practice. By ensuring that citizen-subjects are adapted to the society in which they were born, by ensuring that they live productively, safely and contentedly, adopting its needs as their own, they prohibit other conceptions of what it might mean to live well in society with others.

22.

To the extent that radical social critiques pose a challenge to well-being as it is currently defined and pose a threat to the good life we have been educated to accept, they are extinguished by default, as negative and inhumane. Radical action, involving a fundamental and violent interruption, entailing some sort of temporary deprivation in order to change how deprivation is perceived and constructed, is rendered unthinkable.

NOTES

1. Closed-circuit television cameras have expanded hugely in recent years, in Britain in particular, to the consternation of some.
2. Psammetichus, who reigned during the 26th dynasty of Egypt (664–610 BCE).
3. In other words, their 'free' time is also invested by capital (see Debord, 2009 [1967]).
4. Michel Foucault develops this concept in a number of places (see Foucault, 1998 [1976], 2003 [1976], 2004 [1978]). I explore some of the ambiguities and potential dangers of the pursuit of population health in Allen (2014).

REFERENCES

Allen, A. (2013). The examined life: On the formation of souls and schooling. *American Educational Research Journal, 50*(2), 216–250.

Allen, A. (2014). *Benign violence: Education in and beyond the Age of Reason.* Basingstoke: Palgrave Macmillan.

Cattell, R. (1933). *Psychology and social progress: Mankind and destiny from the standpoint of a scientist.* London: The C.W. Daniel Company.

Cattell, R. (1937). *The fight for our national intelligence.* London: King & Son.

Cattell, R. (1938). *Psychology and the religious quest: An account of the psychology of religion and a defence of individualism.* London: Nelson.

Debord, G. (2009 [1967]). *Society of the spectacle.* Eastbourne: Soul Bay Press.

Foucault, M. (1991). *Discipline and punish.* Harmondsworth: Penguin Classics.

Foucault, M. (1996 [1977]). The eye of power. In S. Lotringer (Ed.), *Foucault live: Collected interviews, 1961–1984.* New York: Semiotext(e).

Foucault, M. (1998 [1976]). *The will to knowledge.* London: Penguin.

Foucault, M. (2003 [1976]). *Society must be defended: Lectures at the Collège de France 1975–76.* London: Penguin.

Foucault, M. (2004 [1978]). *Security, territory, population: Lectures at the Collège de France 1977–1978.* Basingstoke: Palgrave Macmillan.

Pearson, K. (1901). *The ethic of freethought and other addresses and essays* (2nd (rev.) edn). London: Adam & Charles Black.

Rose, N. (1999). *Governing the soul: The shaping of the private self* (2nd edn). London: Free Association.

Žižek, S. (2009). *First as tragedy, then as farce.* London: Verso.

LEARNING OBJECTIVES

After reading this chapter you should be able to:

1. Develop a basic understanding of ontological constructionism.

2. Identify the importance of language use in constituting people and social practices (ways of being and forms of life).

3. Understand how the concept of ontological constructionism may apply to working as an educational or school psychologist.

Ontological assumptions are fundamental to how we come to understand ourselves, others and the world we share together. However, psychologists rarely question these assumptions, often mystified by the term (probably, more often than not, because the opportunity to reflexively engage its possibilities seems unavailable to them). This chapter begins by venturing into the field of philosophy to bring the concept out from the shadows of abstract thought. Having considered ways in which the term might be engaged, it then focuses on social-constructionist appropriations, specifically highlighting the work of British social psychologist and communication theorist John Shotter (1993, 2013). Throughout, the chapter maintains connection to the work of educational psychologists and how the concept might apply within their own practice.

QUESTIONING ONTOLOGY

Which of the following is true?

(a) There are core traits fundamental to all human beings.

(b) The physical world presents beyond interpretations made by people.

(c) When an individual dies, she or he no longer exists.

(d) All of the above.

Answer: any, all, or none. The way in which you respond to these statements – and the answer just provided – largely depends on how you view ontology. Let's begin with a broad definition. Ontology refers to the study of being or existence. Subsequently, how we understand ontology has direct implications for how we view reality. If you are now or ever have been a student, particularly in the social sciences and especially if you attended a critically orientated programme or were fortunate enough to have a supervisor with a leaning towards criticality, you may have been asked to explicate your ontological position. In my experience, the question often engenders a response ranging from mild uncertainty to utter bewilderment – and this should not be surprising. As already mentioned, while students are often expected to 'critically analyse' information, they are usually not invited to question the very nature of reality!

Reflection point

What is the difference between *finding* and *making*?

This seems a simple question but deserves further consideration, especially if asked in reference to ontology. To prepare the ground, Shotter (1993, pp. 24–26) asks us to reflect on knowledge development. He suggests that as we (researchers, students; in fact, all living people) move about in the world, we generate knowledge and this ongoing process provides us with understandings of how people are and how the world is. Of course, we do not move about the world in isolation. We are constantly checking with others about the suitability of our understandings. For example, if I were to say to you that the world is flat, we would probably disagree, as you would argue that, according to your knowledge (backed up by a large community of scientists and everyday people), the world is in fact round or spherical. The Austrian philosopher Ludwig Wittgenstein (1889–1951) had this to say on the subject of disagreement: '"So you are saying that human agreement decides what is true and what is false?" It is what human beings *say* that is true and false; and they agree in the *language* they use. That is not agreement in opinions but in form of life' (Wittgenstein, 1953, no. 241; emphasis in original).

What Wittgenstein is proposing here is that ontology (i.e., our form of life) is, to some degree, constructed via our use of language. Now let's pause for a moment to consider how we might situate the importance of language use to our ontological understanding. One traditional way ontology is understood claims that the world exists independently of human engagement. This view is known as realism. Here, language is considered to merely represent what already exists in the world. Knowledge and facts considered from this viewpoint can be said to be *found* via our interaction with the world and its people. How often, when perusing a research report, do you read the words: 'The current study found that…'? From this point of view, disagreement occurs because you or I misunderstand the existing conditions before us. Perhaps an example would be useful here.

Kevin's story

Kevin was in year 5 – around 10 years old – when he was referred to me by his school. The school administration and his class teacher reported inattentiveness, distractibility, lack of motivation for academic tasks, among other complaints. Subsequently, staff at the school felt the time was right to call in the district's educational psychologist to investigate their concerns.

The school and Kevin's classroom teacher had reportedly tried numerous pedagogic and curricular strategies and, despite their best intentions, they saw no change in his behaviour. With his parents and Kevin's permission, Kevin and I met at school every two weeks for a term or so. One morning, in conversation, he nonchalantly told me about something he was doing in an effort to s\pend more time with his dad. Kevin's dad was a truck driver and his work took him all over the state, even across the country. In Australia this could mean that Kevin's dad might be away from the family home for several days, sometimes a week or more at a time. Kevin's dad always had this kind of work so this situation was not initially thought to be relevant to what was taking place at school.

As Kevin talked about his desire to spend more time with his dad, we explored what his afternoons were usually like. We got on to talking about what he had for afternoon tea. Kevin reported that on the afternoons dad was home or due home, he would drink one or two cups of coffee. Rather surprised by this, I said to him that the thought of a 10-year-old drinking coffee was unusual. Kevin continued. He explained that the taste of coffee was far too bitter for his palate so to sweeten the drink and at the same time retain the strength of the coffee, he would pile in four or five heaped teaspoons of sugar! I had to ask an obvious question: Did what he was doing have any effect on how well he slept? He said it did make it difficult for him to get out of bed in the morning (something Kevin's mum thought might be connected to his general disaffection with school). But fascinatingly, there was more to Kevin's story. He said he drank the coffee to be 'closer' to his dad. Unsure what he meant by this, I asked him to say more. Kevin said that when his dad was home, his mum and dad would often stay up late watching TV. Kevin saw this as an opportunity to be physically close to his dad by tiptoeing into the lounge room after he was supposed to be asleep. He said he would often wait an hour or so after his bedtime to creep out and hide behind a couch in the lounge room. The coffee helped him to stay awake and thus enabled him to spend more time 'with' his dad.

Reflection point

How does language fit with practice?

Kevin's presentation may appear to match criteria used to construct knowledge around what is known as attention deficit hyperactivity disorder or ADHD. From more dominant psychiatric/psychological paradigms, ADHD is explained pathologically, as a neurobehavioural condition identified via a series of diagnostic criteria. Some staff at the school were already using the term as a possible cause to explain their perception of Kevin and his behaviour. While there are no conclusive biological tests that can confirm the presence of ADHD, the presumed certainty of its existence nevertheless produces tangible (i.e., realised) effects. The percentage of parent-reported diagnosis and treatment by US healthcare providers for ADHD in children aged 4–17 increased from 7.8% in 2003 to 9.5% in 2007 and to 11% in 2011 (Visser et al., 2014). Put another way, that 11% accounts for 6.4 million children, an apparent increase in diagnoses of 42% from 2003/2004 to 2011/2012.

In direct contrast to the position of realism is that of relativism. This viewpoint states that it is impossible to assert truth claims outside a system of language (this is also known as the Sapir–Whorf hypothesis or linguistic relativity). A position of moral relativity similarly suggests that ethical appraisals depend on standards that are in turn supported by particular social groups at specific times and places. The common theme in relativist accounts is the contention that no absolute vantage point exists from which claims to truth can be made. In the social sciences, those looking to refute relativism do so by taking the position to its extreme asking whether life is a context in which 'anything goes'? Of course, radical forms of relativism are difficult to sustain because we do not move about the world in isolation and therefore our actions are accountable in one way or another (e.g., legally, morally, socially, relationally). It is not surprising that Kevin could not do as he pleased within the social mores of his classroom.

But what if we are able to accommodate a position somewhere between realism and relativism, acknowledging the unique role language plays in constituting or interpreting the world, but so too giving due respect to the embodied, material and social aspects of everyday life? How might attending to our own and another's use of language help to know/make/find our way in the world – that is, to live? Let's consider an example pertinent to the work of educational psychologists.

JUSTIFYING A RATIONALE

Educational psychologists are regularly requested to undertake formal assessments of students in schools. Perhaps one of the more widely recognised assessments educational psychologists perform is an assessment of intelligence. The concept of intelligence is a relatively new term in the vocabulary of humankind. In the century prior to the 1900s, a time when psychology as a distinct scientific activity was very much in its infancy, the term intellect was commonly used by evolutionists as a static referent to one's capacity for knowing. Charles Darwin's (1809–1882) studies, for example, posited variability in 'mental powers' between species and among human groups. Correspondingly, Herbert Spencer (1820–1903) in 1855 published *Principles of Psychology*, heralding psychology as a biological science and introducing intelligence as a central category of study within the newly defined discipline.

If we look closely, interplay between ontology and social practice is evidenced in the possibility of biological intelligence, the development of psychology as a scientific discipline and the institutionalisation of education. In the late 19th century, the industrialisation of working life included changes to the way education was delivered, including the standardisation of curriculum and syllabi and the formalisation of exams in schools. As often is the case, developments in social practice (e.g., schooling) promote correlated advancements in technologies. Historian of psychology Kurt Danziger (1997, p. 75) explains:

> Without the prior development of a rationalised system of school examinations in the nineteenth century there would have been no technology of intelligence testing in the twentieth. It was the new system of schooling that gave universal validity to the notion that intellectual activity could be treated as a kind of performance to be judged against precise standards of achievement.

Students of psychology, particularly those who have not had the opportunity to undertake coursework in the history of psychological theory, would be well served to explore Danziger's work. Two of his acclaimed publications are *Constructing the Subject* (1990) and *Naming the Mind* (1997).

As we continue to contemplate the relationship between ontology and social practice, recall Wittgenstein's statement: 'It is what human beings *say* that is true and false; and they agree in the *language* they use. That is not agreement in opinions but in form of life' (1953, no. 241; emphasis in original). The contention that intelligence exists in a way that can be defined and measured with statistically sophisticated tools standardised to the general population is effectively an agreement about how we conceive of and articulate life or human nature. Drawing on ontological constructionism can help to simultaneously acknowledge not only the content of a claim but also, importantly, processes assisting a claim being made. Attention to both is vital and directly impacts decisions being made by educational psychologists working in schools.

Attending to knowledge creation and development, at the very least, creates the potential to disrupt the status quo, to interrogate processes and practices that can, at times, be insensitive to issues of power, politics and prejudice. Thus, our ontological agreements carry overwhelming consequences for how we understand people and the world in which we live (i.e., our ways of being and forms of life). It is not surprising then that there is a growing mass of observers, both inside and outside the discipline of psychology, looking to address potentially disabling effects of psychological knowledge (Corcoran, 2014; Fox, Prilleltensky & Austin, 2009; Rose, 1999). One strategy that helps me discern between the kinds of knowledge made/found in psychology is to distinguish first and second nature psychologies.

Reflection point

Is it possible to prefer ways of being?

Some time ago, a leading figure in social constructionism made this declaration: 'Rather than "telling it like it is" the challenge for the postmodern psychologist is to "tell it as it may become"' (Gergen, 1992, p. 27). How do you respond to this statement? Does it seem fanciful? Perhaps confounding? Think back to earlier in this chapter and the discussion delineating 'found' knowledge and 'made' knowledge. Does Gergen's position now seem more comprehensible? If it is possible to 'tell it as it may become', is it possible to prefer ways of being? As educational psychologists, we have the capacity to talk about, write about and relate to people in preferred ways. Let's be clear about how and when this distinction is necessary.

The dominant, and to date enduring, way in which psychology creates an understanding of people is via claims to objectivity, rationality, generality and fundamentality. Such claims align closely with the purview of realism and positivism (i.e., knowledge generated from empirically verified evidence to produce scientific laws). Most psychology training in the world today accepts knowledge of this kind as representing the natural state of human being. I call this first nature psychology (Corcoran, 2009). Ontological assumptions from this perspective allow psychologists (e.g., clinical, educational, health, counselling) to extricate the life out of the people they write about to make certain pronouncements about the phenomena they study. Billig (2011, p. 15) elaborates: '[B]y turning processes rhetorically into things, scientists routinely are creating "fictional things" – namely entities, which cannot actually exist as things, but which are treated as if they were things.' For example, first nature psychologies take processes occurring over time (phenomena such as acting or thinking) and reduce these to static objects (e.g., attitudes). How easy is it to then take these captured snapshots as representative of whom others see a person to be? Would I be considered an anti-authoritarian (an attitudinal state) if I joined in public protest about the rising level of university student fees? Would I be thought to possess an attention deficit if I showed little interest in the curriculum taught at my school?

In contrast, second nature psychologies are open to forms of ontological constructionism. What this means is, in certain contexts, definitive claims about a person and their circumstance might be the most appropriate way to come to a situated understanding of the person. For instance, in contemporary education systems, funding for in-class student supports are explicitly tied to diagnostic categories. An assessment that contributes to establishing a diagnosis has the potential to ensure benefits (i.e., funding to support learning) as well as harbour reservations (e.g., labelling or pathologising the student). But second nature psychologies offer more than the option to fall back on first nature accounts. Being open to the prospect of second nature psychologies permit educational psychologists to orient to ways of being standing outside the normative arrangements of institutional practice. This is because second nature psychologies are open to:

- Shifting from generalised theories to practical, situated instructive accounts;
- Interest on activities rather than things (i.e., internalised psychological phenomena like motives or attitudes);
- Relational activity as opposed to individual behaviour;
- Embedded constructions developing within a flow of situated historical practice;
- The capacity for language to constitute practice and coordinate activity, not merely to represent the known world;
- Critical examination of the social processes that inform how we construct experience (e.g., diagnoses for funded support);
- Investigations validated from within local circumstances that need not be founded on external authority. (Shotter, 1993, p. 20)

As practitioners we must ready ourselves for the opportunities emerging before us in our professional practices by being receptive to second nature accounts of human being. Relating to the world and others in this manner requires us to carefully reflect on the form of life we might find while also through our interventions actively and purposively help to make the world the kind of place we want it to be. While this may sound idealistic to some, you only need to ask yourself what alternatives are available? To continue with first nature accounts categorically 'telling it like it is'?

CONCLUSION

This chapter discussed the importance of how, as practitioners and participants in the commotion that is everyday life, we orient and contribute to the flow of psychosocial action in which we are embedded. My own awareness for the significance of such matters is indebted to the work of John Shotter. As he reminds us, we must always be anticipating:

> how we might orient ourselves bodily towards events occurring around us, how we can relate ourselves to them, and to get ourselves ready for seeing, hearing, experiencing, and valuing what we encounter as we move forward with our lives – for these are the ways that will organise our lookings and listenings, our sense-makings and judgements of value, and thus, ultimately, determine the lines of action we resolve on carrying out further. (2013, p. 142)

As an educational psychologist, my intent is to create ways I can be of assistance to others (e.g., students, teachers, parents, schools, communities, readers). The support I provide, whether assessment, counselling, consultation or other kind of professional service, or presently as an academic through writing chapters like this, strives to collaboratively construct preferred outcomes. Individual preferences can at times struggle to align in collective action. In Kevin's case, the 10-year-old boy who developed a unique strategy to spend more time with his dad, it was gratifying to see the line of action everyone pursued worked towards creating and sustaining preferred relationships. Being aware of their ongoing individual responsibility to relational action brought those connected closer together – Kevin, his parents, his teacher and his school – to ensure the required resolution was directed by the preferences of those involved.

This textbook presents a series of debates pertinent to current practices in educational psychology. What this chapter adds is an opportunity to (re)consider the ways in which you interact with others and the world, and, ultimately, how you choose to engage in relationships as a professional. The heterogeneous nature of our contemporary globalised and multicultural world calls out for orientations that do justice to issues of diversity and equity, engagement and inclusion. Ontological constructionism presents you with options for proactive participation, not only to 'tell it as it may become' but also to work in support of preferred ways of being and forms of life. Through engaging second nature psychologies and the alternative ways of speaking and writing these invite, we move to bettering our capacity to effectively assist those we serve.

REFERENCES

Billig, M. (2011). Writing social psychology: Fictional things and unpopulated texts. *British Journal of Social Psychology, 50*(1), 4–20.

Corcoran, T. (2009). Second nature. *British Journal of Social Psychology, 48*(2), 375–388.

Corcoran, T. (Ed.) (2014). *Psychology in education: Critical theory-practice.* Rotterdam: Sense.

Danziger, K. (1990). *Constructing the subject: Historical origins of psychological research.* New York: Cambridge University Press.

Danziger, K. (1997). *Naming the mind: How psychology found its language.* London: Sage.

Fox, D., Prilleltensky, I. & Austin, S. (2009). *Critical psychology: An introduction* (2nd edn). London: Sage.

Gergen, K.J. (1992). Toward a postmodern psychology. In S. Kvale (Ed.), *Psychology and postmodernism* (pp. 17–30). London: Sage.

Rose, N. (1999). *Governing the soul: The shaping of the private self* (2nd edn). London: Free Association.

Shotter, J. (1993). *Cultural politics of everyday life: Social constructionism, rhetoric and knowing of the third kind.* Buckingham: Open University Press.

Shotter, J. (2013). Agentive spaces, the 'background', and other not well articulated influences in shaping our lives. *Journal for the Theory of Social Behaviour, 43*(2), 133–154.

Visser, S.N., Danielson, M.L., Bitsko, R.H., Holbrook, J.R., Kogan, M.D., Ghandour, R.M., & ... Perou, R. (2014). Trends in the parent-report of health care provider-diagnosed and medicated attention-deficit/hyperactivity disorder: United States, 2003–2011. *Journal of the American Academy of Child & Adolescent Psychiatry, 53*(1), 34–46.

Wittgenstein, L. (1953). *Philosophical investigations.* Oxford: Blackwell.

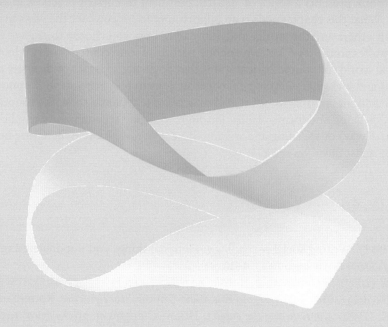

LEARNING OBJECTIVES

After reading this chapter you should be able to:

1. Develop an understanding of narrative theory, in particular how narrative techniques can support a shared exploration of meaning, in conversations and consultations, in educational psychology practice.

2. Understand the importance of identity (the self story), in experience and in relation to change.

> *'An army? More like a resistance movement'*, says David Epston.
> *'And you're the general?'*
> *'No, I'm the archivist – the person who went around collecting and exchanging stories. I have no desire to lead anything.'* (Barton, 2006)

In the above quotation David Epston is referring to his narrative-orientated work with those struggling with anorexia and bulimia as part of his clinical practice in the United States. His positioning of himself as therapist has, I feel, some relevance to the educational and child psychologist in the UK, working across systems and with people who have various perspectives on 'problematic' situations. As a psychologist I am aware of having a somewhat paradoxical role. I often feel uncomfortable about 'leading' in the sense of exercising power directly: for example, if I were to claim an authoritative view. However, through the largely discursive process of establishing a 'shared understanding' and a view of the 'way forward', I might hope to be influential.

As Epston's reference to 'resistance' and 'archives' suggests, a narrative approach to problem-orientated dialogue acknowledges the importance of both power and language in determining outcomes. For the peripatetic psychologist, exploring a child's / children's experience (how I interpret my purpose and frame my activity), moving across contexts, this might be particularly evident: for there is usually a need to synthesise a number of stories told, perhaps in 'feedback' for a meeting, or report writing for statutory assessments. Determining the trustworthiness and usefulness, to the child (not always the consultee but always the client), of each story heard, can be conceived as a process of deconstructing the implicit questions, how and why has meaning been made this way? The process might also involve the exploration of psychological narratives and a reflexive concern with theory being applied. Through such deconstruction and reconstruction, as question why particular meanings are privileged over others, the workings of power (interpersonal, institutional, governmental), may become more visible while oppressive, marginalising and unjust interpretations might be more easily understood and addressed.

In this chapter I will articulate a 'narrative' rationale for the 'doing' of educational psychology. I will begin by providing a background of narrative theory, examining how meanings are generated from experience through narrative construction, and, in particular, examining how a person's identity is constructed through this process. I will then explore some of the possibilities for casework, drawing upon my own practice, the existing theory and evidence base emerging from narrative therapy / practice, as well as the emerging evidence base within educational and child psychology.

STORIES OF EXPERIENCE

Catharsis and poiesis: Emotional expression and meaning making

Aristotle (384–322 BC) believed that witnessing a tragic story provoked 'fear' and 'pity' resulting in the release and transformation of these emotions in the spectators (Aristotle, 2006). Since the development of psychoanalysis, the term catharsis has been used to describe the expression of emotion through the narration of experience. This understanding is continued in modern psychotherapy in the idea that emotion and traumatic memories are 'processed' through dialogical co-construction (Dimaggio & Semerari, 2004). Aristotle

(2006) also conceived of a related term, poiesis: a person's desire for immortality. He proposed that creativity, in the soul, and in life, allows a sense of the transcendent value of human experience, a meaning which is perhaps echoed in modern constructs of personal growth and self-actualisation (Rogers, 1961). Heidegger (1971) defined poiesis as a coming into being, with a focus on thresholds, transitions and transformations. In different cultures storytelling traditions may function to provide opportunities for meaning-making in ways which meet our psychological need for emotional expression and personal continuity (White, 2000).

Interpretation of experience

Bruner describes narratives in cognitive terms, as interpretative frames which help us to make sense of our experience of the sensory world. In the following example he likens narratives to cognitive schema which, once in place, shape subsequent experiences.

> I have developed a feel for what to expect and I usually see what I am looking for, no matter what else I may miss. I use my model to guide my behaviour and drive, or walk, defensively in terms of that model. (Bruner, 1986, p. 47)

Bruner goes on to describe how a narrative can alter where experience contradicts, a position which speaks of a kind of empiricism as well as pragmatism, and resonates with my practice as an educational psychologist. Flexibility and openness to uncertainty may allow us to negotiate our narratives in complex social circumstances. This understanding of the relationship between our sense of the world and language rests, variously, and sometimes controversially, on critical realist or social-constructionist ontological ideas (Bhaskar, 1991; Gergen, 1999; Nightingale & Cromby, 2002). Arguably, such ontologies facilitate a particularly human empathic engagement. Gergen associates this with 'appreciative inquiry', an approach to consultation in which efforts are made to hear all voices, in particular, the voices of those who experience marginalisation. Narratives draw us into the perspective of the storyteller. An empathic criticality allows us to question our own valued positions, our 'truths', and engage with those of others.

> Here we find we can abandon concern with the hidden reservoirs of motivation or ideological bias said to be lurking behind people's words. We need not impute evil intent to the other... Rather our attention moves to the forms of life that are favoured (or destroyed) by various ways of putting things. (Gergen, 1999, p. 38)

I find this perspective encouraging, as a psychologist more comfortable in meetings as facilitator than 'expert', preferring to encourage reflection, reflexivity and collaborative problem solving, rather than making diagnoses and giving prescriptive solutions.

Focus on language: The 'linguistic turn'

As Gergen highlights, *how* things are said is important. Deconstructive analysis of texts, popular in literary theory (Eagleton, 2008), has become important within narrative theory. A fundamental assumption is that meanings are not intrinsic to words; rather, they become meaningful in relation to other words and the contexts in which language is used. Meaning is never static or equivocal, but always up for negotiation and renegotiation (Bruner, 1986). The role of 'power' in determining the value attached to particular language forms is explored in the work of Foucault, who had much to say about psychology's part in categorising and stigmatising various aspects of persons, and its gentle facilitation of state power (Foucault, 1973). Since its emergence as a discipline, educational psychology has been very involved in the identification and description of 'difference'. Such narratives can legitimise 'special' and separate educational placements, which stigmatise and further reduce opportunities for full participation in mainstream communities (Billington, 2000). Educational psychologists in the present day, in our modern/postmodern culture, will be conscious of pressures in their role to collude with such intentions. For example, we are often invited by our employers (and others) in a quiet, Foucauldian fusion of power and knowledge, to recommend educational placements, apply reductionist labels and to claim a knowledge and expertise that often does not sit well with social-constructionist epistemologies and inclusive aspirations.

Also relevant to the psychologist, conscious of wanting to work creatively and collaboratively with the meanings of others, is Bakhtin's notion of intertextuality (Bakhtin, 1981; Todorov, 1984). Narratives are formed in relation to other narratives which invoke past, present and future. In seeking to influence the narrative around a child it is necessary to hear and engage with what others have to say about them.

> A single voice can make itself heard only by blending into the complex choir of other voices already in place. This is not only true of literature, but all discourse. (Todorov, 1984, p. x)

Example: Narrative meetings

When I first began to practise as an educational psychologist, I found meetings very challenging as it was in this context that power differentials were most evident in discourses and ways of talking which I felt did not support collaborative problem solving (pathologising, within-child, blaming). Drawing on the work of Todd (2000, 2003) and Morgan (2002) I started to ask participants if I could facilitate meetings in a 'narrative' way, explaining a little about this. I would usually invite each person present to talk about, and name, the problems the child was being 'bothered' by and on a large sheet of paper note these down in 'problem bubbles' beneath a scale. In relation to the scale I'd ask them to say how much influence this problem was having in the child's life, and also if there was a time it had been less influential, or even absent. I also asked what strengths the child could draw upon, and about their own hopes and ambitions. I'd note this down above the scale, writing words and statements which seemed particularly evocative of the shared experience of the situation. I would contribute the views of the child I had obtained previously.

This process often stimulated collaborative talk and, perhaps because the focus was on 'the problems', staff and parents seemed to relax, their fears of 'blame' with its associated 'shame' possibly subsiding. Having heard from everyone in the room who wanted to speak I would invite the group to consider exceptions to the problem (when it wasn't around) and what this might mean for our understanding of the child and the situation. Usually at this point of the meeting people would be referring to the diagram as they talked. Towards the end of the meeting the problem bubbles would become the focus. How could they be 'shrunk'? What would the day be like without them? Could we cope with them better now that we understood how the problems were working to make us feel helpless and de-skilled? Could we become more skilled at defeating the problem? Did we need to meet again to talk about how we were doing?

IDENTITY: KNOWING WHO WE ARE

Bruner (2004) observes that within narrative accounts there is always an 'I' as well as an 'other'. In attempting to explain the importance of 'selfhood' and why 'we portray ourselves through stories', Bruner suggests that conceiving of a 'self' allows us to 'take a perspective' on experience, a perspective which strengthens agency:

> Selfhood can surely be thought of as one of those 'verbalised events' (Slobin 2000), a kind of meta-event that gives coherence and continuity to the scramble of experience. (Bruner, 2004, p. 7)

However, when our world is disturbed, where our experience in some way fails to match our expectations, we are forced to construct another through an inner search of memory and experience, and an appraisal of the meanings available in culture (Bruner, 2004). Selfhood is thought to be integral to a transformative process of narrative reconstruction.

A change in our experience or perceptions of the world and an altered relationship with the world can bring about a change in identity. Part of this, of course, is what is said about us. We become defined by the narratives that we internalise. The available meanings in discourse and culture provide both constraints and possibilities. We may not be conscious of this. We may not be aware of our relationship to narratives and our potential alternatives. However, increasing our consciousness of the narratives we tell ourselves, the narratives told about us and the narratives we prefer might lead to an emerging agency in relation to choices and actions (Winslade & Monk, 1999).

WORKING WITH STORIES: DOING NARRATIVE PRACTICE

> I noticed that narrative conversations were not about giving advice, solutions, or opinions. They were not about normative judgements or evaluations or positions of authority. (Morgan, 2002, p. 86)

Acknowledging personal and social history

The intention to hear a 'story' might be considered different to gathering information, an everyday activity in educational psychology: there is an acknowledgement of the validity of subjectivity and experience. A story communicates a perspective in a form which can be understood and considered by others but not in a way which gives us direct access to experience: stories do not function as 'a mirror for life' (Epston & White, 1992, p. 123). Rather, the narrative form provides a frame, a 'dual landscape' in which 'action' and 'consciousness' can be represented. Within a story, events unfold in relation to the interpretations, thoughts, feelings and beliefs of the narrator and characters within the story (Bruner, 1986; Epston & White, 1992, p. 123).

Deconstructing narratives: Externalisation and the nurturing of agency

Those who work with narratives are interested in the cultural resources and discourses which shape them, and the hopes, dreams and fears of those who create them. For example, the dominant narratives of culture may position a young person within a story of dysfunction or pathology, such as 'damaged child', 'ADHD'. Such descriptions can operate as reductive explanations which disallow alternative meanings and contribute to exclusionary practices. Alice Morgan believes that 'people live their lives by stories' and that to understand this we need to deconstruct the narratives they share with us. This is always a collaborative process characterised by 'curiosity' and an attitude of respectful and empathic 'wondering'. The narrative practitioner is 'decentred, but influential' as a consequence of inviting a story and developing a style of questioning which centralises the meanings of the teller (Morgan, 2002, p. 86).

It is all too easy to feel taken over by a problem identity. When a person's life becomes 'problem saturated' it can be difficult to experience the agency and the hope required to work towards change (Winslade & Monk, 1999, p. 32). A key narrative technique is 'externalisation'. Simple conversational questions, such as, 'When did you first notice that this problem was around?', with its subtle language shift (*the* problem, not *your* problem), can change a person's relationship with a situation (Morgan, 2002, p. 88). The problem is separate rather than part of who they are.

Narrative practitioners have developed externalisation in creative and playful directions (Dykes & Neville, 2000). I have drawn on the ideas of Liz Todd (2000, 2003) and encouraged children to think of their 'struggle with trouble', for example. Other 'problems' I have externalised are 'nasty moods', 'fear of maths', 'anger', 'difficulty with reading and writing', 'worry at bedtime'. With teachers I have externalised 'fear of Ofsted' in the context of a discussion about the dilemmas of teaching in the present day.

Example: Working with parents

In my own practice I am used to talking in a 'narrative' way in my first meeting with parents who are struggling with their relationships with their children who are themselves on the verge of school exclusion. My overarching story/question is: What is the history of this problem? While the story is told I listen carefully for parents' intentions and purposes, often embedded within the talk, and I ask about these. I ask them if they can remember when family life was easier and to retrieve some memory of themselves as the parent they prefer to be. In these conversations, rather than establishing a relationship through the primary task of gathering information, perhaps guided by a questionnaire, I am privileged to enter parents' stories and to see things from their point of view. This seems to foreground our relationship and support our future collaboration.

Mapping the influence

Externalisation of a problem and naming a problem easily leads to what Winslade and Monk (1999, p. 8) describe as 'mapping the influence'. They suggest that we ask, 'Where is this problem most around, where is it big and where is it smaller?' At its simplest level this allows us to consider the multiple contexts of a child's life and to identify the particular situations in which a problem thrives. However, if we ask, 'What helps the problems to grow in this context?' this allows us to connect problems to ideas and cultural practices; for example, those which circulate in school or at home. We can see how particular problems join up in a synergistic way and analyse how a young person might feel overwhelmed and misunderstood in certain situations.

Example: Sam and his struggle with anger and nasty moods

Sam, in year 4, was referred to educational psychology because he was thought to need 'anger management'. He was getting into fights and arguments in the playground and refusing to do much of his work in class, especially where it involved writing. He had twice run out of school. There was little sympathy for Sam in school and staff expressed frustration and concern that he 'showed no remorse'. I had an initial consultation with him and opened our conversation by telling him I had heard that he was 'having some trouble' and asking if he wanted to tell me anything about it. I was fairly sure that Sam perceived my non-blaming construction of trouble. He looked surprised and less wary. He began to talk quite freely and together we drew the 'trouble bubbles' and where they followed him around. Sam's story was quite simple. He was very anxious about writing and he also didn't have friends. When people wouldn't let him join in their games he felt 'angry' and 'wanted to hurt them because they had hurt him'. He said no one cared about him. I asked what helped him to feel less anxious about writing. He said, 'when someone sits with me and helps me'. Sam identified an adult who would notice him trying to 'squash the anger' when he was rejected. This was discussed in a separate consultation with staff and parents where solutions to the anxiety and social exclusion were explored.

Please note that details of practice have been altered to ensure anonymity.

Re-membering and re-authoring

Hearing the exceptions to problem stories allows us, collaboratively, with others, to begin authoring an alternative story (Epston & White, 1992; Morgan, 2002; Winslade & Monk, 1999), a story preferred by the young person with its origins in their lived experience and witnessed by others. The witnessing or sharing of the alternative story, through dialogue, written documents, such as letters or reports, is important within narrative-orientated educational psychology practice, so that others, teachers, friends, family, can support the young person in their purposes, by noticing their efforts and showing respect and support where possible.

Several writers describe narrative practice as an inclusionary therapeutic approach. The therapy room is extended into contexts: the locus of change is not within the young person, or between themselves and the therapist, but within the community in which the young person finds themselves. White (2000, p. 98) uses the term 're-membering' to describe the psychological and social process of welcoming someone back into a community which the problems they have struggled with have previously isolated them from.

CONCLUSION

An emerging body of practice-based evidence suggests that narrative practice is currently influential within educational psychology. Imaginative applications of narrative principles suggest that they have the potential to provide a framework for practice, a framework in which different aspects of educational psychology practice can be contained. Recent examples are a study by Hannen (2012) which evaluates a narrative therapy intervention with a young person struggling with 'self-harm and depression' and a study by Hobbs et al. (2012) who write of their work in developing a narrative-orientated educational psychology service. In addition there are many unpublished theses by doctoral educational psychology students who have evaluated narrative interventions or used a narrative method in their research.

A concern is often expressed in the profession that educational psychology lacks a clear ontology and epistemology in which to locate our professional activity, that we are consequently too eclectic in our knowledge base (Todd, 2009). It is my view that narrative provides a strong theoretical and ethical grounding for our practice. Perhaps most importantly, a focus on narrative reminds us that we ourselves are tellers of stories, and to take care that our stories recognise the dilemmas and limitations that psychology faces when it claims expertise and knowledge.

Reflection points

- What kind of evidence building/research activity would recognise the expertise of clients in their own experience?

- In collaborative work what ethical actions do we need to take to ensure we are transparent about the structural constraints on our work (e.g., statutory legislation, service delivery agreements)?

- What unique contribution might we, in educational psychology, make to children, families and schools if we adopted a narrative approach to service delivery and evaluation?

REFERENCES

Aristotle. (2006 [335 BCE]). *Poetics*. Trans. J. Sachs. New York: Pullins Press.

Barton, C. (2006). Waging war against a deadly disorder. Online at www.nzherald.co.nz/ (accessed 16 October 2014).

Bakhtin, M.M. (1981). *The dialogic imagination: Four essays*. Ed. M. Holquist, Trans. C. Emerson and M. Holquist. Austin and London: University of Texas Press.

Bhaskar, R. (1991). *Philosophy and the idea of freedom*. Oxford: Blackwell

Billington, T. (2000). *Separating, losing and excluding children: Narratives of difference*. London: Routledge Falmer.

Bruner, J. (1986). *Actual minds, possible worlds*. Cambridge, MA: Harvard University Press.

Bruner, J. (2004). The narrative creation of the self. In L.E. Angus & J. McLeod (Eds.), *The handbook of narrative and psychotherapy: Practice, theory and research*. London: Sage.

Dimaggio, G. & Semarari, A. (2004). Disorganised narratives: The psychological condition and its treatment. In L.E. Angus & J. McLeod (Eds.), *The handbook of narrative and psychotherapy: Practice, theory and research*. London: Sage.

Dykes, M. & Neville, K. (2000). Taming trouble and other tales: Using externalised characters in solution focussed therapy. *Journal of Systemic Therapies*, 19(1), 59–73.

Eagleton, T. (2008). *Literary theory: An introduction*. Minneapolis: University of Minnesota Press.

Epston, D. & White, M. (1992). *Experience, contradiction, narrative and imagination: Selected papers of David Epston and Michael White, 1989–1991*. Adelaide: Dulwich Centre.

Foucault, M. (1973). *The birth of the clinic*. London: Tavistock.

Gergen, K. (1999). *An invitation to social construction*. Thousand Oaks, CA: Sage.

Hannen, E. (2012). Narrative therapy with an adolescent who self-cuts: A case example. *Educational Psychology in Practice*, 28(2), 187–214.

Heidegger, M. (1971). *Poetry, language, thought*. Trans. A. Hofstadter. New York: Harper & Row.

Hobbs, C., Durkin, R., Ellison, G., Gilling, G., Heckels. T., Tighe, S., Waites, B. & Watterson, C. (2012). The professional practice of educational psychologists: Developing narrative approaches. *Educational & Child Psychology*, 29(2), 39–51.

Morgan, A. (2002). Beginning to use a narrative approach in therapy. *The International Journal of Narrative Therapy and Community Work*, 1, 85–90.

Nightingale, D. & Cromby, J. (2002). Social constructionism as ontology: Exposition and example. *Theory and Psychology*, 12(5), 701–713.

Rogers, C. (1961). *On becoming a person: A therapist's view of psychotherapy*. London: Constable.

Todd, L. (2000). Letting the voice of the child challenge the narrative of professional practice. *Dulwich Centre Journal*, 1 & 2, 73–79.

Todd, L. (2003). 'Talking to trouble', Liz Todd 'Talking to Trouble' workshop, Centre for Narrative Practice, Manchester.

Todd, L. (2009). A response to Billington. *The Psychology of Education Review*, 33(2), 21–23.

Todorov, T. (1984). *Mikhail Bakhtin: The dialogical principle*. Trans. W. Godzich. Manchester: Manchester University Press.

White, M. (2000). Collaborating with the family: The approach of narrative therapy. In C. Smith & D. Nylund (Eds.), *Narrative therapies*. New York: Guilford Press.

Winslade, J. & Monk, G. (1999). *Narrative counselling in schools: Powerful and brief*. Thousand Oaks, CA: Sage.

4 Post-Conventionalism: Towards a Productive Critical Educational Psychology

DAN GOODLEY

LEARNING OBJECTIVES

After reading this chapter you should be able to:

1. Tease out a number of key applications of post-conventionalist theories to critical educational psychology.

2. Employ these theories to examine the experiences of disabled children and children labelled as SEN.

3. Examine children's embodiment and pedagogy in schools.

In this chapter I seek to introduce a post-conventionalist perspective as a possible foundational theoretical position for critical educational psychological work. This perspective emerges from the nexus of disability, queer, feminist and crip studies (Goodley, 2014). Following Shildrick (2009, 2012), a post-conventionalist perspective can be described as an affirmative consequence of post-structuralism. While post-structuralism is brutal in its deconstructionist tendencies – and one might say necessarily so – post-conventionalists orientate towards affirmative possibilities. If post-structuralism leads to the death of the subject, post-conventionalism seeks to explore what alternative ways of being and becoming might emerge out of this death. Changes in culture, economics, society and technology have had massive impacts on our bodies and subjectivities. The human being is increasingly constituted through a complex array of material, discursive and embodied formations. One post-conventionalist approach – post-humanism – attends to the folding into one another of culture and bodies. Post-humanists, such as Braidotti (2003, 2006, 2013), are sceptical about the centrality of the individual in our everyday thinking. The idealised fully functioning person is an entity psychologised, internalised and rationalised: autonomous, capable and a distinct self, bounded and separated from others. Increasingly, however, social sciences and humanities have revealed this individual to be an outdated, classic modernist humanist trope that emerges today as more fiction than fact. In contrast, the post-conventionalist self is an assemblage, collectivity and enmeshment with other human beings, non-human animals and technologies. To be human is not to be a solitary individual but a complex enmeshment of wetware and hardware (Braidotti, 2013, p. 145).

> **Reflection point**
>
> What do you understand by the concepts 'body', 'the child' and 'school'? In your answer think about the ways in which different psychological theories would influence and shape the kinds of answers you provide.

POST-CONVENTIONALIST STARTING POINTS

Post-conventionalists challenge how we might normatively understand concepts such as 'the child', 'the school', 'psychology' and 'education'. Post-conventionalists are highly critical of the kinds of bodies, emotions and cognitions associated with the preferred human valued and promulgated by nation-states, institutions of society and the capitalist free market. Indeed, as I explore in a recent publication, what it means to feel and act human is also a matter of how one is *meant to* feel and act as a human in contemporary society (Goodley, 2014). Post-conventionalists, then, roll back to take another look at those things we think we 'know' about ourselves as human beings. The child, at least of Global North, rich Western European and North American societies, is normatively understood to be a human developing between the ages of 0 and 18, educated rather than working, living in some kind of family or kinship network, progressing in a typical, normal, advancing trajectory. Children, we are told, are society's future. When children veer away from these normative trajectories – due, for example, to the presence of disability – then these children disrupt comfortable, traditional and anticipated ideas associated with the child and childhood. Educational psychological practice often has at its professional centre an idealised conception of the developing child. One might argue that the discipline of educational psychology has, traditionally, engaged itself with the identification of childhood deficiencies and the promotion of educable and re/habilitative interventions that seek to render the deficient capable. A post-conventionalist approach intervenes in this psy-complex in a number of important ways.

First, the notion of an individualised capable (or incapable) personhood is rejected. The self and others are actually intimately linked to the extent that neither can exist without the other. This, of course, is a common idea underpinning humanist and psychoanalytic ideas. We need others to recognise our selves. Post-conventionalist ideas extend the relationship: viewing the self and others as interconnected, assembled and mutually dependent on one another. In this sense, then, we are asked to consider the self as a decentred and distributed phenomenon deeply embedded in relationships with others. Second, the normative child-as-national-future is contested. Cooley's (2011, p. 315) post-conventional analysis employs the queer theory analysis of Edelman's 2004 book *No Future* to evaluate the position of people with the children of intellectual disabilities in wider cultural politics. Cooley observes that any society that stakes its perpetuity on the symbol of the child will ultimately be hostile to those of its citizens who threaten this future. Disabled children, then, are viewed as a threat to these idealised versions of the child. Post-conventionalists, in contrast, seek alternative, more broadened conceptions of the childhood that include young people traditionally exiled from the normative child (including disabled children). Third, the child as productive, affirmative and disruptive agent is celebrated; especially those children on the margins of normative childhood. Rather than understanding 'disabled', 'difficult' or 'disruptive' children as lacking, we seek to ask what educational possibilities are raised by their presence in the classroom, community, school and playground. What does disability give to our understandings? Such a question has resonances with the disability scholar Tanya Titchkosky's (2011) wonderful turn of phrase that thinking about the human being through disability has the potential to spark a *politics of wonder*. We are asked to wonder about what it means to be human, an exercise that I think will not be lost on those engaged with educational psychology. Let us turn now to two post-conventionalist considerations. The first will explore how we might approach understandings of children's embodiment. The second asks us to think again about pedagogy in the school.

POST-CONVENTIONALISM AND CHILDREN'S EMBODIMENT

In a recent paper, Katherine Runswick-Cole and I (2012) employ a post-conventionalist approach to make sense of the embodied lives of disabled children. We were drawn to this perspective because of the post-conventionalist tendency to reframe the disabled body along the lines of capacity, potential, interconnection and possibility (for examples, see Gibson, 2006; Goodley, 2007a, 2007b; Hickey-Moody, 2009; Overboe, 2007; Roets, 2008; Shildrick,

1999, 2009, 2012). The work of Donna Haraway (1991) has been incredibly influential and she describes social theory as providing subtle understandings of emerging pleasures, experiences and power with serious potential for changing the rules of game. What people are experiencing, she argues, is not always immediately clear, because we lack subtle concepts for collectively building effective theories of experience. This is especially so when bodies challenge normative standards of embodiment: an intervention often made by the presence of disabled bodies. Shildrick (1999) reminds us that many social scientific theories of the body assume the presence of a normative, biologically given, integrated and fully functioning body. Bodies that sit or stand in opposition to this standard are conceptualised as undesirable monstrous Others (the capital O denoting magnified otherness). Post-conventionalists seek, then, to reinvest in the monstrous and to ask what the embodied Other might actually bring to the theoretical, practical and political table. Different theoretical schema are required to rethink the body of the Other; not in terms of failure but in terms of affirmation. The body is, for Braidotti (2003, p. 44), neither a biological nor sociological category, but an interface, a threshold, a field of intersecting material and symbolic forces; a surface where multiple codes (sex, class, age, race) are inscribed.

> The normative body is understood as being fashioned and materialised through cultural, political and social conditions ranging from surgery to self-help. The non-normative or monstrous body – a body that appears as an object of fear and curiosity – is considered therefore as an opportunity to think through values, ethics and politics that congregate around particular bodies. (Goodley & Runswick-Cole, 2012, p. 5)

Non-normative bodies appear as a moment of disruption and allow us to think again about those bodies that we value and those that we discount. Disabled bodies, as an example, offer much to the post-conventionalist cause precisely because they ask us to think (again) about how bodies should (not) and can (not) be lived (see Overboe, 2007). A post-conventionalist views non-normative bodies not as invalid but in terms of possibility and becoming (Braidotti, 2003). Let us turn to an example from Goodley & Runswick-Cole (2012, pp. 13–14) which contemplates the case of a disabled young person called Kurt.

Kurt's story

For Kurt, being born with no bladder meant that this had been a daily experience for him and 'no big deal', though he had not told any of his close friends. One day he plucked up the courage to tell a couple of pals about his use of a catheter. By the end of the day, his new name around the school was 'wee wee boy'. This had made him very angry. He got his revenge against the main bully of the school, who was using this new name, by emptying his urine bag into the boy's schoolbag, out of sight of the teacher in the maths lesson.

Kurt's story may be read in a million ways. I have shared this story with psychology and education students. Many have expressed sympathy and empathy with Kurt. A number cheered when they have heard about his act of embodied revolution. A few have suggested Kurt is in denial and struggling with his disability. A post-conventionalist reading seeks to ask what Kurt (and his body) contributes to our understandings about the potentiality of bodies. In one sense we could read Kurt as using the urine bag as a form of cyborg activism (Haraway, 1991). Kurt uses his human–prosthesis binary in an innovative way to challenge a bully. He is using the prosthesis in a way that was not originally thought of when the designers were crafting the bag! In our paper, we push the reading further and suggest that:

> Kurt's body work would be seen as a form of what Braidotti (2003, p. 53) terms nomadic subjectivity: where one refutes the settled, fixed labels placed upon one's self and becomes nomadic – learning to 'reinvent yourself and desiring the self as a process of transformation'. However, this nomadic subjectivity first requires claiming a fixed location: something other than 'wee wee boy'. This requires challenging the same of the same–other binary: deterritorialising the dominant (ableist) symbolic (Braidotti, 2003, p. 54). (Goodley & Runswick-Cole, 2012, p. 14)

Part of the ableist symbolic is the desire for bodily control. We know, for example, that in the UK those children starting infant classes in primary school are expected already to be fully toilet trained. Society in general tends to struggle with unruly, leaking and expansive bodies (Vidali, 2010). A post-conventionalist reading, though, looks for possibility in the excluded, outlawed body: Kurt takes control of his leaky body, directing its leakage in ways that lay foundations for possible future interactions with the boys in his school. Kurt demands his leakiness to be acknowledged and, one would hope, accepted.

Reflection point

How might you use Kurt's story as a discussion-provoking vignette to talk through with fellow educational psychologists and/or members of a SENCO? In your discussions consider the ways in which children's bodies and behaviour might disrupt and challenge the ways in which school classrooms are organised.

POST-CONVENTIONALISM, PEDAGOGY AND THE SCHOOL

Post-conventionalist approaches seek opportunities for rethinking our relations with others. One specific example of revisiting relationships is provided by the notion of machinic connection. This phrase, borrowed from the work of Gilles Deleuze and Felix Guattari (1987) (key resources for post-conventional writers), has been especially helpful to researchers focused on analysing the lives of disabled children and their educational, cultural and social encounters (e.g., Gibson, 2006; Goodley, 2007a, 2007b; Hickey-Moody, 2009). Deleuze and Guattari are interested in the ways in which we become (rather than be) through a reaching out for (and desire for) connection with others. As I have written elsewhere, rather than the desire to be a particular kind of subject (e.g., autonomous, functioning, self-contained), they ask:

What might it be like to desire becoming the other? How might we become in the company of others? What kinds of connections might we make in the process of becoming (with) other(s)? (Goodley, 2014, pp. 105–106)

Machinic assemblages constitute one form of connection and are 'composed of multiple and variously embodied parts that interchange and create new relationships, alliances, and communities' (Ramlow, 2006, p. 181). The assumption here is that good teaching and learning – inclusive pedagogy – can often be found in educational contexts when there is an emergence of 'communal becomings; communities of relations, ethics and mappings of togetherness which always challenge the delimitations of borders' (Curti & Moreno, 2010, pp. 416–417). An example of good communal pedagogy is provided by the following vignette.

A school story

Northtown is a co-located special school. The deputy head told me that both the head of Northtown and the mainstream school head were keen to co-locate. They both saw this as an opportunity for inclusion but also saw the potential that sharing resources might have for improving provision for both schools. The schools share the sports facilities, canteen, school hall and theatre. The schools share one reception area but the special school is in one half of the building and the mainstream school in the other. The deputy head told me that the special school parents had accepted co-location as a positive step, partly because they could see that their children would have access to better resources and partly because the school moved only a very short distance.

Many children in the special school come from the local area and are therefore part of the local community, so there is a sense that they share a sense of community with peers. The deputy head said there had been concerns that the mainstream pupils would tease or stare at or name-call the disabled pupils but this hasn't happened. He felt that this had been a very positive outcome of the relocation. The school itself is extremely well appointed with break out areas, interactive whiteboards, sensory room, huge accessible changing/toilet facilities, music, art, science rooms and soft play. The atmosphere in the school when we visited was incredibly calm and purposeful with children engaged in a range of practical activities.

The art room was stunning and I met the art teacher who the deputy head described as 'bonkers but brilliant'. This seemed to be a bit of a theme among the staff. Another teacher was constructing a display that would use lighting to move from day to night and different creatures would emerge throughout the day. This was alongside his construction of a display that glows under UV lights. He uses projectors to display moving pictures of animals and UV paint to bring to life a huge ant. He explained how he had used a projector to take the children to the moon and that they had asked 'where are we?' then speculated on the fact that they couldn't live there because there was no water. He said that there was no way his pupils could have learnt this looking at books. The deputy head said that the science teachers from the mainstream school had said 'why can't we teach science like this?'

(Ethnographic field notes by Katherine Runswick-Cole cited in Goodley & Runswick-Cole, 2010, p. 287)

Reflection point

What examples of socially just pedagogy and forms of inclusive education are present in the 'school story' narrative?

The story in the vignette captures a school working well and a number of examples of innovative pedagogy. A number of machinic assemblages appear to have proliferated throughout Northtown school – across special and mainstream spaces – provoking intense moments of inclusion and exciting pedagogies. These moments feed in to Liasidou's (2012) definition of inclusive education: a sense of belonging and meaningful participation in schools. Inclusive education, she argues, involves fostering new regimes to make schools and teachers redistribute and focus resources on groups of students who are entangled in a complex web of social and educational disadvantage (Liasidou, 2012). Inclusive educational assemblages might be read, then, as moments of redistribution. Such a move fits neatly with Semetsky's (2012) call for pedagogy founded upon an *ethics of integration*. 'Learning' she writes 'presupposes an encounter with something as yet unknown…and in order to make sense for this experience we will have to create new meanings and concepts in practice' (Semetsky, 2012, p. 49). Our brilliant/bonkers teacher (whose practice is admired by science teachers from the mainstream school) and his pupils appear to be experimenting together; encountering new ideas and practices. Our bonkers/brilliant teacher and the pupils call out to all teachers and students from across mainstream and special settings to revisit their practices. At the heart of this inclusive practice is the desire to connect with dis/abled students: for teachers to become-other:

> Such a desire 'emerges from our awareness of moral interdependence, that is, self-becoming-other by means of entering into another person's frame of reference and taking upon oneself the other perspective. In the context of education, to become capable, explicitly or implicitly, of becoming-other, means to confirm the potential best in both oneself and another person' (Semetsky, 2012, p. 55). The disabled student, then, is shifted from a fixed position of incapacity (being disabled) to a dynamic image of potential and becoming-learner (becoming dis/abled). Semetsky (2012, p. 56) relates this shifting pedagogy to an ethics of integration 'that should help us in overcoming the dualistic split between self and other, to integrate "the other" completely'. (Goodley, 2014, pp. 113–114)

Hence, as we discussed at the start of this chapter, the self and other (in this case teacher and pupil) are always dependent on one another, but in an extended sense of connection that can be guided by what Greenstein (2013, pp. 225–226) describes as 'a stance of getting-to-know, openness to communication that recognises differences cannot be erased and that sees conflict and resistance as inevitable within human relations, but as a productive positivity'.

CONCLUSIONS

In this chapter we have encountered a post-conventionalist approach. A number of key messages emerge from the analysis:

1. Bodies and relationships are in a constant state of emergence and interconnection;
2. Bodies that are considered to be disabled, difficult or disruptive can be reconceived of in terms of potentiality and possibility;
3. Innovative pedagogies often emerge through selves encountering and respecting the Other; and
4. Inclusive schools appear to be founded on productive assemblages and collectives of learners, teachers and others community members.

REFERENCES

Braidotti, R. (2003). Becoming woman, or sexual difference revisited. *Theory, Culture & Society*, 20(3), 43–64.

Braidotti, R. (2006). Posthuman, all too human: Towards a new process ontology. *Theory, Culture & Society*, 23(7–8), 197–208.

Braidotti, R. (2013). *The posthuman*. London: Polity.

Cooley, R. (2011). Disabling spectacles: Representations of Trig Palin and cognitive disability. *Journal of Literary & Cultural Disability Studies*, 5(3), 303–320.

Curti, G.H. & Moreno, M (2010). Institutional borders, revolutionary imaginings and the becoming adult of the child. *Children's Geographies*, 8(4), 413–427.

Deleuze, G. & Guattari, F. (1987). *A thousand plateaus: Capitalism and schizophrenia*. London: Continuum.

Edelman, L. (2004). *No future: Queer theory and the death drive*. Durham, NC: Duke University Press.

Gibson, B. (2006). Disability, connectivity and transgressing the autonomous body. *Journal of Medical Humanities*, 27, 187–196.

Goodley, D. (2007a). Becoming rhizomatic parents: Deleuze, Guattari and disabled babies. *Disability & Society*, 22(2), 145–160.

Goodley, D. (2007b). Towards socially just pedagogies: Deleuzoguattarian critical disability studies. *International Journal of Inclusive Education*, 11(3), 317–334.

Goodley, D. (2014). *Dis/ability studies: Theorising ableism and disablism*. London: Routledge.

Goodley, D. & Runswick-Cole, K. (2010). Len Barton, inclusion and critical disability studies: Theorising disabled childhoods. *British Journal of Sociology of Education*, 20(4), 273–290.

Goodley, D. & Runswick-Cole, K. (2012). The body as disability and possability: Theorising the 'leaking, lacking and excessive' bodies of disabled children. *Scandinavian Journal of Disability Research*, 15(1), 1–19.

Greenstein, A. (2013). Radical inclusive pedagogy: Connecting disability, education and activism. Unpublished PhD thesis, Manchester Metropolitan University.

Haraway, D. (1991). *Simians, cyborgs and women: The reinvention of nature*. London: Free Association Books.

Hickey-Moody, A. (2009). *Unimaginable bodies: Intellectual disability, performance and becomings*. Rotterdam: Sense.

Liasidou, A. (2012). Inclusive education and critical pedagogy at the intersections of disability, race, gender and class. *Journal for Critical Education Policy Studies, 10*(1), 168–184.

Overboe, J. (2007). Disability and genetics: Affirming the bare life (the state of exception). In 'Genes and society: Looking back on the future': Special issue of *Canadian Review of Sociology, 44*(2), 219–235.

Ramlow, T.R. (2006). Bodies in the borderlands: Gloria Anzaldua's and David Wojnarowicz's mobility machines. *MELUS, 31*(3), 169–187.

Roets, G. (2008). Connecting activism with academia: A postmodernist feminist perspective in disability studies. Unpublished PhD thesis, Ghent University.

Semetsky, I. (2012). Living, learning, loving: Constructing a new ethics of integration in education. *Discourse: Studies in the Cultural Politics of Education, 33*(1), 47–59.

Shildrick, M. (1999). This body which is not one: Dealing with differences. *Body and Society, 5*(2–3), 77–92.

Shildrick, M. (2009). *Dangerous discourses of disability, subjectivity and sexuality*. London: Palgrave Macmillan.

Shildrick, M. (2012). Critical disability studies: Rethinking the conventions for the age of postmodernity. In N. Watson, A. Roulstone & C. Thomas (Eds.), *Routledge handbook of disability studies* (pp. 30–41). London: Routledge.

Titchkosky, T. (2011). *The question of access: Disability, space, meaning*. Toronto: University of Toronto Press.

Vidali, A. (2010). Out of control: The rhetoric of gastrointestinal disorders. *Disability Studies, 30*(3/4), n.p.

5 Psychoanalysis

ANTONY WILLIAMS

LEARNING OBJECTIVES

After reading this chapter you should be able to:

1. Reflect upon the use of psychoanalytic concepts in the formation of critical psychological work.

2. Reflect upon what assumptions about self and other are implicitly brought to bear when using psychoanalytic concepts to make sense of the social world.

Psychoanalysis is an interpersonal process between two people. The process is a treatment for mental distress developed by Sigmund Freud (1856–1939) in the late 1890s and has been the context in which theories of the mind have been developed. These theories based on the experience of psychoanalysis have had a wide-ranging impact on the modern Western understanding of mind and are often fiercely attacked by critics of psychoanalysis.

This chapter poses a question for the reader to reflect upon throughout:

(a) Of what use are psychoanalytic concepts in the formation of critical psychological work?

What would it mean to incorporate psychoanalytic concepts into practice as a critical psychologist working with children, parents and school staff, particularly bearing in mind the very different social spaces[1] within which practice takes place?

To consider the above question, an associated question is posed. This second question is an ontological one which seeks to illustrate that whatever perspective or theory of knowledge you draw upon in your work with clients, you make assumptions about both them and yourself. A central theme within this book is that it is important to be aware that you make those assumptions and also take some time to think through what they are. As such the secondary question posed is:

(b) What assumptions about self and other are implicitly brought to bear when using psychoanalytic concepts to make sense of the social world?

From a consideration of these questions, learning objectives emerge. Although the learning objectives are not explicitly listed here, the answers you take from considering the above questions when reading this chapter will represent a learning experience that I hope has been meaningful and one you can relate to your professional practice experiences.

INTRODUCTION

To begin by tackling the second question first it is clear that psychoanalysis's subject (the subject or person assumed by psychoanalysis) is a very different one to the subject assumed by the other schools of thought, often referred to as paradigms, within psychology. This difference is one of the factors that prevents psychoanalysis from being subsumed into general psychological approaches. This differing understanding of how minds work also problematises much of the knowledge that psychology produces. To understand this difference it is helpful to begin with a consideration of the model of mind that psychoanalysis presents and what about this model general psychology finds so unpalatable. The key distinction rests on the centrality of the unconscious in psychoanalysis. Frosh (2002) proposes, in *Key Concepts in Psychoanalysis*, the unconscious as the notion that distinguishes psychoanalysis from all other approaches to human psychology. Indeed the unconscious is the central notion within psychoanalytic thought on which the practice and theory of psychoanalysis rests. As early as

1900, in *The Interpretation of Dreams*, Freud articulates an understanding of consciousness in an 'embattled relationship to the larger, more primary and largely unknown phenomenon he called "the unconscious"' (Haughton, 2003, p. ix). Later, in the last years of his life, Freud was to write:

> The concept of the unconscious has long been knocking on the gates of psychology and asking to be let in. Philosophy and literature have often toyed with it, but science could find no use for it. Psycho-analysis has seized upon the concept, has taken it seriously and has given it a fresh content. (Freud, 1938, p. 273)

Stephen Frosh (2002, p. 13) offers a succinct definition in explaining that the unconscious is not a space or place in the mind but rather 'a type of idea, one which is hidden from awareness yet still active ("dynamic"), pushing for release'.

Reflection point

Is the concept that each of us has unconscious ideas which structure how we think and feel about others and ourselves, but of which we are unaware, one that you would agree with?

PSYCHOANALYTIC ASSUMPTIONS ABOUT SELF AND OTHERS

Psychoanalysis presents a model of mind in which the developing conscious sense of self is rather fragile. As such psychoanalytic theory details how the mind develops a range of processes that protect or defend against an acknowledgement of the self as fragile and the overwhelming feeling states that accompany such ideas. From this perspective – the mind as structured to protect against overwhelming uncomfortable feeling states, and has a lack of clarity or insight into how ideas, out of conscious awareness (in the unconscious), shape thoughts and behaviours.

We will now consider the initial question posed in this chapter before reviewing a number of key concepts developed within psychoanalysis to introduce how those working from a psychodynamic[2] perspective understand and think about the mind from this starting point.

Of what use are psychoanalytic concepts in the formation of critical psychological work?

The process of defending against anxiety and the introduction of the concepts of projection and transference to examine how the mind does such defending will follow. However, before this, to show their potential relevance to critical psychological work it may be helpful to clarify the general argument put forward in this chapter. The critical educational psychologist can develop their appreciation of the complex social situations they encounter by assuming a dynamic unconscious, and recognising its sizeable influence on thoughts and behaviour. In adopting this stance there is a recognition that key drivers of thoughts and behaviour generally remain outside the field of view and yet at the same time structure that view.

Psychoanalytic concepts are valuable in that, by giving a name to psychological processes that influence thoughts and behaviour, albeit outside conscious awareness, we are more able to think about such processes and consider their possible influence. Thinking about unconscious processes is not a straightforward task, given that we cannot directly see or quantify the phenomena in question, but can only infer it from what we can appreciate. Behaviour that is out of kilter or unusual, given the context, does suggest that something beyond what is currently understood by you or perhaps others in the room is going on and the suggestion here is that:

1. Appreciating and being able to draw upon a psychoanalytic understanding of mind and develop a psychoanalytic sensibility is potentially helpful for a psychologist working with children, their parents and the school staff that deliver their education.

2. The psychoanalytic concepts of transference, projection and containment may offer a starting point from which to reflect upon the experiences of professional practice.

DEFENCE AGAINST ANXIETY

Given the assumptions outlined above it is perhaps not surprising that from a psychodynamic perspective the key role for the conscious self is to protect itself from feeling overwhelmed, lost and unable to cope with a reality that is presented, while simultaneously trying to make sense or meaning from that reality. Initially we require an other, in the form of a primary caregiver, to do this. An infant will sense some form of unease and react to it, typically crying, and eliciting the response of a caregiver. As a child grows, they develop spontaneous strategies for managing perceived (and/or real) threats. Psychoanalysis has generated an understanding of how the mind develops to enable a person to stay in touch with the reality of their experience, to the extent that is it possible for them to do so at any given time. Psychoanalysis outlines unconscious mechanisms that are produced without the conscious awareness of the individual. These unconscious mechanisms or 'defences' have been studied, thought about and written about by psychoanalysts from Sigmund Freud onwards. Indeed Bion's (1962) psychoanalytic study of thinking suggests that thinking is usefully understood as a human response, a functional defence, to emotional experience.

Anna Freud made a particularly influential contribution to the thinking about defence mechanisms. Her work built on an understanding introduced by Sigmund Freud that defence mechanisms distort reality and by doing so provide a perception that is less anxiety provoking. Anna Freud identified nine defence mechanisms in her influential 1937 book. These included repression, recognised as being central and worthy of distinction due to its role in the constitution of the unconscious, regression, reaction formation, isolation, undoing, projection, introjection, sublimation and identification with the aggressor. While the list offered here is not exhaustive, it is important to reiterate that these mechanisms act in defence of the 'I' and in an unconscious way, and in doing so shape perception.

PROJECTION

As noted above projection is considered a defence mechanism. It is considered worthy of further examination here as it is recognised by many in psychoanalysis to be of primary importance. Despite the variety of meanings that projection has come to represent Freud offers a clear definition, as 'an attribution to another (person or thing) of qualities, feelings or wishes that the subject repudiates or refuses to recognise in himself' (Laplanche & Pontalis, 1980, p. 352). Recognised as a particularly powerful defence that develops early in life, it is a process whose understanding has been particularly developed by the Kleinian school of psychoanalysis. As with other concepts introduced from psychoanalysis projection is a process that is understood to occur outside of conscious awareness.

Projection is of particular interest to the critical psychologist in its potential to give meaning to group dynamics and help practitioners think about the often powerful emotions they experience. The concept of projection may also help practitioners consider their 'lost' emotions in emotive situations. Projection is a concept that can help open-minded practitioners to think about the differing perceptions of a situation those they work with often recall and it can be helpful in encouraging practitioners to remain curious. An acknowledgement of the possibility that feelings and the ideas associated with them can be out of the awareness of someone and also experienced by that person as if they are coming from an external source is a powerful possibility to entertain.

Everyday example 1

It may be that a situation is occurring in a classroom in which a pupil begins to feel anxious – for example, they are finding the learning task challenging and feel unsupported. As a way of coping with these feelings, before they are recognised as feelings the pupil owns – 'I am anxious because this task is really hard' – the emotion is disowned and the idea is got rid of, projected into a classmate. The pupil identifies another who they feel owns those feelings and then looks on that other pupil as the one that anxiously struggles. The projection is not conscious or a cognitive error but an unconscious defence, which gives it particular power and strength. The experiencer lacks awareness of the origin of the feelings, but looks across at his neighbour, sure that it is they that feel increasingly anxious. It is this strength within the projected material that justifies what is then felt to be a conviction that the other feels the disowned feelings.

Recognising the power of such unconscious processes can give critical practitioners a starting point for considering what feelings and ideas can be thought about and by whom in the social space in which they are working.

TRANSFERENCE

The expressions transference and countertransference are terms that along with projection (and there are many other associated terms in the language of psychoanalysis) seek to offer a way of conceptualising how the affect we fail to recognise within ourselves can shape our perception in ways that we fail to recognise at the time. Freud considered transference as a particular form of displacement of affect from one idea to another (Laplanche & Pontalis, 1973, p. 457). Sandler, Dare and Holder (1973, p. 47) explain transference as:

> a specific illusion which develops in regard to the other person, one which, unbeknown to the subject, represents, in some of its features, a repetition of a relationship towards an important figure in a person's past.

The effect of transference and thinking through communications within the clinical space for transferences, in effect staying aware of how you are being related to, is a major aspect of the psychoanalytic process. Discussed by Freud as early as 1895 in *Studies on Hysteria*, the concept of transference has been particularly developed within the Kleinian tradition. As Milton, Polmear and Fabricius (2011, p. 11) note, thinking about elements of transference in a psychoanalytic space requires responding to a communication with thoughts such as: Why this? Why now? What am I feeling in response to what was just said/done? What does it feel like to be the other (in this exchange) at this moment?

View of transference outside an analytic relationship

Freud (1940) acknowledged the potential of transference to structure the relationship between teacher and pupil as well as that of doctor and patient along the way to recognising the importance of transference in structuring the analyst–analysand (person in analysis) relationship. Frosh (2002) suggests that transference is a process that is evident in everyday life, being a facet of human communication, albeit an unconscious one.

Particularly helpful for the critical psychologist in thinking through the merits of considering transference outside of a psychotherapeutic relationship are the writings of Thomas Szasz (1963, p. 433) who suggested:

> To define transference in terms of the analytic situation is like defining microbes as little objects appearing under a microscope... As the occurrence of bacteria is not limited to laboratories, so the occurrence of transference is not confined to the analytic situation: however each is observed and studied best, not in its natural habitat, but under special circumstances.

As such the analytic situation is the situation in which transferences can be studied and learnt from rather than acted upon. While the working context of the educational psychologist is much more variable and in many ways more complex than a clinical setting, we can assume that transference remains a factor structuring relations and, while detailed analysis may not be possible, being alive to this fact and the possible effects is a possibility.

Although there are numerous inherent difficulties in thinking/feeling transference, the most fundamental being countertransference which will be discussed next, I suggest nevertheless that considering transference can facilitate an appreciation of the need to think about:

- The feelings that are stirred up, particularly in people that are in close relationship with each other/you.

- The degree to which stirred up feelings can be recognised and thought about rather than acted upon.
- The possibility that feelings evoked by people in close relation to each other (child–parent, child–teacher, psychologist–client) may involve a perception of the other that is rooted in earlier/past relationships.

COUNTERTRANSFERENCE

When introducing the concept of transference it is important to link to it an understanding of countertransference. The 'counter' transference seeks to describe the unconscious responses in you that being with a particular client (teacher, child or parent) may evoke. In effect it draws our attention to recognising when an experience of being with someone provokes an emotional response, which stems from your own unconscious emotional life. As such it is helpful to consider countertransference alongside transference in thinking through and reflecting on how you can draw upon the experience of being with clients in developing an understanding of a professional practice situation.

Everyday example 2

Consider a multi-agency meeting in which a child you have worked with is being discussed. You are there to offer psychological insights into the behaviour that school staff are currently finding difficult to manage. It may well be that your work with the young person has given you something to say which you hope will be of use to school staff. However, in the meeting you find yourself becoming irritated by the class teacher's descriptions. It is said that your contribution is valuable yet for some reason that doesn't feel quite true. At this point there is certainly something important going on. While it may, in such a psychologically complex situation, be difficult to think through the psychological dynamics of the experience, it may well be helpful to recognise that the dynamics of transference involving your emotional self are at play as they may well shape your action – for example, making extra suggestions to be helpful, assuming an overly knowing position to assert authority, placating the disgruntled teacher and so on.

We know powerful emotions are incentives to action rather than thought, and thinking about how the embodied emotional experience shapes our perception in unconscious ways is potentially valuable in working with experience. Such work is of a different order to thinking about the experience in a more abstract way, such as 'the way that teacher went on and on really annoyed me' or 'it was frustrating that the meeting ran over'. As such, seeking to sensitise yourself to the influence of unconscious psychological dynamics will require skilled supervision.

CONTAINMENT

Wilfred Bion (1897–1979) at no time defined the concept he introduced in 1959, despite being at his most productive for some time after this. As Bion developed theories of thinking and knowledge (see, e.g., Bion, 1962) he proposed the establishment of a certain type of relationship[3] as crucial for thinking characterised by insight to take place. Such thinking is at the crux of this chapter and Bion used the term containment to explain the character of this relationship.

O'Shaughnessy (1981, p. 181) in reviewing Bion's contribution to the psychoanalytic understanding of thinking offers an appreciation of his work:

> What does Bion mean by 'thinking'? He does not mean some abstract mental process. His concern is with thinking as a human link – the endeavour to understand, comprehend the reality of, get insight into the nature of, etc., oneself or another.

Such a definition presents a particular sort of challenge for those that have studied psychology at various academic levels, particularly when you have moved from such study into practice with children, parents and school-based practitioners. This is because Bion recognises that understanding can invariably be linked to an overintellectual reaching after facts (Keats, 1817, quoted by Bion, 1970, p. 125). This grasping for certainty is often inherent in the demand for psychological services: a demand for a rationale that names and locates the 'problem', often within the child, at times in the family, the classroom or school. While such naming is a necessary prelude to meaningful work, this chapter introduces psychoanalytic concepts with the aim of helping practitioners and would-be practitioners to develop and sustain a capacity to think about the meaning of such problems. This thinking, thinking as a human link, may be one way the critical psychologist may better look after both their clients and themselves.

NOTES

1. The social spaces in which educational and child psychologists practice are diverse in themselves, this being one of the features of community-based practice. They are also generally very different from the clinical space in which psychotherapy or psychoanalysis takes place.
2. Within this chapter psychodynamic and psychoanalytic are terms used interchangeably to refer to theory and practice from the perspective outlined in this chapter.
3. This relationship begin as an external one; that is, between one person and another, or baby and caregiver. Through a process of internalisation the relationship become an internal one, a capacity that a person has to stay in touch with the range of mixed emotions prompted by experience.

REFERENCES

Bion, W.R. (1962). The psycho-analytic study of thinking. *International Journal of Psycho-Analysis, 43*(4–5), 306–310.

Bion, W.R. (1970). *Attention and interpretation.* London: Karnac Books Ltd.

Freud, A. (1937). *The ego and the mechanisms of defense.* London: Hogarth Press/Institute of Psycho-Analysis.

Freud, S. (1938). *Some elementary lessons in psycho-analysis* (standard edn, 23). London: Hogarth Press.

Freud, S. (1940). An outline of psycho-analysis. *The International Journal of Psycho-Analysis, 21,* 27.

Frosh, S. (2002). *Key concepts in psychoanalysis.* London: British Library, Science Reference and Information Services.

Haughton, H. (2003). Introduction. In S. Freud, *The uncanny.* London: Penguin.

Laplanche, J. & Pontalis, J.-B. (1973). *The language of psychoanalysis.* London: Hogarth Press.

Milton, J., Polmear, C. & Fabricius, J. (2011). *A short introduction to psychoanalysis* (2nd edn). London: SAGE.

O'Shaughnessy, E. (1981). A commemorative essay on W.R. Bion's theory of thinking. *Journal of Child Psychotherapy, 7,* 181–192.

Sandler, J., Dare, C. & Holder, A. (1973). *The patient and the analyst: The basis of the psychoanalytic process.* London: Allen & Unwin.

Szasz, T.S. (1963). The concept of transference—I. A logical analysis. *International Journal of Psycho-Analysis, 44,* 432–435.

Part II Ethics and Values in Practice

This part of the book takes seriously ethics as an undergirding concern of practice and intervention. Ethical questions addressed include: How do educational psychologists understand and justify their professional role? In what ways does educational psychology risk constructing conceptions of children through its very practice? What are the ethical challenges and responsibilities of educational psychologists to the individuals that they work with? Can psychology per se – and educational psychology more specifically – ever practise in ethically justifiable ways? Should educational psychology exist and, if so, why?

6 Critical Educational Psychology and Disability Studies: Theoretical, Practical and Empirical Allies

DAN GOODLEY AND TOM BILLINGTON

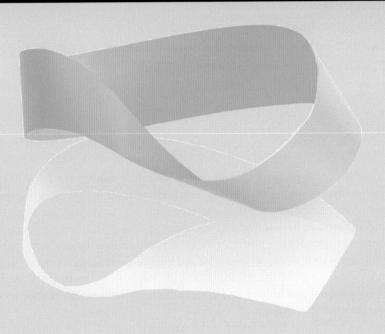

LEARNING OBJECTIVES

After reading this chapter you should be able to:

1. Engage with some overlapping aims of critical disability studies and critical educational psychology.

2. Develop an understanding of the processes of psychologisation and medicalisation.

3. Have some insight into the processes and practices of neoliberal education.

4. Engage with critical psychological and disability studies' emphasis on the impact of the external environment on individual people.

5. Centralise disabled young people at the centre of consideration.

6. Challenge the processes of developmentalism.

This chapter is underpinned by a strong belief on the part of the authors: that critical educational psychology and critical disability studies have much in common and much to share with one another. As we shall demonstrate, the development of *critical* educational psychology and *critical* disability studies heralds a new era of theory, politics and practice. One key task, at least as we see it, is to theorise and engage with the educational opportunities of disabled and/or non-normative children. We argue that there are five areas of alliance for critical educational psychology and disability studies that will support theorisation and contestation of the education of non-normative childhoods. These are:

1. Against psychologisation and medicalisation;
2. Challenging neoliberal education;
3. Contesting interiority and emphasising exteriorities;
4. Placing disabled/non-normative children at the centre of consideration;
5. Illuminating and contesting developmentalism.

INTRODUCTION

Both critical educational psychology and critical disability studies are fairly new, emerging areas of scholarship, research and activism. Yet, each, in their own way, is responding to key problematics of contemporary political and economic life, including the increased labelling of childhood difference; breakdowns in educational and community settings as a consequence of government cuts and austerity measures; and an ever-expanding psychologisation of life that threatens to obscure wider social and economic reasons for personal distress and augment individualised and pathological accounts. We have come to the shared conviction that critical educational psychology and critical disability studies can reinforce one another in contesting these problematics.

Hitherto, the two areas have failed to be explicitly linked. Too often psychology and disability studies have been cast as enemies: the former interested in pathologising difference, the latter engaged with the emancipation of difference (for a discussion, see Goodley & Lawthom, 2005). Such a simplistic binary fails to recognise the main ways in which psychology has always had politicised potential while disability studies has increasingly become more engaged with the register of human life that we might call the psychological. As we shall demonstrate in this chapter, the development of *critical* educational psychology and *critical* disability studies heralds a new era of theory, politics and practice. One key task, at least as we see it, is to theorise and engage with the educational opportunities of disabled and/or non-normative children. We argue that there are five areas of alliance for critical educational psychology and disability studies that will support theorisation and contestation of the education of non-normative childhoods. But first, let us sketch out our transdisciplinary areas of engagement, starting with critical educational psychology.

WHAT IS CRITICAL EDUCATIONAL PSYCHOLOGY?

The need for a critical educational psychology arose as a resistance to particular discourses which came to be accepted as something we know now as 'Psychology'. Despite the work of James (1890) and Dewey (1916, 1938), educational psychology ignored those resources which might lead to more complex models of the individual, the social or the relational. Too often, educational psychology focused on models of learning, narrowly conceived; on analyses of behaviour disconnected from experience; and on essentially asocial individuals, somehow fractured from a human world of others. This led to a preoccupation with the identification of individual young people who could be scrutinised according to crude conceptualisations of difference and in which the quantification or categorisation of difference and disability were used as a means of justifying social exclusion on an industrial scale (Billington, 1996, 2000).

Educational psychology in the 20th century, whether as research or practice, became synonymous with the needs of government. Thus a critical educational psychology became necessary, first, as political resistance (i.e., to the inhuman consequences of particular theories and practices). Second, however, resistance has been necessary on epistemological grounds since the social practices of exclusion and segregation, which educational psychology served to construct, were not the product of science but ideology, the application of crude technologies masquerading as science. In aspiring to a critical educational psychology, however, we ultimately maintain that political commitment but look to move beyond resistance and at the same time encourage a more encompassing and ancient tradition of scientific inquiry and inquisitiveness that transcends an application of an oversimplified Cartesianism (Billington & Williams, 2015).

WHAT IS CRITICAL DISABILITY STUDIES?

> **Reflection point**
>
> In a group of five colleagues each answer the following questions: (1) How do you define disability? (2) How does society tend to understand disability?

Following on from a paper by Goodley (2013), contemporary disability studies occupy and agitate for what Carol Thomas (2007) defines as a transdisciplinary space; breaking boundaries between disciplines, deconstructing professional/lay distinctions and decolonising traditional medicalised views of disability with sociocultural conceptions of disablism. Thomas (2007, p. 73) defines disablism as 'a form of social oppression involving the social imposition of restrictions of activity on people with impairments and the socially engendered undermining of their psycho-emotional well-being'. This definition sits alongside other forms of oppression including hetero/sexism and racism. Indeed, as explained below, the intersectional character of disability is one of a number of reasons why we might conceptualise the contemporary state of the field as critical disability studies. Critical disability studies start with disability but never end with it: disability is the space from which to think through a host of political, theoretical and practical issues that are relevant to all (Goodley, 2011, p. 157), assessing where we have come from, where we are at and where we might be going. For Margrit Shildrick (2009, 2012), critical disability studies rethink the conventions, assumptions and aspirations of research, theory and activism in an age of postmodernity.

Disability studies, at least in Britain, were conceived as a modernist project to challenge capitalist conditions of alienation. Critical disability studies builds on these insights but acknowledges that we are living in a time of complex identity politics, of huge debates around the ethics of care, political and theoretical appeals to the significance of the body, in a climate of economic downturn that is leading yet again to reformulations of what counts as disabled. The variegated nature of critical disability studies theory led Lenny Davis (2002) to confidently define the contemporary field as dismodernist: where disability links together other identities at the moment of reflection. For Davis (2002), disabled people are the ultimate intersectional subject, the universal image, the important modality through which we can understand exclusion and resistance. Indeed, the fact that disability absorbs the fetishised and projected insecurities of the precariously 'able-bodied' suggests that disability studies scholars are in a key position to challenge a host of oppressive practices associated with the dominant hegemony of able society (Goodley, 2014). We would also observe that critical educational psychologists and disability studies scholars occupy the left field of mainstream life because they engage with aspects, elements, labels and conditions of humanity that are often made peripheral and external to the central demands of mainstream able-bodied, neoliberal society. In this sense, then, disability studies and critical educational psychology may work together as natural allies.

CONNECTING THEMES

We will now address the challenge we have set ourselves which is to explore the ways in which critical educational psychology and disability studies provide complementary and additive alliances with one another. One key task, at least in our view, is to theorise and engage with the educational opportunities of disabled and/or non-normative children. Our argument is that there are five areas of alliance for critical educational psychology and disability studies that will support theorisation and contestation of the education of non-normative childhoods.

Reflection point

In what ways do disabled and/or non-normative children pose a challenge to the workings of mainstream educational settings? In your answer focus your discussion on the practices of educational setting rather than the potential difficulties within the child.

Against psychologisation and medicalisation

In many ways one could argue that disability studies is a direct riposte to the dominance and medicalisation and psychologisation in the lives of disabled people.

The word 'disability' hints at something missing either fiscally, physically, mentally or legally (Davis, 2002, p. xiii). To be disabled evokes a marginalised place in society, culture, economics and politics. It is concentrated in some parts of the globe more than others, caused by armed conflict and violence, malnutrition, rising populations, child labour and poverty. Paradoxically, it is increasingly found to be everywhere, due to the exponential rise in the number of psychiatric, administrative and educational labels over the past few decades. The key story being peddled is quite simple: disability is an individual problem, either biological or psychological in origin, and therefore the remit of associated medical and psychological professionals is increased and the tyranny of normality is accentuated. Disability is cast as an essentialist condition (with organic aetiologies); disabled people are treated as objects rather than authors of their own lives; 'person fixing' rather than 'context changing' interventions are preferred; the power of health and social care professionals increased and the tyranny of normality is accentuated. Critical disability studies wheels in to intervene, disrupt, dislodge, deconstruct, shake up and contest the individualisation, psychologisation and medicalisation of disability.

Educational psychology provided a means by which that medicalisation and psychologisation could infiltrate education. Alfred Binet had founded the first French psychological journal, *L'annee Psychologique*, in 1894 following the advent of compulsory schooling for all children in France between the ages of 6 and 14. Binet had been handed a specific problem – to assist the authorities in dealing with the problem of the many children in Parisian schools who did not seem well suited to the new mass system of schooling. Rather than look to the structure of the schools themselves, or indeed the nature of what was being taught, the gaze of the regulators fell on the children – the objects (Binet, 1905).

In the UK, the dominant figure in the first 50 years of educational psychology, from the date of his first appointment in 1913, was Cyril Burt. Quite apart from Burt's apparently fraudulent use of his experimental data (Hearnshaw, 1979; Mackintosh, 2013), there were intriguing personal relationships involved which smoothed the transformation of his personal prejudices into public policy. Burt was a family friend of Francis Galton (1822–1911), whom Burt himself regarded as the 'Father of British Psychology' (Wooldridge, 1997, p. 77), and who was one of the most significant figures in the development of statistical tests for use in the social sciences. Shortly after his cousin, Charles Darwin, published *On the Origin of Species* (1859), Galton published *Hereditary Genius* (1869) which was to become a foundation stone for modern psychology and education and which has influenced generations of psychologists and teachers on both sides of the Atlantic:

> The Galtonian conception of mental ability which Burt embraced contained the notion of innately determined limits, differing from one individual to another…intelligence was, in the broad sense of the term, an intellectual quality…it characterized the cognitive. (Chitty, 2007, pp. 68–69)

Burt's close proximity to Galton's positivist, biological and eugenicist arguments (in support of heritability and of a very particular kind of fixed intelligence measured against statistical calibrations of the *normal*) provided the epistemological foundations for psychology in 20th-century UK education.

> **Reflection point**
>
> What was the eugenics movement?

It is testimony to the virulence but also the value of those concepts to government that, despite the accusations against Burt, attempts to rehabilitate his work have continued (Eysenck, 1969; Jensen, 1969), which invariably seem effectively to air-brush:

1. Burt's reductionist and scientifically inadequate conceptualisation of intelligence;
2. His concentration on a biological hereditability as the single most important variable (even to the exclusion of all others); and
3. What we would now regard as the innately racist, sexist and ableist assumptions and consequences of his theories.

However, the die had been cast and that idiosyncratic manifestation of psychology which sought to mimic the experimental methods of a singularly positivist application of a medical science was thus to achieve a preferred status in education too and the conditions were thus in place for a 'perfect storm':

- Capitalised conditions for living;
- The creation of mass schooling on an industrial scale;
- The adoption of positivist methods, which had been honed in the physical or material sciences, to investigate the human.

Some children were not going to stand a chance.

Challenging neoliberal education

Contemporary researchers in critical disability studies and critical educational psychology engage proactively with the work of inclusive educators. One of the biggest challenges to the inclusion of disabled and non-normative children in everyday educational and community settings is the dominance of neoliberal thinking within these contexts. It is now commonly accepted that neoliberalism refers to monetary and trade policies of a pro-corporate free-market economy that has dominated Western European and North American economic and cultural politics and global markets since the early 1980s (Richardson, 2005). The state is 'rolled back', unproductive welfare spending is reduced and public services and social provisions are increasingly taken over by, or aligned with the principles of, business. Public entitlements such as welfare and education have become dismantled through alliance with market freedom and the essence of the Washington consensus, the driving force of global progression and the deregulation of the market. It is linked to a context of austerity; a change of economic context in which countries have to compete internationally and economic rationality overtakes social welfare reform (Rizvi & Lingard, 1996, p. 13). The individual consumer and family unit constitute key sites for private welfare. Neoliberal philosophies are enshrined in the aims of supranational organisations such as the World Bank, the World Health Organization (WHO) and the Organisation for Economic Co-operation and Development (OECD). As Vislie (2003) observes, the OECD represents 30 of the richest, highest income countries, all of which espouse the virtues of Western democracy and the principles of the free market. When these same countries are behind OECD initiatives around inclusive education, questions are raised about the nature of education that is sanctioned and the conditions that are placed on other, poorer countries to enact such educational philosophies. Democracy has now been reduced to a metaphor of the 'free market' (Giroux, 2004, p. 35).

Neoliberal education at its most seemingly benign calls on common standards, assessment and accountability of schools and teachers to pupils and parents. At their most damaging, these values are characterised by shrinking resources and schools are pulled into the competitive marketplace where productivity and accountability (to consumers and government assessment bodies) are paramount. We see too the application of increasingly more stringent academic criteria and higher standards of education, narrowing of curriculum and an increase in educational testing and assessment (Jung, 2002). This 'McDonaldisation of education' (surveillance, testing, targeting, performativity and marketisation, according to Gabel & Danforth, 2008) has led to a splintering of teacher unions and an erosion of morality. In the context of neoliberalism, services are no longer regarded as a civic or human right but as commodities for consumers. The common good equates with free competition, consumer power and profitability (Rizvi & Lingard, 1996, pp. 14–15).

> ### Reflection point
>
> Visit the following website to read the article: http://truth-out.org/opinion/item/12126-can-democratic-education-survive-in-a-neoliberal-society Tease out three key points of the argument.

Schools are high-pressure places; they are subjected to league tables, the children to endless SATs, the teachers to inspection. Curricula are nationalised, allowing comparison between schools, teachers and pupils, and are focused on science, maths and literacy: key requirements of capitalist economies. The major concern for activists of inclusive education relates to the misfit between the ambitions of neoliberalism and disability politics. The latter emphasises belonging, acceptance, community support and interdependence. The former promotes individual achievement, academic excellence and aggressive independence. All children are expected to flourish in the neoliberal school through to accommodation, assimilation and integration: in short they are expected to fit into existing schooling arrangements. In contrast, inclusive education demands educators to rethink education and disability. As Slee (1997, p. 412) puts it: 'Are we talking about where children are placed and with what level of resource provision? Or, are we talking about the politics of value, about the purpose and content of curriculum, and about the range and conduct of pedagogy?'

Inclusion is therefore a response to special education, an integration in which children with special educational needs (SEN) are understood as comprising a group constituted by a 'bureaucratic device for dealing with the complications arising from clashes between narrow waspish curricula and disabled students' (Slee, 1997, p. 412). Inclusive education:

- Is a process by which a school attempts to respond to all pupils as individuals;
- Regards inclusion and exclusion as connected processes; schools developing more inclusive practices may need to consider both;
- Emphasises overall school effectiveness;
- Is of relevance to all phases and types of schools, possibly including special schools, since within any educational provision teachers face groups of students with diverse needs and are required to respond to this diversity. (Vislie, 2003, p. 21)

However, in a world of fast-changing technologies, it will soon presumably occur to government to question whether schools are indeed the most efficient manner of executing a system of mass education which is, let's face it, little more than a hundred years old. There had been two important drivers for the development of mass schooling in the UK from 1800 onwards: first, economic concerns, with advocates emphasising that education should be technological and provide an 'introduction in reading, writing and arithmetic' (Peel, 1802); second, moral concerns, with its proponents seeking to minimise their feelings of disgust at the ways in which children were suffering those economic demands and circumstances – children who, often as young as six to eight years, were forced into 'labour [which] was so excessive that it took away all opportunity of moral and mental improvement' (*Hansard*, 1832, June).

In contemplating what an education system might be like John Dewey (1859–1952) provided a model for liberal, progressive education and he took a particular kind of psychology into the classroom, one which emphasised individual experience but also broader moral, social and human concerns (Dewey, 1916). Dewey emphasised the importance of community in his classrooms, and his progressive spirit remains alive today – just. Paulo Freire's (1972) more piercing educational and political critique, however, directed us away from the individual and towards a more community-based social activism.

Contesting interiority and emphasising exteriorities

> The science of relationships has yet to be established. (Bion, 1970, p. 53)

It is precisely in the materiality of the exchanges between, for example, teachers and young people that something unique about the importance of relations in learning is revealed. Kenneth Gergen assembled a huge array of collaborators in constructing his challenge to what he termed *bounded being*. Drawing on Vygotsky's challenge to the 'dominant view of isolated minds', he envisaged a 'process of relational flow' which, informed by Bakhtinian linguistic analyses, linked to the Deweyan tradition that 'the cultivated mind was essentially a social mind' (Gergen, 2009, pp. xviii, 46, 242). Gergen begins to reconstruct his arguments in such a way that the theorisations become accessible and relevant to practitioners not only across mental health but across education too, sharing with Dewey and Bruner the belief that 'the primary aim of education is to enhance the potentials for participating in relational processes...that can ultimately contribute to the continuing and expanding flow of relationships within the world more broadly' (Gergen, 2009, p. 243).

Gergen makes the case for the fundamental importance of relationships and, in particular, the importance of our relationships in education. He critiques the legacy of a Cartesian model of scientific practice as applied to human beings; for example, in challenging its implications for how we relate to individuals, its assumptions concerning simplistic, linear understandings of cause and effect. Instead, he constructs a hypothesis which generates challenges to that notion of 'bounded being' in all conceivable situations and makes his arguments relevant to professional practice. He suggests a model of relationally embodied action, in which 'knowledge emerges from the process of co-action', and uses this understanding of a mutuality of engagement to challenge the traditional positivist methods employed by the physical sciences to say anything at all about our psychological selves: 'biology tells us nothing about what psychological states, if any, are related to psychological activity' (Gergen, 2009, pp. 138, xxviii, 116). He thus proposes an education whose aims should be revisited 'in a relational key' (see Gergen, 2009, pp. 240–269).

Gergen takes us from a Cartesian model of 'bounded being' towards a model of the person which is conceptualised by the term 'multi-being' and in which our potentials are not considered as primarily 'biological but social' (Gergen, 2009. pp. 134, 139). The terrain being mapped in Gergen's thesis is one of social engagement in which all everyday ideas, feelings and actions are constructed not in isolation but always in relation to the world of others. We achieve together with, and because of, others and crucially for our work in critical educational psychology and critical disability studies, Gergen suggests that all 'disorder' is created socially within our cultural situatedness in ways that he describes as 'crippling' (Gergen, 2009, p. 278).

Critical disability studies and inclusive education merge meaningfully around the question of register. When we are thinking about promoting inclusion the collectivist registers of community, relationships and teacher–learner engagement are evoked over the more individualistic registers of cognition, psychological well-being, intelligence. Following Wedell (2008, p. 131), in this collectivist community, a child's learning problem becomes a teacher's teaching problem. Jarman (2008) suggests that a feminist ethics of care approach complements a disability studies perspective in that support, teaching, facilitation and guidance are refigured in terms of their emotionality, mutuality and interdependence (see also McLaughlin et al., 2008).

Reflection point

Review an informal introduction to the ethics of care literature by visiting the following Wikipedia entry: http://en.wikipedia.org/wiki/Ethics_of_care

Wedell (2008) suggests that the issue for inclusion is not about treating everyone the same but treating everyone equally. The label of SEN is considered primarily as the means to access support that increases the meaning of education for pupils rather than simply being a commodity that is exploited and used by an ever-growing panoply of professionals. But, in line with Apple's (1982) stance, teachers become more in tune with the kinds of relationships that already exist – and work – in the 'hidden curricula' of pupils, promoting a horizontal pedagogy.

A personal anecdote

In school, 7-year-old Danny has social and emotional behaviour difficulties, ADHD and dyslexia. The educational psychologist has advised that Danny has 'wrap around support'. A support worker is with him all day, every day, even when he visits the washrooms. At the end of each day, it has been decided that Danny must wait in a separate room, until the other children have collected their coats and school bags. The school fears Danny might harm one of his classmates. When the other children have finally spilled out into the playground to their waiting parents and childminders, and then left the playground, Danny is then allowed to leave the school. Each day, every day, Danny and Mum leave the school grounds alone. Meanwhile, to his classmates Danny is…? Rosa says: 'He is naughty, sometimes. He pulls my hair'. But he is also 'funny Danny, he makes us laugh. He is good at football. He's good at sorting things out when my friends argue. Can he come to my birthday party, Dad?'

Reflection point

What does the above anecdote tell you about (1) the practices of schools and (2) the values of children and young people?

Inclusive education might involve working alongside pupils as agents of their own learning, permitting more 'unruly' behaviour (like that of Danny) to be permitted while not violating the rights of other children. This contrasts with the vertical model of teaching – the technical/administrative style of pedagogy that is actually more in keeping with the style of management in corporate organisations (Apple, 1982, p. 34). Critical pedagogies are also caring pedagogies. This may well involve elucidating those everyday happenings that constitute social justice: caring, reciprocity in the educational relationship, ordinariness, extraordinariness, intuition and personal shared understandings between the agents of pedagogy. It also involves accepting and facilitating 'becomings' rather than beings. Is Danny allowed 'to become' in the company of his peers like Rosa? Or is he always 'being': a difficult, deficient, SEN being? Inclusive schools require all their staff to be trained to support children with labels of SEN and disability. This would include inclusive education and disability studies being key elements of teaching training programmes. Moreover, the actual professional role of teachers and their teaching assistants might be recast in more embracing ways. As Ferri (2008) argues in relation to Italian education, the 1971 legislation specified the rights of disabled children to be educated in regular classes, making Italy a model of inclusive education, according to UNESCO and OECD. There is now 99% inclusion of disabled students. Key to this inclusion has been the role of the *sostegno*, a teaching position equivalent to teacher dual certificate in the USA, who works for the class not the individual, modifying the curriculum where needed. They consider the classroom as a family or community and address whole class issues not just a specific population (Ferri, 2008). This approach to teaching and learning is what Wedell (2008, p. 134) defines as 'co-production – treating everyone equally but not necessarily the same'.

Placing disabled/non-normative children at the centre of consideration

One of the key contributions of critical disability studies has been to the social and educational research literature. Indeed, one could argue that disability scholars have, on one hand, been among the most vocal critics of positivistic social science while, on the other hand, advocated for the use of post-positivistic research encounters including action research, participatory methodologies and qualitative forms of analysis. As an example, in Banister et al. (2011) disability studies emerges as one of the guiding voices – alongside feminist and Marxist analyses – towards politicised qualitative research approaches. Such an emphasis on storytelling and subjectivity, the co-production of research with our participants and the importance of the researcher's positionality in relation to the subject matter and object of research, has huge implications for how we theorise, research and understand disabled and/ or non-normative children. For example, in a study centred around the experiences of families with disabled babies and young children, McLaughlin and colleagues heard numerous stories from families about disability. Here is one:

> If there were a magic pill, that could 'cure' Roberto of his disabilities, I'm not at all sure that I'd want him to have it. His disabilities are part of him. If you took them away, Roberto would no longer be Roberto. He wouldn't be my child any more…if I had another child like Roberto I wouldn't change that neither (Helen, mother). (McLaughlin et al., 2008, p. 132)

> **Reflection point**
>
> How would you explain Helen's response?

Narratives may be used in resistant ways in order to challenge dominant discourses that exist around particular objects and subjects. Indeed, as Allport and Postman (1947, p. 40) observed, it is possible to trace social progress in relation to the deployment of vivid stories of personal experience. The historical, creative and analytical elements of story can combine to shift thinking. In the case of Helen she reminds us of the complexities associated with children that exist behind the simplistic tendencies of childhood labels. Her story demands that we put children first, above psychological complexes.

> where children are able to talk more openly about the processes of change that affect their lives they are more likely to develop coping strategies themselves. This has been seen as a major contributor to resilience in childhood. (Dowling & Barnes, 1985, p. 67)

An important feature of narrative research and practice is that it 'respects each individual story and whatever shape of life that emerges...' (Parker, 2005, p. 72). However, it is not merely individuals who are at the centre of analysis: it is the contexts in which particular kinds of narratives can emerge that are important; for example, in the relationships between young people and their teachers or, indeed, educational psychologists.

Narrative lies at the core of our lives and is central to the ways in which children learn to think, feel and learn in the form of the stories, which they see others construct about them and which they construct about themselves. Rather than construct stories of deficit *about* children, it is incumbent upon us to work *with* the young people and the adults in their lives to engage in their own 'preferred stories' (White & Epston, 1990). As part of that process it will be important to bear in mind three *critical distinctions*:

> Between a diagnosis and a child,
> between a knowledge of children generally and our interpretations of the child before us,
> between any descriptions of the child we construct and the descriptions the child might potentially construct for themselves. (Billington, 2006, p. 158)

Illuminating and contesting developmentalism

In recent years, qualitative research studies have become increasingly sophisticated in their attempts to represent the human (e.g., Parker, 2005; Burman, 2008a; Willig & Stainton Rogers, 2008; Banister et al., 2011). Much of this activity has been influenced by debates originating in philosophy and spreading throughout the social sciences, in particular focusing on language (e.g., Wittgenstein, 1961 [1921]) and connected to analyses of knowledge and power (Foucault, 2002 [1969]). Such approaches to qualitative research were a response to a dissatisfaction with a paradigmatic hegemony (positivism) which ultimately was incapable of detecting its own unscientific tendencies. The hitherto positivist inclinations of much research in the social sciences in the 20th century are now being challenged and doubts emerging as to its claims to truth when applied to human processes and situations; we need a 'qualitative psychology...[which has] its place in the project of trying to make psychology more scientific' (Harré, 2004, p. 4).

Approaches to qualitative psychology have exposed the ways in which development discourses and developmental psychology have allowed capitalised economic structures to penetrate lives through a focus on the individual as the prime target of governmentality. In performance of its duties, developmental psychology focused on the measurement of difference as opposed to an exploration of quality which, of course, would provide a completely different basis for study, not merely of learning but of the human.

Both William James and Henri Bergson were interested in the kinds of human inquiry which were less amenable to measurement and were critical of attempts to apply such techniques in situations for which it was clearly ill-equipped: 'Physics, whose particular function it is to calculate the external cause of our internal states, takes the least possible interest in those states themselves...' (Bergson, 2001 [1913], p. 70). Bergson continued his own distinctive critique of the dangers inherent in the mis-application of positivist methods and pinpointed a fundamental error: 'the moment was inevitably bound to come at which science, familiarised with this confusion between quantity and quality, between sensation and stimulus, should seek to measure one as it measures the other...' (Bergson, 2001 [1913], p. 71). Our consciousness, our minds are beyond simple measurement. This, of course, reveals difficulties should we accept rather than challenge developmental discourses which are, at root, dependent solely or primarily on a quantitative assessment of what it is to be human.

Reflection point

Outline up to six cognitive, behavioural and emotional indicators of development comparing primary and secondary school children. In what ways might we argue that these indicators are a product of the society in which we live?

Critical disability studies, neoliberal conceptions of education and the neoliberal child find their way into the subjectivities of children, parents and professionals. As Burman (2008b, p. 50) notes, parents worry about 'whether our child is doing well enough, is developing at the right pace, is "going through the milestones correctly"'. This not only isolates each mother and treats her as the originator or responsible agent of the 'problem' but also sets her in competition with other mothers. Education and citizenship are closely related. Questions arise about the restricted image of the 'ideal citizen' that the norms of developmentalism embody (Baker, 2002, p. 688). Developmentalism is wedded to the structure of schooling and provides a restricted image of the ideal citizen/learner. In contrast, following Burman (2008b), disabled children are deemed to be appalling (so to be excluded) and appealing (so to be an endless source of fascination) and this 'disavowal of children' lies at the heart of debates about the inclusion of disabled children. There is a cultural imperative to fit in, under the rubric of normality, to strive to be normal (Davis, 2002). Marks (1999, pp. 170–171) mischievously draws our attention to the psychoanalytic idea of 'normotic illness' developed by Bollas (1987). Individuals with this 'illness' are abnormally normal [sic]: overly stable, secure, comfortable and socially extravert; ultrarational, objective, lacking imagination and empathy. But normotic illness might be seen more correctly as the logical subjectivity of neoliberal education: hyper-normal rather than normal. This point is developed further by Harwood and Hymphry (2008) who suggest that a new norm is emerging in the Global North. Parents are no longer worrying about whether or not their child is normal – they are becoming interested and anxious about whether or not their children are 'exceptional' or 'gifted and talented'. This heightened sense of normality is not only exclusionary to those disabled and marginalised children it leaves behind; it also fans the flames of competition, assessment and testing around all children. Critical disability studies may function as a necessary antidote to the ubiquitous nature of developmentalism. It can intervene to ask: Where does this seemingly naturalised process come from? Who benefits from developmentalism? To what extent is the progress of global capitalism and economic progression marked in a more singular way on the body of the 'normatively developing child'?

CONCLUSIONS AND FUTURE CONNECTIONS

In this chapter, we have considered a number of overlapping themes that demonstrate the potential for alliance between critical approaches to educational psychology and disability studies. We believe that not only can each approach feed into one another but, at the same time, they can contest and challenge the assumptions at play. Hence we might ask if a focus exclusively on disability might ignore wider processes of ableism that require our attention (Goodley, 2014). We might also ask of educational psychology whether an overreliance on the disciplinary location of psychology will always, inevitably, limit the politics of one's criticality. How each approach morphs and changes will be interesting to observe: what we urgently need now, in the name of education, children and learning communities, is a continued debate between critical disability studies and critical educational psychology.

ACKNOWLEDGEMENT

Dan would like to thank Sage for giving permission to draw on Chapter 9 of Goodley (2011) for this paper © 2011 Sage Publications.

REFERENCES

Allport, G.W. & Postman, L.J. (1947). *The psychology of rumor*. New York: Holt, Rinehart & Winston.

Apple, M. (1982). *Education and power*. Boston: Routledge & Kegan Paul.

Baker, B. M. (2002). The hunt for disability: The new eugenics and the normalization of schoolchildren. *Teachers College Record*, *104*, 663–703.

Banister, P., Bunn, G., Burman, E., Daniels, J., Duckett, P., Goodley, D., … & Whelan, P. (2011). *Qualitative methods in psychology. A research guide* (2nd edn). London: McGraw-Hill.

Bergson, H. (2001 [1913]) *Time and free will: An essay on the immediate data of consciousness*. New York: Dover Publications.

Billington, T. (1996). Pathologizing children: Psychology in education and acts of government. In E. Burman et al. (Eds.), *Psychology discourse practice: From regulation to resistance*. London: Taylor & Francis.

Billington, T. (2000). *Separating, losing and excluding children: Narratives of difference*. London: Routledge Falmer.

Billington, T. (2006). *Working with children: Assessment, representation and intervention*. London: Sage.

Billington, T. & Williams, A. (2015). Education and psychology: Change at last? In I. Parker (Ed.), *Handbook of critical psychology*. London: Routledge.

Binet, A. (1905). New methods for the diagnosis of the intellectual level of subnormals. *L'année Psychologique*, *12*, 191–244.

Bion, W. (1970). *Attention and interpretation*. London: Karnac Books.

Bollas, C. (1987). *The shadow of the object: Psychoanalysis of the unthought known*. London: Free Association Press.

Burman, E. (2008a). *Deconstructing developmental psychology* (2nd edn). Hove: Routledge.

Burman, E. (2008b). *Developments: Child, image, nation*. London: Routledge.

Chitty, C. (2007). *Eugenics, race and intelligence in education*. London: Continuum.

Darwin, C. (1859). *On the origin of species*. London: John Murray.

Davis, L.J. (2002). *Bending over backwards. Disability, dismodernism and other difficult positions*. New York: New York University Press.

Dewey, J. (1916). *Democracy and education: An introduction to the philosophy of education*. New York: The Macmillan Company.

Dewey, J. (1938). *Experience and education*. New York: Collier Books.

Dowling, E. & Barnes, C. (1985). *The family and the school: A joint systems approach to problems with children*. London: Routledge & Kegan Paul.

Eysenck, H.J. (1969). The rise of mediocracy. In C.B. Cox & A.E. Dyson (Eds.), *Black paper two: The crisis in education* (pp. 34–40). London: The Critical Quarterly Society.

Ferri, B.A. (2008). Inclusion in Italy: What happens when everyone belongs. In S. Gabel & S. Danforth (Eds.), *Disability and the international politics of education* (pp. 41–52). New York: Peter Lang.

Foucault, M. (2002 [1969]). *The archaeology of knowledge*. Trans. A.M. Sheridan Smith. London and New York: Routledge

Freire, P. (1972). *Pedagogy of the oppressed*. Harmondsworth: Penguin.

Gabel, S. & Danforth, S. (2008). Foreword. In S. Gabel & S. Danforth (Eds.), *Disability and the international politics of education* (pp. i–ix). New York: Peter Lang.

Galton, F. (1869). *Hereditary genius: An inquiry into its laws and consequences*. London: Macmillan.

Gergen, K.J. (2009). *Relational being: Beyond self and community*. New York: Oxford University Press.

Giroux, H. (2004). Critical pedagogy and the postmodern/modern divide: Towards a pedagogy of democratisation. *Teacher Education Quarterly, Winter*, 31–47.

Goodley, D. (2011). *Disability studies: An interdisciplinary introduction*. London: Sage.

Goodley, D. (2013). Dis/entangling critical disability studies. *Disability & Society, 28*(5), 631–644.

Goodley, D. (2014). *Dis/ability studies*. London: Routledge.

Goodley, D. & Lawthom, R. (Eds.) (2005). *Disability and psychology: Critical introductions and reflections*. London: Palgrave.

Hansard (1803–2005). Online at http://hansard.millbanksystems.com/sittings/1832/ (accessed 29 May 2016).

Harré, R. (2004). Staking our claim for qualitative psychology as science. *Qualitative Research in Psychology, 1*, 3–14.

Harwood, V. & Humphreys, N. (2008). Taking exception: Discourses of exceptionality and the invocation of the ideal. In S. Gabel & S. Danforth (Eds.), *Disability and the politics of education: An international reader* (pp. 371–384). New York: Peter Lang.

Hearnshaw, L. (1979). *Cyril Burt: Psychologist*. London: Hodder & Stoughton.

James, W. (1890). *Principles of psychology*. London: Macmillan.

Jarman, M. (2008). Disability studies ethics: Theoretical approaches for the undergraduate classroom. *Review of Disability Studies, 4*, 5–13.

Jensen, A.R. (1969). How much can we boost IQ and scholastic achievement? *Harvard Educational Review, 39*(1), 1–123.

Jung, K.E. (2002). Chronic illness and educational equity: The politics of visibility. *NWSA Journal, 14*(3), 178–200.

Mackintosh, N.J. (2013). The Burt affair: 40 years on. Perspectives on Sir Cyril Burt and 100 years of British educational psychology. Special edition, *Education and Child Psychology, 30*(3), 13–32.

Marks, D. (1999). *Disability: Controversial debates and psychosocial perspectives.* London: Routledge.

McLaughlin, J., Goodley, D., Clavering, E. & Fisher, P. (2008). *Families raising disabled children: Enabling care and social justice.* London: Palgrave.

Parker, I. (2005). *Qualitative psychology: Introducing radical research.* Maidenhead: Open University / McGraw-Hill.

Peel, R. (1802). *Health and Morals of Apprentices Act.* Online at http://www.parliament.uk/about/living-heritage/transformingsociety/livinglearning/19thcentury/overview/earlyfactorylegislation/ (accessed 13 November 2013).

Richardson, D. (2005). Desiring sameness? The rise of neoliberal politics of normalization. *Antipode, 37*(3), 515–535.

Rizvi, F. & Lingard, B. (1996). Disability, education and the discourses of justice. In C. Christensen & F. Rizvi (Eds.), *Disability and the dilemmas of education and justice* (pp. 9–26). Buckingham: Open University Press.

Shildrick, M. (2009). *Dangerous discourses of disability, subjectivity and sexuality.* London: Palgrave Macmillan.

Shildrick, M. (2012). Critical disability studies: Rethinking the conventions for the age of postmodernity. In N. Watson, A. Roulstone & C. Thomas (Eds.), *Routledge handbook of disability studies.* London: Routledge.

Slee, R. (1997). Imported or important theory? Sociological interrogations of disablement and special education. *British Journal of Sociology of Education, 18*(3), 407–419.

Thomas, C. (2007). *Sociologies of disability, 'impairment', and chronic illness: Ideas in disability studies and medical sociology.* London: Palgrave.

Vislie, L. (2003). From integration to inclusion: Focusing global trends and changes in the Western European societies. *European Journal of Special Needs Education, 18*, 17–35.

Wedell, K. (2008). Confusion about inclusion: Patching up or system change? *British Journal of Special Education, 35*(3), 127–135.

White, M. & Epston, D. (1990). *Narrative means to therapeutic ends.* New York: Norton.

Willig, C. & Stainton Rogers, W. (Eds.) (2008). *Handbook of qualitative research in psychology.* London: Sage.

Wittgenstein, L. (1961 [1921]). *Tractatus logico-philosophicus.* Trans. D. Pears & B. McGuinness. London: Routledge & Kegan Paul.

Wooldridge, A. (1997). *Measuring the mind: Education and psychology in England, c.1860–c.1990.* Cambridge: Cambridge University Press.

LEARNING OBJECTIVES

After reading this chapter you should be able to:

1. Reflect on the meaning of 'ethics' and what the term 'professional ethics' means to you.

2. Examine critically the role of published codes of ethics and conduct.

3. Consider why professional psychologists might behave 'unethically'.

In our secular and culturally relativist society, discussion of the framework of values within which we act, of the moral indicators of our behaviour, and of the dispositions of character that drive our actions, seems to lag behind the drive for pragmatic solutions to problem solving and target setting in a climate of financial austerity.

Psychology as a discipline embraces the need for evidence-based practices, robust methodologies and peer review, but does it also reflect sufficiently critically on its own theories of knowledge? On its susceptibility to being hijacked by certain dominant politicised educational and medical discourses? On its own contribution to the maintenance of existing frameworks of power and governance?

Can a discussion of ethics contribute to the conversation about what is a critical psychology?

The problem with this apparently innocuous question lies in the word 'ethics' itself. Can ethics be defined – or, rather, which of the multiplicity of definitions available do we personally adhere to, if any? Whose ethics? What ethics? What is it to be an ethically aware practitioner?

Although deriving from different classical roots, 'ethical' and 'moral' are terms frequently used interchangeably. All of us are called upon to make moral decisions in life and ethics is a branch of moral philosophy. It is, very broadly, the rational, systematic and critical study of how we ought to live and why; the pursuit of the 'good' on all levels ranging from the individual 'good life' to the governance of an institution or society.

If ethical practices rest on beliefs and values about what it is right to do, then are they temporally, culturally and societally relative? Different cultures, societies and historical eras have different conceptions of right and wrong, of how we should act. Does the lack of universally accepted belief systems preclude, therefore, any debate about core values and whether, in spite of differences in customs and beliefs, there may be commonalities in the kind of values we hold, the role of the 'good' in how we live and, professionally, how we should act?

PROFESSIONAL CODES OF ETHICS AND CONDUCT

In the years after World War II, following documented atrocities in which doctors and psychologists alike had participated, psychological societies and professional associations attempted to impose standards through the development of normative codes of practice or codes of ethics and conduct. Academic and practitioner psychologists have since contributed a voluminous body of literature and research on the subject. However, those original codes have since been rewritten many times. A comparison of the first code of the American Psychological Association produced in 1954 with its latest publication attests to ethical norms that have changed to reflect the prevailing narratives of the era. Tubbs and Pomerantz (2001), for example, found that there was a need to assess ethical norms frequently, given that they found different prevalences in behaviours of varying ethical appropriateness over a mere 14 year timespan. Codes of ethics have been developed by the professional psychological associations of Europe, North America and worldwide, with the production in

Europe of a cross-national metacode (2005) to which all member organisations are expected to have regard when drawing up their own national ethical codes (Lindsay et al., 2008). The European Federation of Psychologists Associations (EFPA) oversees the ethical codes of its member associations (in the UK, the British Psychological Society) by ensuring that individual national codes of ethics adhere to certain fundamental principles. These principles are *respect*, *responsibility*, *competence* and *integrity*. Educational psychologists work especially closely with teachers, who have their own professional 'Teachers' Standards' (DfE, 2011).

So is that how psychologists decide what is ethical? Do we adhere to the ethical norms, to the latest consensual validation of our profession, as set out in the codes of ethics and conduct, and periodically adjust our behaviour whenever these codes are amended in the light of societal value shifts? The biomedical framework of practice, where internal review boards or professional committees monitor ethical performance, is the most prevalent. A code is both a point of reference for practitioners and the basis for the accumulation of 'case law' – that is, an attempt to determine the correct response to an ethical dilemma by drawing parallels with previously agreed cases. For heterogeneous groupings of people, whose only common bond might be the profession they practise, this has the advantage that agreement on any specific metatheory of ethics is not required in order for policy to be determined. Codes illuminate the desirable relationships expected between practitioners and clients, researchers and the researched, and between professionals in their relationships with each other. Codes can protect the interests of the researched against the interests of the researchers and can guide and protect the psychologist faced with resolving both individual and institutional ethical dilemmas.

SO WHAT'S THE PROBLEM?

These codes enshrine a wide range of ideas taken from across history: they embody Western liberal post-Enlightenment concepts such as human rights, individual autonomy, equality and social inclusion. These derive from a potpourri of beliefs deriving from utilitarian philosophies; Kantian (1995) influences in the formulation of the 'categorical imperative' to 'treat humanity in your own person and in others always as an end and never only as a means'; and may incorporate elemental notions of virtue theory in exhorting practitioners to exercise integrity, beneficence, trustworthiness and other qualities of character. In other words, codes of ethics are artefacts grounded in a historical narrative; they have predecessors and will have as yet unknown successors.

As professional codes are usually and necessarily general rather than specific in nature (since they cannot foresee every ethical problem that might arise), their application in specific situations is left for the psychologist to resolve. How this happens will be discussed below.

If we look at professional codes of ethics through a critical psychological lens, we might observe that codes do not of themselves protect either clients and the objects of research, or the integrity of the profession, because individuals are motivated to act, for better or worse, by more than any systems imposed by exterior bodies.

Interpretation of the codes can depend on the particular worldview of the individual practitioner, the members of the review board, or ethics committee. In the case of the latter, a legalistic or institutional approach to ethical practice, with its tendency to box ticking and defensive practice, may shift the emphasis away from applied ethical practice by the practitioner towards rule making and rule observing. The existence of codes and committees should not obviate the need for reflective vigilance. This is essential with regard to the regulation of the shifting balance of power within discourse; the potential for abuse of rights that exists in all relationships; but, in particular, in the relationships between client and practitioner, researched and researcher.

Anonymity

In seeking to research the voices of young people in a research project, a trainee psychologist completes a university ethical review application form with the standard assurances of anonymity for all participants, and the application duly passes the review board. Subsequently, the young people researched[1] request that their real names be used in the write-up, as they are proud of their contribution and want their names included in the publication. The young people are 'persuaded' to agree to pseudonyms because the ethical 'rule' is that research participants should not be identified and the trainee psychologist then publishes the paper under his or her own name only.

Reflection point

We commonly use the phrase 'political correctness'. Is 'ethical correctness' the new hegemony? Will the young people in the vignette consider that they have been treated ethically? The institution of the university, for perfectly well-intentioned reasons designed to protect research participants in general, has overruled, in the name of their own ethical research practice guidelines, the wishes of these particular willing participants to have their real names published, and has imposed its own condition that their names should be anonymised, taking advantage of its power vis-à-vis the participants. In the three-way tension that can exist between the personal ethical standards with which people enter a profession, institutionalised codes of practice and the expressed wishes of participants (the subjects or objects of research), whose wishes should be followed? A power relationship is thus laid bare.

ETHICS AND POWER

The pursuit of professional expertise can be compared to the colonial settler doctrine of *terra nullius* where, just as the first colonists to cultivate a land could claim possession of it, dispossessing the indigenous population, so researchers and psychologists access information and intellectual property and claim ownership of it, dispossessing the original participants of their joint ownership; for example, see Meskell and Pels (2005).

Hegemonic power relations can militate against reflection on first principles and against ethical scientific and therapeutic practices by dominating the professional discourse. In assuming the power to decide for themselves what is and is not ethical, without negotiation with the client or the researched, professional committees and individuals can perpetuate power differentials. Apparent adherence to an ethical code cannot per se protect the client or the researched from coercive practices.

Similarly, a lack of negotiation can maintain the relationship between practitioner and client, or researcher and researched, in dyadic terms, thereby maintaining a presupposed distinction between the expert and the lay person (i.e., the ability of the former to produce propositions which are more valid than those of the latter). In the practice of a critical psychology, ethical decisions would be negotiated between parties, thus implying a redefinition of the locus of expertise and power relationship.

One of the dangers of professional codification of ethics can lie in the loss of the dynamic process of debate and the potential fossilisation of an ethical code as a rule-based instrument that exists to impose the consensual standards of the institution on those who are the mere clients or objects of research. As such, ethical authority can be usurped by institutions and practice and research judged accordingly.

The question was asked earlier in the chapter: What can a discussion of ethics contribute to the conversation about what is a critical psychology? Critical psychology practice and research offers an ethical lens onto bodies of knowledge and into areas of institutional ethical authority. It revitalises the dynamic process of problematising existing concepts dependent on the medicalisation and categorisation of childhood, one example being in the debate surrounding the biopsychosocial nature of childhood diagnoses such as attention deficit hyperactivity disorder (ADHD). It similarly considers those ethical issues which emerge in a political climate of financial austerity, child poverty and swingeing changes to schools and medical services. However, there are pressures to accept prevailing codes of governance and it can require not only critical reflection but also the virtue of courage to resist hegemonic power relationships.

A critical psychological approach would also permit challenges to routine application of codes of ethics and expose the complexity of ethical dilemmas faced by individual educational psychologists. It would not accept a restricted view of ethics as limited to conventional proscriptions but support standards that induce proactive behaviour to avoid ethical lapses of omission. It would be alert against a psychology which designs ethical codes and guidelines merely for the defence and protection of itself as an institution rather than for the benefit of those people who are the recipients of our practice.

There may be occasions when, in full cognisance of an ethical code, a psychologist may decide to act otherwise than in accordance with one or more of its principles if to do so would address the jointly negotiated best interests of the client. Dancy (2004), for example, argues that the possibility of ethical thought and judgement does not rest necessarily on the assumptions of predetermined principles to which practitioners and researchers subscribe. He advocates a position whereby it can be ethical to eschew the principles approach to being a moral agent (i.e., having ethical principles which necessitate a 'prima facie' duty to behave in a certain way) in favour of a particularist approach whereby one might have a 'duty proper' to do what is considered right in a particular instance.

When institutional requirements, such as for empirically supported interventions, begin to infiltrate ethical frameworks, some recognised or innovative psychological practices may become stifled, marginalised or considered unethical against an ethical code designed primarily to protect the institution. The language of ethics and the tool of ethical codes can be usurped by an epistemological or ontological hegemony, dangerously introducing ethical codes into debates which are essentially bureaucratic or professional.

I argue, then, that critical psychological practice is synonymous with, and cannot be disentangled from, what, by analogy, can be called critical ethical practices (ethical code creation and decision making) where attempts by institutional interests to colonise the territory of professional ethical practice should be challenged where necessary, in order to keep open the possibility of dynamic debate, changes of narrative and the inclusion of the voices of clients and the researched.

Reflection point

Is my ethical dilemma the same as your ethical dilemma? What is an ethical dilemma? Are there circumstances where we might deceive ourselves into thinking that we are acting ethically when in fact we are pursuing our own self-interest?

ETHICAL DILEMMAS

Psychologists' personal and professional characteristics (including gender, class, race, religion and dis/ability), competence and emotional awareness feed into our ethical decision making. Other determinants of ethical professional conduct may be related to personality and traits such as proneness to anxiety, depression or shyness. Individual differences in idealism on the relative–absolute continuum can be another dimension as can organisational constraints and dual loyalties to client and employer. The above factors can all result in different individual approaches to ethical practice, in spite of the existence of professional codes. The ethos of the social setting (workplace) can also influence the ethical behaviour of the individual.

Authors disagree on what is an ethical dilemma. Some, such as Francis (2002, p. 12), appear to define an ethical dilemma in terms of a potential violation of an aspect of a code: 'The first [issue to be addressed] is to identify that the problem is an ethical (and not some other sort) of dilemma. If it is, one would want to know exactly what part of the code had been breached.' Others, such as Jacob-Timm (1999), include 'difficult situations', 'ethical tugs' and 'ethically troubling situations' in addition to direct violations of a code. There can be a three-way tension that exists between the personal moral standards with which people enter a profession, professional/institutional ethical norms and the levels of morality underpinning the general public and/or our research participants, as exemplified in the earlier vignette.

Several authors recommend pragmatic solutions in the form of staged problem-solving frameworks; for example, Bond (2000), Fisher (2003), Flanagan, Millar and Jacob (2005). There is one in the British Psychological Society's *Code of Ethics and Conduct* (2009). Such frameworks can be useful in structuring reflection on the ethico-legal aspects of a dilemma, consultations with colleagues, and an evaluation of the rights, responsibilities and welfare of the affected parties. Decisions that have been reached through transparent use of a recognised framework are less likely to be challenged. However, if the existence of a code of professional practice is treated merely as a checklist to be ticked off, primarily in pursuit of defensive practice, then it may create more rather than less unethical behaviour.

It is considered a 'given' to act in accordance with a recognised ethical system. One approach is to base such a system on an understanding of a universal reason with rules applied consistently. However, it can also be argued that while it is a good thing to follow principles which produce good outcomes we need to break these principles if they produce bad outcomes. Bond (2000) argues that there may be occasions when, in full cognisance of a code, the practitioner decides to act otherwise than in accordance with one of its principles if to do so would be to act in the best interests of the client. For educational psychologists, the role of situated judgement within a relationship is crucial. For example, in spite of the expressed wishes of parents and children, a psychologist may set aside the general principle of respect for views of the person and, in exceptional circumstances, report that, in their opinion, it would be in the best interests of the child to be removed from the parents' care. Another example would be where the psychologist has to balance the duty of care and advocacy of the rights of an individual child who has been displaying sexualised behaviours to other children, with the duty of care and advocacy of the rights of those other children in the classroom. In the vignette above, should the researcher have overridden the normal practice of the university that research participants' names should be anonymised, and allowed them to be published?

Reflection point

How can psychologists who believe that the authority of the legal and ethical codes are not absolute ensure that their actions are based on sound professional judgement rather than self-interest, prejudice, rationalisation and the sense that one is above the law? (Pope & Vasquez, 1991, p. 82)

Do our ethical sensitivities 'fade' through insufficient critical self-reflection? A body of literature (see, e.g., Bandura, 1999; Bazerman & Banaji, 2004) has examined how we might engage with self-deception – that is, behave self-interestedly while simultaneously believing that we are behaving ethically. Tenbrunsel and Messick (2004) call this an *internal con game*. Self-interest and concern for others can provoke a conflict of interest in us in which self-deception can lead us to believe that we have acted ethically when this is not necessarily the case. Moore and Loewenstein (2004) argue that professional responsibilities can clash with our own self-interest and can tend to be processed differently, the former being processed through conscious controlled processing (cognition) and the latter being an automatic influence tending to occur outside of conscious awareness (e.g., see Freud, 1957). It can then be argued that ethical professional practices require supervisory practices which are sufficiently sophisticated to allow us to negotiate the subtlety of our responses. Eraut (1994, p. 155) states that:

> there is a need for professionals to retain critical control over the more intuitive parts of their expertise by regular reflection, self-evaluation and a disposition to learn from colleagues. This implies from time to time treating apparently routine cases as problematic and making time to deliberate and consult. It is partly a matter of lifelong learning and partly a wise understanding of one's own fallibility.

The complacency of long practice can be as dangerous as the naivety of the new entrant to a profession. Proactive behaviour is needed to avoid ethical lapses of either omission (failure to be aware that an instance has an ethical dimension at all) or self-deception (believing falsely that one's moral principles have been upheld while behaving self-interestedly).

SUMMARY

Ethical codes, practice guidelines, disciplinary and regulatory committees are useful and necessary structural supports to professional practice that might be consensually regarded as ethical. However, they cannot alone ensure the integrity of the individual practitioner or the welfare of the client and their existence should not lead either the individual or the profession to become complacent. Within the dyadic discourse of practitioner and client there is a continually shifting balance of power and potential for abuse of rights and in this relationship power can find its justification in the privilege of expertise. Unquestioning and complacent adherence to codes, lack of awareness of the power of 'ethical fading' and self-deception, and blindness to the processes of self-interest can, in the absence of critical self-reflection and supervision, lead psychologists to practice unethically. I argue that a critical psychology requires a critical reflection on its ethical underpinnings.

NOTE

1. The young people are deemed by the researcher to have Gillick competency (i.e., to be capable of giving their considered and informed opinions).

REFERENCES

Bandura, A. (1999). Moral disengagement in the perpetuation of inhumanities. *Personality and Social Psychology Review*, 3, 193–209.

Bazerman, M.H. & Banajai, M.R. (2004). The social psychology of ordinary ethical failures. *Social Justice Research*, 17(2), 111–115.

Bond, T. (2000). *Standards and ethics for counselling in action*. London: Sage.

British Psychological Society. (2009). *Code of ethics and conduct*. Leicester: BPS.

Dancy, J. (2004). *Ethics without principles*. Oxford: Oxford University Press.

Department for Education (DfE). (2011). *Teachers' standards*. Online at www.education .gov.uk/government/collections/teachers-standards (accessed 8 June 2016).

Eraut, M. (1994). *Developing professional knowledge and competence*. London: Falmer.

Fisher, C.B. (2003). *Decoding the ethics code: A practical guide for psychologists*. Thousand Oaks, CA: Sage.

Flanagan, R., Millar, J.A. & Jacob, S. (2005). The 2002 revision of the American Psychological Association's ethics code: Implications for school psychologists. *Psychology in the Schools*, 42(4), 433–445.

Francis, R.D. (2002). The need for a professional ethic: International perspectives. *Educational & Child Psychology*, *19*(1), 7–15.

Freud, S. (1957). *Splitting of the ego in the defensive process.* Collected papers, Ed. and Trans. J. Strachey. London: Hogarth.

Jacob-Timm, S. (1999). Ethically challenging situations encountered by school psychologists. *Psychology in the School*, *36*(3), 205–217.

Kant, I. (1995). *Ethical philosophy: Grounding for the metaphysics of moral and metaphysical principles of virtue.* Indianapolis: Hackett.

Lindsay, G., Koene, C., Ovreeide, H. & Lang, F. (2008). *Ethics for European psychologists.* Gottingen: Hogrefe.

Meskell, L. & Pels, P. (2005). *Embedding ethics.* Oxford: Berg.

Moore, D.A. & Loewenstein, G. (2004). Self interest, automaticity and the psychology of conflict of interest. *Social Justice Research*, *17*(2), 189–201.

Pope. K.S. & Vasquez, M.J.T. (1991). *Ethics in psychotherapy and counselling: A practical guide for psychologists.* San Francisco: Jossey-Bass.

Tenbrunsel, A.E. & Messick, D.M. (2004). Ethical fading: The role of self-deception in unethical behavior. *Social Justice Research*, *17*(2), 223–235.

Tubbs, P. & Pomerantz, A.M. (2001). Ethical behaviours of psychologists: Changes since 1987. *Journal of Clinical Psychology*, *57*(3), 395–399.

Impossible Profession

NIALL DEVLIN

LEARNING OBJECTIVES

After reading this chapter you should be able to:

1. Understand the nature of microethics.

2. Reflect on the nature of the ethical demand in the encounter with clients.

3. Offer an introduction to Levinas's concepts of 'said' and 'saying'.

The aim of the chapter is to trouble and disturb educational psychology through being open to the voice of the Other (Todd, 2000). The phrase 'to trouble' has been chosen carefully to signal that the intention is not to reject or refute educational psychology. Rather, troubling educational psychology means adopting both a problematising and critiquing attitude, which are simultaneously methods of analysis and self-forming activities. Problematisation is the process of questioning and making problematic the everyday assumptions and discourses that define the limits of freedom. It is in the moment of problematic disruption that ethical choice becomes possible as a reflexive act.

The chapter examines the ethical demand present in everyday encounters with clients in two moves. Firstly, it provides a theoretical overview of the microethics present in educational psychologist–Client relations. This is followed by an examination of my meeting with a 14-year-old male pupil at a high school (hereafter referred to as M) in which I reflect on notes made at the time. Levinas's (1981) ethics of responsibility is introduced as a possible corrective for the traditional bioethics that underpin educational psychology and some provisional conclusions are offered at the boundary of personal and professional ethical responsibility.

> ### Definition
>
> **'Other', 'other' and 'just another other':** In this chapter the terms 'other' and 'Client' are spelt with either a capital or lower case 'o' and 'c'. This is to signify different ontological positions towards the other/client. For example, the capital letter 'O' is used to acknowledge that the Other is unique and beyond crude classification, transcendent and ultimately unknowable. The lower case letter 'o' is used to signify when the other is not seen as unique but as an example of a category or label. The phrase 'just another other' signifies that the Other has been reduced to a faceless object and is considered as such.

AN ETHICAL VOCABULARY FOR THE 'EVERYDAY'

In this chapter the term ethics is employed as a way of discussing the relations (including power relations) between the educational psychologist (EP) and Others including the decisions, reflections, considerations, judgements and choices taken. The focus is on everyday ethical practice; a microethics of practice as opposed to the more dramatic *'big'* ethical dilemmas (Brinkmann & Kvale, 2008; Komesaroff, 1995). A range of terms and overlapping approaches are used in literature to describe and examine everyday ethical practice:

- Situational ethics (e.g., Fletcher, 1997)
- Care ethics (e.g., Benner, 1997)
- Ethics of intersubjectivity (e.g., Popke, 2003)
- Practical ethics (e.g., Singer, 1993)
- Ethics of care (e.g., Tong, 1998)

- Ethics of responsibility (e.g., Tauber, 2005)
- Ethics of ambiguity (e.g., De Beauvoir, 1948)
- Proximity ethics (e.g., Nortvedt & Nordhaug, 2008).

The above microethics negotiate tensions between a number of apparent binaries: of autonomy and dependence, self-determination and paternalism, interference and abandonment, the particular and the universal, rationality and emotion, and justice and care. The microethical approaches also position themselves, in varying degrees of proximity, in relation to bioethics (Komesaroff, 1995). The negotiations of ethical tensions occur in discussions about rights, responsibilities, needs and obligations between professionals and Others (Zur, 2005). Unlike the quandary style of professional ethics/bioethics, founded on the discourse of the autonomous, non-emotional, neutral, rational individual, microethics might not involve questions about clinical choices or patient confidentiality (Benner, 1997; Brinkmann & Kvale, 2008; Popke, 2003; Tauber, 2005; Tong, 1998). Rather, as Giroux (1997, p. 219) argued:

> Ethics, in this case, is not a matter of individualized choice or relativism but a social discourse grounded in struggles that refuse to accept needless human suffering and exploitation. This ethics is taken up as a struggle against inequality and a discourse for expanding human rights.

Giroux's ethics is radically different from that traditionally expressed in professional codes. Microethical challenges frequently arise when professionals know what to do, but are unable to do it because of organisational or resource issues. This is sometimes referred to as an ethical tug (Campbell 2004; Davis & Mickelson 1994; Lamb Enquiry, 2009; Raviv et al., 2003). Austin and Fitzgerald (2007) suggested 'moral distress' as a more relevant concept than ethical dilemma to characterise this everyday experience of professionals. During periods of moral distress, evidence-based practice was less useful and effective resolutions were more likely to be achieved through dialogue.

Definition

Bioethics is the dominant ethical paradigm in the healthcare professions and is concerned with the ethics and philosophical implications of certain biological and medical procedures, technologies and treatments. Bioethics tends to be the leading principle when making treatment decisions, described by Beauchamp and Childress (2009) as including:

1. Principle of respect for autonomy,
2. Principle of non-maleficence,
3. Principle of beneficence, and
4. Principle of justice.

The principles appear to be virtuous; however, difficulty arises when the needs of the one are balanced against the needs of the many. For example, the needs of one child against the needs of the all the other children in the classroom: one child's right to be included and the other children's right to learn.

> **Definition**
>
> **Said:** Levinas (1981) uses the term 'said' to describe the theme that is intended to be understood in a dialogue. This includes rational acts such as naming, describing, comprehending, analysing, rationalising and thematising.

EPs frequently find themselves in a microethical space betwixt and between the demands of different clients – for example, parents, local authorities, national governments, schools, and children and young people (CYP) (Ashton & Roberts, 2006; Farrell et al., 2006; Fox, 2003; Love, 2009). This liminal space feels like having to take sides and challenges the supposedly neutral space inhabited by EPs (Bennett, 2008; Devlin, 2013; Guiney, 2009). Rather, EPs inhabit the 'swampy lowlands', which comprise uncertainty, risk, interdependence and multiple interconnecting parts (Schön, 1987; Wendell, 1996).

The dominant bioethical response to this complexity usually privileges personal, individualised, responsibility that in turn privileges the rational decision maker who is accountable for their judgements. Traditionally, professional ethics argues that knowledge of what would enhance client's development and well-being should be based on the values of 'good psychology' as set out in a code of conduct which acts as the 'conscience' of the profession (Webster & Bond, 2002). Here the arrow of ethics points from the EP to the client. It is the EP who offers consent and the client who consents, it is the EP who respects and the client who is respected and it is the EP who guarantees confidentiality and the client who has a sensitive history. There is merit in this position underpinned by an asymmetrical and paternalistic power relation; however, there is also a cost and a need for a corrective.

Levinas's (1981) ethics of responsibility radically challenges the traditional foundations of professional directed ethics by shifting the focus from the self (professional) to the Other (Client). During a face-to-face encounter the self is made vulnerable to the Other's vulnerability. The role of the self is not to understand the Other but to be addressed by them. The Other is not understandable or a subject to be made thematic and categorised. The Other, by being profoundly Other, 'unsays' the desire of the self to reduce the uniqueness of the Other to the same (i.e., to be just another other). Levinas's Other always escapes being reduced to themes, categories, labels, developmental histories or being made known by being measured, weighed, compared or traded. The radical conclusion is that it is the Other (Client) and not the self (EP) that resists. Resistance is found

> **Definition**
>
> **Saying:** Levinas (1981) uses the term 'saying' to describe what is meaningfully expressed in a dialogue and is therefore concerned with the non-semantic dimensions of meaning. Saying is not present in the words but the intention behind them. For example, if I say 'hello' this would address myself to the other and acknowledge their proximity. However, 'hello', as well as addressing the other, also says 'here I am'. Saying reminds us that there is always more that can be said by a word or proposition.

in the Other's ability to 'unsay' what psychology has 'said' about them. The 'said' can be understood as the theme that was intended to be understood in a dialogue. This included rational acts such as naming, describing, comprehending, analysing, rationalising and thematising (Levinas, 1981) The Other/Client as a singular opaque and unknowable Other remains more than, and additional to, what the professional discourses could ever have 'said' about them.

The EP is always free to eschew the ethical demand; however, the ethical content of the demand and its authority are not derived from the EP. This time the arrow of ethics is pointing from the Other to the EP. These obligations are in tension to the 'role-relationships' EPs have with clients. For example, the role of EPs can include measuring attainment and capacity and identifying the nature and severity of special educational needs. Acknowledging the Other's opacity changes the ethical question from 'what am I to do?' to 'what does the Other want from me?' (Eagleton, 2009). The Client, by resisting the thematic and categorisation processes of the professional, just by being Other, places the professional and their practice in question. The encounter between the self and Other, therefore becomes one of intense and unbearable alterity in which the self is responsible for the Other (Levinas, 1981).

Reflection points

- Would it ever be possible for educational psychology to be considered ethical in the Levinas sense? And, if yes,
- What would need to happen in order for educational psychology practice to be ethical in the Levinas sense?
- What are the dangers of not employing bioethics?
- Could bioethics and microethics both have a role in supporting and understanding EPs' relationships with clients or are they mutually exclusive?

TROUBLING EDUCATIONAL PSYCHOLOGY: 'M'

So far the chapter has focused on setting out the concepts and theories that underpin micro-ethics. This section examines a meeting with a client (referred to as 'M') to illustrate the concepts discussed above.

Before meeting M, I had already encountered him as a set of descriptors provided by the school. The things said included: as school refuser, as having hygiene problems, being a loner, victim, attention seeker, pupil with special educational needs, having mental health problems, attachment issues and belonging to a dysfunctional family. The adequacy of these descriptions did not survive the first meeting with M. Meeting M questioned the processes by which clients were made visible and the role of educational psychology in warranting, regulating, producing and fabricating those visibilities. The meeting invited the question: What can I say about the other that would not be excluding/limiting/reductive?

The above ethical question arose from an anxiety about the EP–Client power asymmetry and the role that educational psychologists have in labelling, categorising and measuring (e.g., see Billington, 2002). As a consequence of the unease I felt following the meeting I wrote a reflective account and the quotes below are taken from this account.[1] I consider three acts of resistance by M. The first was to verbally suggest an alternative hypothesis, the second was not to respond and the third was to unsay what was being said about him by being a living contradiction.

RESISTANCE IS NEVER FUTILE

This section is interested in the micro acts of relational resistance that are typically performed through being silent, offering an alternative category, redefining a clinical category, changes in tone of voice and explicitly stating a disassociation to the offered category (Austin & Fitzgerald, 2007; Fitzgerald & Austin, 2008). Relational resistance or agitation is played out in the interaction between the 'said' and 'saying' (Levinas, 1981).

Resisting by providing an alternative category/story

During our meeting, there were several examples of M resisting categorisation by offering alternative categories (Austin & Fitzgerald, 2007). For example, M resisted my medical categorisation of his appearance by suggesting that the smell and dirty fingernails resulted from poverty and having a coal fire. In the discussion about school attendance I had framed the problem as poor attendance. However, for M the problem was one of bullying. I also attempted to frame M's case using systems theory:

> M said that when something was not right or someone was going to make the wrong decision he would let them know. I asked if this was his job in the family but M said that it wasn't and that he had to let them know. I tried to explain how everybody in a family could have a role and perhaps he saw his as stopping bad things happening.

M challenged this formulation by suggesting that his actions were simply 'something that needed to be done'. Therefore, M was offering common sense as an alternative explanation for his behaviour. M's re-authoring of his account was akin to what Billington (2002) calls user's stories. M's common sense presentation normalised (as opposed to pathologised) the professionals' account. In the example below I attempted to get M to make the connections between his beliefs and his behaviour:

> M explained that his brother and sister were not going to CAMHS and were not having the same problems as him. I asked why this was. M explained that his brother and sister did not worry as much as he did and did not think so deeply about things. I asked which was better: worrying or avoiding.

I was calling M to have agency and attempted to give M responsibility for his actions. M was thus being asked to govern himself and consider himself as an object to be watched (evaluate his thoughts). Through asking the question, I was calling M to discern which was 'better, worrying or avoiding', establishing an economy of values by offering 'worrying' and 'avoiding' as a moral choice.

Resisting by not engaging

The second form of resistance offered by M was non-responding to questions or changing the subject. For example, I asked M about his literacy needs. Again, M did not answer directly and changed the subject several times. When I continued this line of questioning M de-individualised the literacy issue by talking about his family. M explained that:

> although his brother had difficulties with spelling and reading he did not have a problem with his speech and that his sister was good at reading.

The above example of 'non-compliance' could be seen as attempts to refuse categorisation by a dominant other (Austin & Fitzgerald, 2007; Billington, 2002). This micro act of resistance challenges the pervasive passive description of Clients (Gabe, Calnan & Bury, 1991; Hoeyer, 2006; Laidlaw, 2002).

In the meeting hypotheses were frequently framed as suggestions: for example:

> I then asked M about his fingernails and M explained that he had a bath every night but that his fingernails, because they were long, got dirty very quickly. I explained that I had asked because sometimes people who had been badly bullied did not always take care of themselves and look after their hygiene, adding if M knew what hygiene meant.

The above could be read as a neutral and exploratory dialogue; however, this forgets the power inherent in professional and Client relationships (e.g., Benwell & Stokoe, 2006; Butler, 1997; Dillard, 1982). The positing of hypothesis can be read as interpellation where M was being called to recognise (identify) himself as a set of deficits and needs that were normalised and valorised. This interpellation was also located in medical and educational discursive formations which warranted both the categories and the speaker (Billington, 2002). M was therefore being asked to recognise (identify with) his clienthood (Murry, 2007).

Unsaying by being a living contradiction

The phrase 'living contradiction' refers to M's resistance to being made thematic, being labelled or by being beyond (not reducible to) labels and themes (Buber, 1959; Critchley & Bernosconi, 2002; Levinas, 1981). While meeting with M begged ethical questions of my practice, M himself did not explicitly ask those questions, my ethical reflection being a response to the way his vulnerability was being both acknowledged and avoided in the meeting. M's vulnerability was continually pointed to in my account of the meeting, for example, in respect of his appearance:

> M is 14 years old. I noticed that M was unkempt and that his long finger nails were dirty, his hair looked unwashed and there was a slight smell.

M also told me about his father saying he was going to the shops but in fact he was leaving with the family's savings; descriptions of his family being continually harassed by their community were also evocative. I was bearing witness to M's account of his suffering.

M's vulnerability had asked previously unarticulated questions of my practice and reversed the asymmetry. I continually attempted to (re-)author what M was saying using the language of the 'said' but positioning M in the language of the 'said' pursued closure and avoided the unrelenting experience resulting from the ethical demand that recognises the radical otherness of the Other in their vulnerability (Levinas, 1981). However, the language of the 'said' opened up a tension between a psychology, informed by bioethics, that insists on emotional distance, and the ethical tug presented by the Other. In particular, attempting to become emotionally distant suggests there is something that requires emotional work. The ethical tug occurred when I recognised M as a singular Other and not just 'another other'. Awareness of M's singularity engendered tensions between self-determination (autonomy) and paternalism and between the fear of abandonment and the danger of colonisation (Ellwood, 2006; Verkerk, 2001). Educational psychology practice experienced this way is inherently complex, socially embedded and emotionally engaged. This complexity and engagement challenges the trope of the emotionally neutral, abstract and rational professional–Client relationships (Arras, 1990)

CONCLUSIONS

The meeting with M was not unique and EPs frequently experience ethically challenging situations (Bennett, 2008; Devlin, 2013; Guiney, 2009). EPs also recount stories of how Others (children, parents) transgress the relational space that was demarcated by procedures that establish emotional distance, objectivity and authority and the collapsing of this space by the presence of the Other (Devlin, 2013). The ethically challenging situations encountered by EPs provide opportunities for emotional and identity work. The challenge here is for the EP to be more than their role. It is the resolution of the demand placed on the EP by the Other which enables the potential for the EP to return to a shifted praxis. It is at this moment of disruption that EP practice becomes the object of work. This can result in a tension between the ethics of responsibility and technical competence/instrumental rationality. This can be crudely characterised as the tension between being-with and doing-to. The choices we make and actions we take position us as much as they position the Client. The encounter with a Client is not a straightforward mirror into the wider world of educational psychology or a window into the inner life of the Client. Rather, the encounter is a performative act, speaking a world into being (Dillard, 1982). The institutional nature of the EP–Client encounter works to alienate both the EP from their non-EP identity and the Client from their non-Client identity. The account suggests that I continually attempted to make M an example of a category and a target for care. Caring provided the opportunity for control and closure. This is because the professional discourses attempted to make M manageable and bounded within a category already shaped for treatment or intervention.

It could be asked if it is possible to be an EP and practice ethically. I could even be accused of having a perversely cynical and overly suspicious attitude towards EP–Client relations.

However, adopting a suspicious disposition is necessary if the familiar is to be made unfamiliar and to challenge the taken for granted in my practice. Rather than seeing this as a barrier it should be accepted as a challenge that requires ethical work. This ethical work should not just be grounded on the ethical principles found in professional codes but on a vigilant relational microethics that presents ethico-political choices. I would suggest the following aphorism:

> *If you are going to survive as an educational psychologist, you have to learn to accept that there are things you cannot change but if you are going to survive as a person then you cannot stop trying to change things that you cannot accept.*

NOTE

1. This was also a period when I was in search of a theme for my doctoral dissertation.

REFERENCES

Arras, J.D. (1990). *Common law morality, Hastings Center Report, 20*(4), 35–37.

Ashton, R., & Roberts, E. (2006). What is valuable and unique about the educational psychologist? *Educational Psychology in Practice, 22*(2), 111–123.

Austin, H. & Fitzgerald, R. (2007). Resisting categorisation: An ordinary mother. *Australian Review of Applied Linguistics, 30*(3), 1–36.

Beauchamp, T.L., & Childress, J.F. (2009). *Principles of biomedical ethics.* (6th edn). New York: Oxford University Press.

Benner, P. (1997). A dialogue between virtue ethics and care ethics. In D. Thomasma (Ed.), *The moral philosophy of Edmund Pellegrino* (pp. 47–61). Dordrecht: Kluwer.

Bennett. P. (2008). An investigation into educational psychologists' views of and experience in ethical decision making. Unpublished EdD (Educational Psychology) thesis, University of Sheffield.

Benwell, B.M. & Stokoe, E. (2006). *Discourse and identity.* Edinburgh: Edinburgh University Press.

Billington, T. (2002). Children, psychologist and knowledge: A discourse-analytic narrative. *Education and Child Psychology, 19*(3), 32–41.

Brinkmann, S. & Kvale, S. (2008). Ethics in qualitative psychological research. In C. Willig & W. Stainton Rogers (Eds.), *The SAGE handbook of qualitative research in psychology* (pp. 263–279). New Delhi: SAGE.

Buber, M. (1959). *I and thou* (2nd edn). Trans. R.G. Smith. New York: Scribner.

Butler, J. (1997). Contingent foundation: Feminism and the question of postmodernism. In S. Benhabib, J. Butler, D. Cornell & N. Fraser (Eds.), *Feminist contentions: A philosophical exchange* (pp. 127–143). New York: Routledge.

Campbell, M.A. (2004) What to do? An exploration of ethical issues for principals and school counsellors. *Principia: Journal of the Queensland Secondary Principals' Association, 1,* 7–9.

Critchley, S. & Bernasconi, R. (2002). *The Cambridge companion to Levinas.* Cambridge: Cambridge University Press.

Davis, J.L. & Mickelson, D.J. (1994). School counselors: Are you aware of ethical and legal aspects of counseling? *School Counselor, 42*, 5–14.

De Beauvoir, S. (1948). *Ethics of ambiguity*. Trans. B. Frechtman. New York: Citadel Press.

Devlin, N. (2013). A critical examination and analysis of the processes by which educational psychologists constructed themselves as ethical professionals: To be what I am not. Unpublished EdD thesis, Newcastle University.

Dillard, A. (1982). *Living by fiction*. New York: Harper & Row.

Eagleton, T. (2009). *Trouble with strangers: A study of ethics*. Chichester: Wiley-Blackwell

Ellwood, C. (2006). Coming out and coming undone: Sexualities and reflections in language research. *Journal of Language Identity and Education, 5*(1), 67–84.

Farrell, P., Woods, K., Lewis, S., Rooney S., Squires, G. & O'Connor, M. (2006). A review of the functions and contribution of educational psychologists in England and Wales in light of 'Every child matters: Change for children'. London: DfES Publications.

Fitzgerald, R. & Austin, H. (2008). Accusation, mitigation and resisting guilt in talk. *The Open Communication Journal, 2*, 93–99. Online at http://www98.griffith.edu.au/dspace/bitstream/handle/10072/23059/51615_1.pdf?sequence=1 (accessed 4 August 2016).

Fletcher, J.F. (1997). *Situation ethics: The new morality*. Louisville, KY: John Knox Press.

Fox, M. (2003). Opening Pandora's box: Evidence-based practice for educational psychologists. *Educational Psychology in Practice, 19*(2), 91–103.

Gabe, J., Calnan, M. & Bury, M. (1991). Introduction. In J. Gabe, M. Calnan & M. Bury (Eds.), *The sociology of the health service*. London: Routledge.

Giroux, H. (1997). *Pedagogy and the politics of hope: Theory culture and schooling*. Oxford: Westview Press.

Guiney, D. (2009). Educational psychologists' accounts of ethically troubling incidents at a time of rapid change in their workplace. Unpublished DEd thesis, University of London.

Hoeyer, K. (2006). Ethics wars: Reflections on the antagonism between bioethicists and social science observers of biomedicine. *Human Studies, 29*(2), 203–227.

Komesaroff, P.A. (1995). *Troubled bodies: Critical perspectives on postmodernism, medical ethics, and the body*. Durham, NC: Duke University Press.

Laidlaw, J. (2002). For an anthropology of ethics and freedom. *Journal of the Royal Anthropological Institute (MAN)* 8, 311–332.

Lamb, B. (2009). Lamb Inquiry: Special educational needs and parental confidence. Report to the Secretary of State on the Lamb Inquiry review of SEN and disability information.

Levinas, E. (1981). *Otherwise than being or beyond essence*. Trans. A. Lingis. Pittsburgh: Duquesne University Press.

Love, P. (2009). Educational psychologists: The early search for an identity. *Educational Psychology in Practice, 25*(1), 3–9.

Murry, S.J. (2007). Care and the self: Biotechnology, reproduction and the good life. *Philosophy, Ethics and Humanities in Medicine, 2*(6). Online at http://www.ncbi.nlm.nih.gov/pmc/articles/PMC1868753/ (accessed 7 January 2011).

Nortvedt, P. & Nordhaug, M. (2008). The principle and problem of proximity in ethics. *Journal of Medical Ethics, 34*(3), 156–161.

Popke, E.J. (2003). Poststructuralist ethics: Subjectivity, responsibility and the space of community. *Progress in Human Geography, 3*(3), 298–316.

Raviv, A., Raviv, A., Propper, A. & Fink, A.S. (2003). Mothers' attitudes toward seeking help for their children from school and private psychologists. *Professional Psychology: Research and Practice, 34*(1), 95–101.

Schön, D. (1987). *Educating the reflective practitioner. Toward a new design for teaching and learning in the professions.* San Francisco: Jossey-Bass.

Singer. P. (1993). *Practical ethics.* Cambridge. Cambridge University Press.

Tauber, A.I. (2005). *Patient autonomy and the ethics of responsibility.* Cambridge, MA: MIT Press.

Todd, T. (2000). *Letting the Voice of the Child Challenge the Narrative of Professional Practice.* Adelaide: Dulwich Centre.

Tong, R. (1998). The ethics of care: Feminist virtue ethics of care for healthcare practitioners. *Journal of Medicine and Philosophy, 23*(2), 131–152.

Verkerk, M.A. (2001). The care perspective and autonomy. *Medicine, Health Care and Philosophy, 4*(3), 289–294.

Webster, A. & Bond, T. (2002). Structuring uncertainty: Developing an ethical framework for professional practice in educational psychology. *Educational & Child Psychology, 19*(1), 16–29.

Wendell, S. (1996). *The rejected body: Feminist philosophical reflections on disability.* New York: Routledge.

Zur, O. (2005). The psychology of victimhood. In, R.H. Wright & N.A. Cummings (Eds.), *Destructive trends in mental health: The well intentioned path to harm* (pp. 65–86). London: Routledge.

9 EP Becoming *Phronimos*: The Virtue of *Phronêsis* in Educational Psychology

DANIELA MERCIECA AND DUNCAN P. MERCIECA

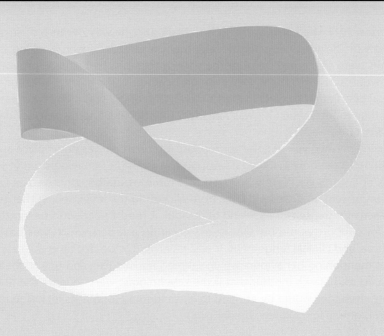

LEARNING OBJECTIVES

After reading this chapter you should be able to:

1. Develop an attitude towards practice with reference to the question: 'What kind of educational psychologist am I becoming?'

2. Appreciate *phronêsis* in terms of educational psychology.

3. Work with, rather than against, uncertainty.

4. Critique issues of decision making and responsibility of educational psychologists.

INTRODUCING MARK, HIS FAMILY AND THE EP

This is a narrative of one of the authors who is an educational psychologist (EP) and her involvement with a little boy and his family. Both authors engage in critical work within education and educational psychology.

21 September 2011: I had been working with Mark since he was 2 years old. He presented as a child with delayed language development and with sensory-seeking behaviour. His parents were concerned because the speech therapist had already pronounced the dreaded word 'autism' to them. However, on hearing Mark's story, I questioned such a categorical declaration so early in Mark's development. He was a boy who was adopted from another country when he was already 5 months old, and his sensory deprivation was apparent.

Following my involvement, the appropriate intervention was put in place and I pulled back, waiting to see how Mark would respond. Most of his behaviours did fit within the diagnosis of autism, yet I firmly believed that more would be conceived as possible in terms of improvement if we held back from allocating the label, seeing that there were other reasons for the sensory-seeking behaviour. A report needed to be written so that funding for support would be allocated. I drew up a report which was based on my observations and clinical judgement. It was received by the deciding board who noted that I was mentioning behaviours which seemed autistic-like, and one of the members of the board told Mark's mother that if the psychologist were to write the diagnosis in the report, then they would be entitled to extra funding for Mark's inclusion in an after-school programme for children with autism.

The parents called me immediately afterwards, asking for my take on the issue. I had discussed the matter with them prior to submitting the report and had shared with them my beliefs on the political nature of diagnosing and on the weight that the shadow of such a diagnosis would cast on Mark's life. They had agreed that there was plenty of time for the label to be definitely placed on Mark and that it would serve Mark better if we were more open to his potential progress than we otherwise would if the label was stuck to him. Yet they were now concerned that Mark would miss out on intervention which might benefit him. Its very existence challenged both my judgement to hold back, and their acquiescence to it. They looked towards me for guidance.

We believe that one of the guiding principles of the profession of the educational psychologist is that of advocacy for children in the educational arena, as in the above narrative. Yet EPs often find themselves in situations where the actual carrying out of such a role presents seemingly insurmountable difficulties. It is easy to resort to the convenient stance that 'reality out there' is very different from the idealisms which were imparted in the safety of the university lecture room where training took place. This kind of thinking is reinforced by the numerous demands made on professionals in the workplace, so that they sometimes wonder at the displacement which occurred since they emerged, bright-eyed and full of good intentions, from their training.

Elsewhere we have written extensively (Mercieca, 2009, 2011; Mercieca & Mercieca 2012, 2013) about how such situations involve dilemmas, where we also suggest the possibility of viewing the uncertainty in these situations as a state of being from which we should not hasten to escape, since in so doing we would precipitately re-create the situation into one which fits the solution rather than one where the course of action is tailor-made for the case at hand.

This chapter, however, does not involve a discussion of the possible merits or otherwise of early diagnosis. The issues accompanying labelling are beside the point; by this time we are all aware of the politics within labelling of pathology (see, e.g., Parker et al., 1995). This writing concerns the processes within the narrative recounted above, the to-ing and fro-ing of decision making and the responsibilities which accompany it. We would like, here, to revisit an old term that Aristotle (384–322 BCE) developed extensively in his book *Nicomachean Ethics* (1984), which term is not often heard in the realms of psychology in general nor educational psychology in particular, despite its incredible relevance to how one's beliefs are translated into practice. This term, the virtue *phronêsis*, is after all what had allowed one of the authors to think outside the box and to consider uncertainty as possibly helpful rather than debilitating. The temporal spaces in the narrative are significant in this chapter. Mark and his story are situated in time, place and space in the psychologist's life. We want to draw awareness of readers of particular forces that are present in the EP's life: knowledge, skills and practical wisdom. Our main focus is on the latter, which ties in with the good life of the psychologist, as explained further below.

Reflection point

Is the practice of the EP to be valued quantitatively, or are there other elements that influence practical wisdom?

Our reading of MacIntyre (2000) and Smith (2003) helps us see how the good life of the EP comes through her practice – her actions and decisions, her very being within the activities which constitute her practice. The practice itself is seen as a moral source (Higgins, 2003, p. 289) and is where she encounters the good, not merely where she applies it. Considering that the EP's interventions span over a 2-year period, the reader might ask about the nature of the practice which she has encountered and how she has changed as a result of these encounters.

If the good life of the EP is linked to her practices, then we question the role of practice in our work. One of the authors was once reassured that her relationship with uncertainty need not be a burden, since it was only the result of a lack of experience. Increased confidence and certainty in practice was promised with time. Our argument here is that the life of the EP is linked to her practice, how the work of an educational psychologist is a complex interaction between the child and the psychologist, as well as a number of other factors, in which the flourishing of all is aimed at, not least of which that of the psychologist. This is in line with the idea that the psychologist is in a constant process of becoming. This chapter revisits the concept of practice within an Aristotelian framework, as we believe in the value that is given to practice and wisdom that emerges in acting, so that flourishing can also take place when failures are encountered (Mercieca, 2011, p. 118). As will be argued later, the above reassuring colleague was not referring to practice in terms of *phronêsis* as much as he was referring to knowledge and skills. Educational psychology is not self-contained but has purposiveness: 'without this element of purposiveness it is difficult to see what prevents a practice from falling into self-indulgence and self-absorption, from coming in this respect to resemble an endlessly sophisticated tea-ritual' (Smith, 2003, p. 315).

Reflection point

How is *phronêsis* intellectual and yet practical?

Phronêsis refers to practical wisdom, the virtue of thinking in terms that are practical: 'a true and reasoned state of capacity to act with regards to the things that are good or bad for man' (Aristotle, 1984, III.3, II12b11). It is particularly interesting because it is an intellectual virtue, yet is one that involves practice. The word *phronêsis* has been translated into English in various ways: practical wisdom, moral discernment, prudence and practical reasoning. None of these translations capture the Greek word fully, but each one emphasises an aspect of the word. *Phronêsis* is not knowledge in itself, but is the capacity to act. The focus of *phronêsis* is the process that is 'concerned with how knowledge and experience are brought to bear in particular situations' (Halverson & Gomez, 2001, p. 3). It is the capacity 'to see' and be sensitive to a situation, discern, deliberate, reflect, judge and act (see Carr, 2006). Richard Halverson and Louis Gomez (2001, p. 5) remind us that 'to see' a situation requires 'an intimate familiarity with the characteristics of a particular situation...it grows out of intensive interaction and familiarity with particular situations'.

The focus here is on the 'good life' of that particular situation and context. Just a note on the idea of the 'good life': for Aristotle, the good life for a person is the active life of functioning well in those ways that are essential and unique to humans. We emphasise 'those ways that are essential and unique to humans' as this idea is fundamental to Aristotle. What distinguishes us from animals is the capacity for rational thought – this is uniquely human. Therefore, the good life for a human is the active life of exercising the rational capacity. In this light we have to think that fundamental to *phronêsis* is the character in action. 'According to Aristotle the excellence of character and intelligence cannot be separated' (MacIntyre, 2000, p. 154). *Phronêsis* is the ability to think about how and why one should act in order to change things, and especially to change one's life for the better. '*Phronêsis*, to simplify a complex picture, is characterised by sensitivity to situated particulars and concrete cases, and by flexibility; it is the property of people of a certain character, who have relevant experience and know how to use it wisely' (Smith, 2006, pp. 166–167).

Phronêsis is an ethical project: it 'allows the person who has *phronêsis* – the *phronimos* – to be able to ascertain what is good for humankind and then deliberate about how best to reach that good' (Noel, 1999, p. 279). It asks the question: What should I do in this situation? Joseph Dunne refers to the concept of *phronêsis* as 'ethical goodness': he argues for a 'circle between *phronêsis* and character' (Dunne, 1993, p. 275). In order to be considered *phronimos*, one must be able to show 'ethical goodness' when engaging in practical reasoning. However, in order to have this as one's character, the *phronimos* must have experiences involving *phronêsis* that develop this ethical character. 'We have in the notion of *phronêsis*, then, ethical knowledge in a very full sense: not just knowledge that directs ethical action, but knowledge that must itself be constantly protected and maintained by good character' (Dunne, 1993, p. 227). Therefore, *phronêsis* and character are not prior to one another, but they are in coordination to develop and shape each other. 'To be able to engage in *phronêsis* that is informed by "ethical goodness", the *phronimos* must already have a character that is informed by and is coexistent with ethical goodness' (Noel, 1999, p. 280). It is in this light that we have to note another Aristotelian distinction that he makes in relation to *phronêsis*: *technê* gives technical knowledge and skill. It does not involve the character, neither is it involved in judgement. With *technê*, a judgement is ready-made; it is read off from the evidence at hand – this effectively reduces judgement to complying with procedure.

Reflection point

Policy – source of tension?

> The guidelines offer general principles and their implementation is intended to assist and clarify the judgements of individual practitioners subject to their particular circumstances. (DECP, 2002, p. 3)

Some codes of ethics and professional guidelines, such as those published by the British Psychological Society, make reference to attitudes and judgements, and practitioners are required to develop certain character traits or dispositions that influence not so much their doing as their being. At the same time, being a code of conduct, a thread of defensiveness can be noted, mostly in language which is rather managerial and procedural. This puts the onus on the professional persona of the EP, and does not address the character of the person. The EP recounting her involvement with Mark is familiar with these guidelines. She knows that if she were to act so as to comply with the well-intentioned guidance of the member of the Statementing Board, and if she were to agree with the therapists who did not question whether Mark fit in the diagnosis of autism, her actions would still be well within such guidelines. She is still functioning effectively as an EP. Yet is she living the good life through such motions and actions? Is it contributing to her *eudaimonia* and that of Mark? Or is she silencing her doubts as she does not tolerate the anxiety which accompanies them? The risk which accompanies judgement, particularly when the EP is alone in such thinking and action, can be frightening. Yet these attitudes and judgements are formed through practice and reached through the living of it – it 'cannot be read off from tradition, dogma, creed or community, although each of these may provide guidance' (Nixon, 2004, p. 117). In fact, Standish (2004, p. 494) speaks of the virtuous person who never feels that she has done enough.

> A professional character is a character formed and informed by the profession and one that reflects an aspiration for the ideals of that profession. The ideals of professional psychology must include conscientious decision making, but they also must include virtuous deciders, who emphasise not so much what is permitted as what is preferred. (Jordan & Meara, 1990, p. 112)

> **Reflection point**
>
> How does the educational psychologist become *phronimos*?

Mark's story involved the EP in a constant revisiting of the question as to whether one should intervene or let him be; to involve him and his family in a heavy influx of professional involvement, or to keep one's touch as light as possible so that the caring and love which these parents clearly felt for Mark would be allowed to work its own magic. The risks were frightening: would he lose out on critical intervention if the time was missed because the EP insisted on letting him be? But she could not think it wise to risk upsetting the delicate balance which could be seen in his growing attachment to his family. How much could his mother be told to 'persuade' him to comply with the homework given by different therapists? Could intervention/interference be harmful to Mark's development, rather than helpful?

At the same time, it had been the parents who had sought guidance from the EP about their son's development. Having invested in their growing relationship since his adoption at 5 months, at 2 years of age they had decided that it was time to allow outside input into their life. Yet, there was the EP, still questioning the wisdom of whether and how much to encourage outside involvement. Through her experience, she is aware of how bright the spotlight shines on a child once he is seen as a client receiving a service from a provider. Every movement is isolated and questioned, every coincidental happening is possibly viewed as fitting under some diagnostic title, so that the appropriate intervention could be recommended. The eagerness with which this is done is commendable, as it stems from an earnest wish to serve the family, to support. However, we believe that it is within educational psychology that the questioning of whether involvement can constitute more harm than good is allowed and addressed. It is as though educational psychology is the place where persons can be critical, even of their own roles, at the risk of seeming to devalue their skills, their box of tools, indeed their very magic wand. *Phronêsis* helps EPs question this; that form of reasoning 'acquired by practitioners who, in seeking to achieve the standards of excellence inherent in their practice, develop the capacity to make wise and prudent judgments about what, in a particular situation, would constitute an appropriate expression of the good' (Carr, 2006, p. 426).

We are still here faced with the question of how one becomes *phronimos*. How critical is the dimension of character and the good life (*eudaimonia*) to the EP's becoming? These lead to another question: can anyone become an EP, or can we have EPs who are not *phronimos*? It is a question which we return to and evaluate constantly. This can be reflected in measures taken to ensure personalised and individual formation. Trainees undergo interviews, reflections on prior experience is evaluated, practice is heavily supervised, and in certain routes even personal therapy is expected.

Yet, what is all this in aid of? Are these safety nets, put in place to safeguard that entrants into the profession have the basic requirements of the ethical code of conduct? Are they aimed at making sure that the skills of assessment, of interviewing, of analysis and reporting are sharp? Is the fundamentality of character at all at the forefront of these measures?

We are calling for an awareness of the necessity of the above measures but also that this awareness needs to be put in terms of the language of *phronêsis*. It is not possible to say that such and such amount of hours of supervised practice are surely enough to form an educational psychologist, that so many thousands of hours of course work lead to this intellectual virtue. We agree that the above are important but think it is essential to keep in mind that they cannot guarantee the formation of *phronimos*. While knowledge (*epistême*) and skill (*technê*) can be taught and learnt, *phronêsis* is not something where the initiate can learn to copy the master. It is through her actions, through her voicing of deliberation, that the master can inspire the initiate so that the latter can start to find her own *phronêsis*.

> The 'student' cannot copy the master, for the master is a different person, with different skills and abilities, in a different situation. The master's courageous action may well be rash and foolhardy if undertaken by the student. So neither simply instruction not faithful mimicry will work for cultivating virtues [the virtue of *phronêsis*]…The *phronimos* is not someone to be imitated in the sense of *copying* but someone who inspires those who are not yet virtuous to attempt to act virtuously themselves, and, indirectly, guides them in doing so. (Treanor, 2010, p. 187).

In *phronêsis*, the act and the character go hand in hand, so that the doing informs the character and the character influences the action. When carrying out the initial interview, prior to the commencement of training, this needs to be done with the search for such a character in mind. We need to remember that:

> *phronêsis* owes its inception and growth chiefly to instruction and habituation. Therefore, it is 'very important, indeed all-important' to be inculcated into the right sort of habits from youth (Aristotle, p. 35 [1103b])…That is, although *phronêsis* is an intellectual disposition…it is, in a sense, also a habit which gradually kicks in through performance of the activities that the habit embodies. (Kristjánsson, 2005, p. 464)

Thus, at the risk of sounding too serious, we feel the need to highlight the delicacy of *phronêsis*; that it is something to be valued and cherished, and above all not to be taken for granted. Continuous professional development cannot be attended for the sake of ticking the right box so that one's licence may be renewed. We need to be open to ways in which our sense of judgement and sensitivity can be whetted, even by going to literature, film, drama or other creative arts for inspiration, if at times supervision seems to be a question of 'more of the same'. Furthermore, an awareness of life experiences and their various possible influences on character is essential, so that what could have a debilitating effect on one EP could also be fortifying to another. We all have different skills, different backgrounds, different relationships and continually different working contexts and situations, but we all need to be encouraged to pursue the good life. It is critical that professional and life experiences start to be seen in terms of the discourse of *phronêsis* so that EPs can think again about the question, 'What kind of educational psychologist am I becoming?'

CHAPTER SUMMARY

This chapter draws on a narrative of an EP's involvement with a child and his family to highlight the constant revisiting of decisions taken and judgements formed. This attitude, which espouses uncertainty towards practice, is seen as enabling the flourishing and becoming of the EP, so that soundness of character and rationality are presented as vital for good practice. While commending the emphasis placed on supervision, continuous development and training, the authors call for such to be thought about in terms of the language around *phronêsis*. Such awareness leads towards the rethinking of the question: 'What kind of EP am I becoming?'

REFERENCES

Aristotle. (1984). *Nicomachean ethics*. Trans. David Ross. New York: Oxford University Press.

Carr, W. (2006). Philosophy, methodology and action research. *Journal of Philosophy of Education*, 40(4), 421–435.

Division of Educational and Child Psychology (DECP). (2002). *Professional practice guidelines*. Online at http://www.bps.org.uk/sites/default/files/documents/professional_practice_guidelines_-_division_of_educational_and_child_psychology.pdf (accessed 12 June 2016).

Dunne, J. (1993). *Back to the rough ground: Phronêsis and technê in modern philosophy and in Aristotle*. Notre Dame, IN: University of Notre Dame Press.

Halverson, R. & Gomez, L. (2001). Phronêsis and design: How practical wisdom is disclosed through collaborative design. Paper presented at American Educational Research Association Annual Meeting, April, Seattle, WA.

Higgins, C. (2003). MacIntyre's moral theory and the possibility of an arêtaic ethics of teaching. *Journal of Philosophy of Education*, 37(2), 279–292.

Jordan, A.E., & Meara, N.M. (1990). Ethics and the professional practice of psychologists: The role of virtues and principles. *Professional Psychology: Research and Practice*, 21(2), 107–114.

Kristjánsson, K. (2005). Smoothing it: Some Aristotelian misgivings about the phronêsis-praxis perspective open education. *Educational Philosophy and Theory*, 37(4), 455–473.

MacIntyre, A. (2000). *After virtue: A study in moral theory* (2nd edn). London: Gerald Duckworth.

Mercieca, D. (2009). Working with uncertainty: Reflections of an educational psychologist on working with children. *Ethics and Social Welfare*, 3(2), 170–180.

Mercieca, D. (2011). *Beyond conventional boundaries: Uncertainty in research and practice with children*. Rotterdam: Sense.

Mercieca, D. & Mercieca, D.P. (2012). How can the use of petit narratives create space and possibility when short-hand is used in educational psychology practice? *Education & Child Psychology*, 29(2), 67.

Mercieca, D. & Mercieca, D.P. (2013). 'How early is early?' or 'How late is late?': Thinking through some issues in early intervention. *Educational Philosophy and Theory*, 46(8), 845–859.

Nixon, J. (2004). Learning the language of deliberative democracy. In J. Nixon & M. Walker (Eds.), *Reclaiming universities from a runaway world*. Maidenhead: Open University Press.

Noel, J. (1999). Phronêsis and phantasia: Teaching with wisdom and imagination. *Journal of Philosophy of Education, 33*(2), 227–286.

Parker, I., Georgaca, E., Harper, D., McLaughlin, T. & Stowell-Smith, M. (1995). *Deconstructing psychopathology*. London: Sage.

Smith, R. (2003). Thinking with each other: The peculiar practice of the university. *Journal of Philosophy of Education, 37*(2), 309–323.

Smith, R. (2006). As if by machinery: The levelling of educational research. *Journal of Philosophy of Education, 40*(2), 157–168.

Standish, P. (2004). Europe, continental philosophy and the philosophy of education. *Comparative Education, 40*(4), 485–501.

Treanor, B. (2010). Emplotting virtue: Narrative and the good life. In B. Treanor & H. Isaac Venema (Eds.), *A passion for the possible: Thinking with Paul Ricoeur* (p. 187). New York: Fordham University Press.

Non-Expert Binary: The Fluid and Contested Nature of Expertise

CATHERINE BEAL

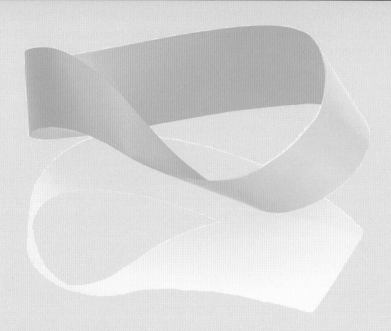

LEARNING OBJECTIVES

After reading this chapter you should be able to:

1. Reflect on the role of listening within professional practice and within construction of self.

2. Extend knowledge of phenomenological research.

3. Critically engage with expertise as an outsider to the phenomenon researched.

4. Construct yourself as a critical practitioner.

This chapter is written with the aim of prompting thinking and emotion that enable the reader to engage in further individual and shared reflection to consider the following questions about critical educational psychology practice:

1. Can we develop models of service delivery which enable us to meaningfully engage with the intersubjective and dynamic nature of expertise about education in context?
2. Can we create the intersubjective space for young people to recognise their expertise in their own perceptions of self and their experience?
3. Can we engage with others to enable change without constructing fixed perceptions of others as in need of change?
4. Can we engage with others over time as they experience life and significant experiences within this? Can this time commitment be valued in practice as well as research?
5. Can we reflect on our knowledge base as applied psychologists as a positive aspect of our embodied engagement in the intersubjective activity of interacting with others to improve outcomes for young people?

In practice, educational psychologists (EPs) often oscillate between being positioned as experts and positioning themselves as facilitators of others' expertise through the application of ideas informed by psychological theory. This chapter uses episodic narratives of 17-year-old Shaun's experience of transition (Beal, 2012) from an 18-month sentence in a young offenders institute to deconstruct the role of EP as expert and to highlight the fluid nature of expertise. I question whether, in the absence of developing 'experience close' (Smith, 2011) narratives – stories that are grounded in an individual's expressed perceptions of that experience – we are drawn to evidence-based narratives – stories based on researching shared experiences which tend to be constructed from reading or from one's own experience of practice rather than co-construction with individual young people. I note the contradiction between positioning myself as non-expert within casework while adopting a position of expertise in my work to improve outcomes for young people.

A PHILOSOPHICAL STARTING POINT

Phenomenology is a philosophical discipline which 'aims to describe in all its complexity the manifold layers of the experience of objectivity as it emerges at the heart of subjectivity' (Moran & Mooney, 2002, p. 2). In practice this means focusing on lived experiences as they are subjectively experienced by individuals and noting that one cannot stand outside of phenomena to understand them (Heidegger, 1962/2002). This chapter uses narratives from Shaun to prompt personal and public reflections on the fluid and contested nature of expertise in educational psycology practice. Readers are enabled to sit alongside interactions with Shaun's narratives of self as three interactions between Shaun and me (a practitioner-researcher) are presented. Within these interactions I was an academic female EP engaged in research, who was interested in listening to Shaun's experience and had no direct influence over decisions affecting his life. I did not request information about Shaun's offences or personal history, so my perspective was based only on the three interactions discussed here, which are presented as a series of extracts structured under themes that emerged through my use of interpretative phenomenological analysis (Smith, 2011). It is hoped that the reader will listen to Shaun and his experience and reflect on the act of listening as a person, a student and/or a professional. I am critically reflective about my interactions with, and interpretations of, Shaun (Merleau-Ponty, 1965 [1945]).

INTERACTION 1

My first meeting with Shaun as a recorded conversation about his experience of transition is shown below. This occurred within the young offenders institute (YOI).

Loss and separation

Shaun: It's like in there you're with loadsa people and then you're on your own in that one.

Catherine: Can you give me some examples of things that change?

Shaun: Erm, like your area changes, all the people what you know move to different places an that. Erm, like new things would come out and like you don't know what they are.

Catherine: So is planning quite a big part of transition?

Shaun: That's part of the reason why I breached before cos when I got out, when I fell out wi me dad I ant spoke to him for 4 years and when I lived with him my national insurance card would've gone to his house.

Helplessness

Shaun: I dint have ID so I couldn't open a bank account or anything.

Expectation

Catherine: How do you think you'd feel?

Shaun: I'd feel happy. I'd feel good cos I've never stuck to it before.

Catherine: So if I was to ask your mum to talk about what she thinks of your transition what do you think she'd say?

Shaun: I reckon she'd [mum] say yeah he'll probably stick to it for a few days and then just breach like he normally does. That's what sh…that's what she thinks I'll do every time.

Catherine: What do you think about those people?

Shaun: They're my mates but when we get together we just do stupid things.

Catherine: Why do you think they're doing that?

Shaun: To try an keep me out of trouble cos that list of people is every person that I've ever been arrested with.

Shaun: Just because I've been in before they think oh he's gonna go out an do something else so we'll stop an see what he's doing.

Shaun: Like cos I just got out. Cos I'm known.

Conflict

Catherine: You want this one yeah [point to 'good transition']? But what could make it go that way?

Shaun: Erm, if I got into an argument with my mum or summat or my sisters I'd. One of the times when my mum was arguing with me I snapped me tag off. I got recalled for that as well. So if like I fall out with my mum or summat.

Catherine: So you've got other people but they're harder to get to?

Shaun: Yeah. So I see em around buts its harder cos most of them are in college an that.

INTERACTION 1: TRAVERSING THE EXPERT NON-EXPERT BINARY

This interaction prompted reflection about my knowledge as an EP of the assumed importance of connections and relationships for adolescent identity development and outcomes (see above themes labelled 'loss and separation' and 'expectations'). Listening to Shaun in my role as a practitioner-researcher was a different perspective to my everyday experiences within practice as an EP. I question whether the role and time parameters that EPs operate within encourages elicitation of narratives framed around potential for change rather than meaningful rich descriptions of experience (Moran & Mooney, 2002); focusing on the practitioner's needs over the client's need to explore hopes, fears and anxieties that shape his sense of self and his future possibilities (see above themes labelled 'loss and separation', 'helplessness', 'expectation' and 'conflict').

I question whether my understanding of offending behaviour and YOIs is too shaped by my community, experiences and construction of self as a person and a practitioner. Giving Shaun power over the content of the interaction in his position as expert in his own experience enabled me to listen to ambiguity and conflict within his dialogue about whether non-offending could form part of his future. In typical practice I might have intervened to enable more use of language to construct possibilities for positive change (challenging 'helplessness'), assuming that this articulation could have an impact on his experience (Rees, 2008). This highlights the dilemma of positioning myself as either 'expert' or 'listener'.

> **Reflection point**
>
> How do you position yourself in interactions with young people? And how does this position them?
>   I have intentionally presented listening to, and intervening with, young people as polar opposites within EP practice, but in practice the boundaries are blurred.

INTERACTION 2

My second recorded conversation with Shaun was in the YOI 3 weeks before his expected transition into the community.

The YOI in the community

Catherine: So what does it [living in the community] feel like?

Shaun: It's like being in here really. Cos I can leave but if I leave I'll come back in here cos I've breached. Coming round in marked up police cars all the time. Through the middle of the day just doing welfare check. All the neighbours are thinking 'oh why are the police always at her house all the time?' They'd…think it's to do with my mum all the time.

Shaun: Me licence conditions were pretty bad. Three month ISSP [Intensive Supervision and Surveillance Programme], 3 month 25 hours a week, 91 day tag. Er, non-association with about 20 of me mates. Er, to live at a hostel, all that stuff.

Return to the YOI

Catherine: What do you want?

Shaun: If I got recalled though I'd still be out for my 18th birthday, cos my licence finishes in November but I don't wanna get recalled. But if I reoffend and then I get back in here and I got another sentence I'd be in for me 18th and they'd keep me in here for the whole sentence instead of shipping me out to a YOs [Young Offenders Institute for 18–21-year-olds]. Even if I was 18 I came here and then I had my 18th birthday in here I'd stay in here because I committed the crime while I was 17. So they'd keep me here on a DTO [Detention and Training Order].

Catherine: What do you think about that?

Shaun: …cos that's what I've done my other time. Especially ISSP cos I do my induction and I don't go back. I do the induction after I, the day that my youth offender takes me when I get released and then I don't go back the next day. And I get, I get a letter through the post saying oh you're been breached there's your court date so I snap my tag off. Then I get breached for, erm, breach of tag. And then YOT put out a warrant for me.

Catherine: What do you think is going to happen this time?

Shaun: Like before I dint really, I wasn't, I was bothered but I dint care if I came back cos its nothing in here. But now I know, now I know it is. There's no point in coming back cos it just upsets me mum and me family and that.

Loss

Catherine: How do you feel about that?

Shaun: I feel bad, I've tried, I've tried to speak to him [dad] load of times but he doesn't want to speak to me. Cos he's proper against drugs and that, and crime and all that stuff.

Offending behaviour

Catherine: So you think that'll be a hard thing not to do?

Shaun: I should be able to stop, I shunt, I should be able to stop myself from doing it.

Catherine: How does that sound?

Shaun: Hard. So if I get caught for drugs getting at least 2, if I get caught burgling getting at least 3 years. That's why I don't wanna come back now. Cos…I got convictions for drugs, burgling, stealing cars and assault. So if I get locked up for any of them I come back as well.

Catherine: So what did you think when they [police] came to you?

Shaun: I expected them to cos I'd just been in for, cos I was like last year I was doing burglaries all the time. But now I been, I, I, I ant been doing none I stopped now I started selling weed [marijuana] instead of doing burglaries. It's just as bad but, erm, it's not as it, I don't know burglaries are lot worse. Cos you're robbing of people and I think that's tight. But selling weed it's not really, you're not really robbing off anybody you're just selling a bit of twifter.

INTERACTION 2: TRAVERSING THE EXPERT NON-EXPERT BINARY

Reflecting on my developing expertise as an EP, I wrestled with the dilemma of listening as a practitioner-researcher rather than intervening as an EP in practice. To have listened as an EP, this return to the YOI was a negative outcome, but as practitioner-researcher I focused on listening to Shaun's construction of a return to the YOI as positive or negative. My professional assumptions connected to literature which framed Shaun as vulnerable to repeated transition and increasing institutionalisation, thus providing impetus to intervene rather than to listen (Social Exclusion Unit, 2002). Listening to Shaun's understanding of the YOI, on the basis of direct experience, provided insight into how Shaun felt about where he lived and where he felt most at home (most understood and cared for). This offered an alternative view of the challenge of the transition ahead. This view related to my professional view of lack of provision in the community, but was subjectively rooted in Shaun's experiences both inside and outside the YOI.

Listening to Shaun's narrative of his release to a bail hostel, I felt injustice on his behalf and empathy for his situation. This form of accommodation for young people leaving YOIs has been negatively highlighted in the media (*The Guardian*, 2011) as being equivalent to release to homelessness because bail hostels are not deemed to be stable or appropriate accommodation for young people.

> **Reflection point**
>
> Do we (society) construct the YOI as negative? Would young people who have experienced it construct it differently?

Intersubjective engagement with Shaun made me experience helplessness and guilt about not actively promoting self-efficacy or proxy agency (Bandura 2001; 1977) as an EP with potential to create opportunities for him. I questioned whether my phenomenological practice is embodied within therapeutic constructions of the EP's role. By listening to understand, rather than to change, and positioning Shaun as expert, a cycle of interpretation was initiated in which I began from a not-knowing position. This produced a space between us within which I began to sense the enormity of his struggle. It is important for me to continue to reflect upon whether my typical practice as an EP enables or disenables such interactions with young people and whether the experience was significant for Shaun.

Reflection points

- How do you listen as a practitioner?
- What are you listening for; do your expectations shape what is said and what you are open to hear?

INTERACTION 3

My third conversation with Shaun: this interview (post-transition) was conducted within the YOI because Shaun had been sentenced to complete the remainder of his sentence within custody for breaching conditions of his release into the community.

Return to the YOI

Shaun: Now I've been in six times I know if I do summat wrong I'm just gonna come back, get out, be on licence, breach that, come back again, get out on licence, come back again.

Catherine: What did it feel like when he [Youth Offending Team (YOT) worker] was giving you chances?

Shaun: Better but I don't know it's the same when I get out, all I'm gonna do whenever I get out it's hard.

Catherine: This last one is different because you haven't offended?

Shaun: If I wasn't on ISSP I think I'd still be out. Cos like I were sticking to my tag while I was breaching my ISS. Cos if I got out and they put me on tag I think I'd stay out and finish the 6 weeks…but it's ISS really that I can't do. Once you've breached that you might as well breach your tag cos you've already know you're coming back.

Successful transition

Catherine: What do you think other people think about the transition you've had?

Shaun: They think it were good. Me mum and me sister were saying that they were proud cos I were not going out grafting [burgling] and carrying on selling weed and that. She knew I were coming back for breaching.

Catherine: How do you feel about that?

Shaun: Good. Loads of people asked me to, er, sell weed for em or if I wanted to come out, go out grafting with them. I said no.

Catherine: Is there anything else that could describe what transition was like?

Shaun: I don't know. I'm still, erm, trying to get in colleges as well while I was out. I went to Connexions looking for courses to get on and I started claiming jobseekers allowance as well.

Catherine: How do you feel about the next transition?

Shaun: Last one I did I was saying oh I'll stick to me tag stick to my ISSP and that and then I stuck to it for about 2 days. This time ant got nothing to stick to. Only thing I ant got to do is just keep meself out of trouble. That's all I'm going to do. Cos it's not that hard, I've done it for a month.

Others maintaining offending behaviour

Catherine: What do you hope for the future?

Shaun: Make my own choice instead of just saying yeah I'll do it. I'll do this, I'll do that. Like when I was in court you know_____? She [YOT worker] was saying 'he's easily influenced' and that. Like if someone asks me to do summat I'll do it for them. So obviously stopped doing that as well.

Catherine: What made you think you weren't [being recalled]?

Shaun: Erm, they didn't, they didn't adjourn it they just recalled me. Said we think 'we don't think you're even going to try so we're just recalling you for the rest of your licence'. No one will stick to it. I don't know why they put people on it cos not many, it's hardly anyone is gonna stick to it, just gonna breach and come back. And the jails are getting full and they're sending people back on recalls and that for stupid things.

Catherine: How did you feel about that?

Shaun: Annoyed. No, once they'd done that tried, they were saying that 'oh you've got no lights on it, no brakes, you've got bald tyres, there's no reflectors on it'. And they were saying 'oh can we arrest him for that?' The sergeant were saying 'nah you can't arrest him for it cos it's not really that dark'…Winding me up anyway, I went fuck off. They went 'oh I can do you for section for public order as well'. So they were just trying to arrest me for anything they could.

New connection outside the YOI

Catherine: How do you feel about that?

Shaun: So when I'm off licence I can do it. Cos when I'm on licence I can't go down there cos I'm on tag and if I go down there I've breached straight away. I come back they'll arrest me. So I can go down there see the rest of my family is what I haven't seen for like 3 years.

Shaun: Last year I was in for my birthday, my little sister's birthday, Christmas, my other sister's birthday and me mum's birthday. So this year I want to be out for them all.

INTERACTION 3: TRAVERSING THE EXPERT NON-EXPERT BINARY

Engaging with Shaun's narrative showed his perception of professionals and systems within youth justice as maintaining, rather than preventing, his offending behaviour (see above themes labelled 'return to the YOI' and 'others maintaining offending behaviour'). Offending appeared to be constructed as part of his identity (who he was) rather than behaviour (what he did). Shaun expressed that people's expectations of him as an offender were not altered by disengagement from offending on release. As a systemic EP, I work with others to construct challenging behaviours as the product of interacting systems around young people rather than as part of their identity. This made me feel frustrated and confused about how Shaun could construct and enact an alternative future while he perceived that others labelled offending as a fixed part of who he was rather than what he did. I also reflected on whether professional involvement constructs and maintains narratives of difference or deficit rather than of inclusion and potential. Within Shaun's narrative he constructed police involvement as part of his engagement with offending behaviour. His perception highlights the importance of reflecting on his understanding of what these interactions mean for who he is and who he can become. I continue to question whether I would have heard these narratives if my role had been to intervene. Following this interaction I perceive that systemic/phenomenological EPs need to adopt a critical stance to who is included in the system of support around and with young people.

> **Reflection point**
>
> Do your interactions influence how young people are constructed?

Shaun's reflection on his stepped progress and evaluation of progress on his own terms may have been important for development of self-efficacy around engagement with offending behaviour. I wonder whether our interaction enabled him to reflect on his experiences and understand himself in terms of his thoughts and feelings about transition and whether this would enable him to achieve what he wanted to achieve rather than what others think would be 'a positive outcome' for him.

Reflecting on my interactions with Shaun has enabled continued critical awareness of the intersubjective and dynamic nature of expertise in professional and personal interaction. This awareness enables the practitioner to question assumptions about the role of EPs. Shaun's narratives highlight assumptions about professional involvement constructing need and identities of others as 'needy'. Engaging in open and active listening to Shaun highlights his role as an expert in himself and the role of the professional in enabling him to consider self. This chapter should have prompted critical reflection on how we engage with young people, our role and ourselves. I encourage the reader to consider the questions at the outset of this chapter about future EPs' practices and how they can be embedded in critical foundations.

REFERENCES

Beal, C. (2012). Insider accounts of the move to the outside: An interpretative phenomeno-logical analysis of three young people's perceptions of their transition from the secure estate (custody) into education, training or employment. Unpublished doctoral disserta-tion, University of Sheffield.

Guardian, The. (2011). Young offenders leaving custody for life of homelessness and reof-fending. Online at http://www.guardian.co.uk/society/2011/Feb/28/young-offenders-released-homelessness-crime (accessed 21 November 2012).

Heidegger, M. (1962/2002). On time and being. In D. Moran & T. Mooney (Eds.) (2002). *The phenomenology reader*. London: Routledge.

Merleau-Ponty, M. (1962 [1945]). *Phenomenology of perception*. Trans. C. Smith. London: Rou-tledge.

Moran, D. & Mooney, T. (Eds.) (2002). *The phenomenology reader*. London: Routledge.

Rees, I. (2008). A systemic solution-oriented model. In B. Kelly, L. Woolfson & J. Boyle (Eds.), *Frameworks for practice in educational psychology: A textbook for trainees and practitioners*. Lon-don: Jessica Kingsley.

Smith, J.A. (2011). Evaluating the contribution of interpretative phenomenological analysis. *Health Psychology Review, 5*(1), 9–27.

Social Exclusion Unit. (2002). *Reducing offending by ex-prisoners*. London: Crown.

11 Joining the Q: What Q Methodology Offers to a Critical Educational Psychology

MARTIN HUGHES

LEARNING OBJECTIVES

After reading this chapter you should be able to:

1. Gain an understanding of Q methodology.

2. Appreciate the case for Q's contribution towards a critical psychology.

> *Because isn't that the point of every relationship: to be known by someone else, to be understood? He gets me. She gets me. Isn't that the simple magic phrase?*
> (Flynn, 2012, p. 33)

In this chapter, I shall briefly explain what Q is, why I think Q is an *ethical methodology*, good at hearing marginalised voices, before concluding by considering how Q contributes to a critical educational psychology. As this chapter seeks to present some of the strengths of Q and ways in which my interpretation of it has influenced my attempts at a more critically inclined practice, I shall start with a brief introduction of what has been described as 'perhaps the ultimate mixed method' (*The Psychologist*, 2008, p. 481).

Q IN BRIEF

Q is 'unusual' in a number of ways. Although nearly 80 years old, few have heard of it. It is both qualitative *and* quantitative – it relies on the interpretation of factors that are arrived at following statistical analysis. William Stephenson developed Q in 1935 when factor analysis was being developed (by Spearman, for instance) to explore correlations between test scores across populations of people, serving psychology's approach to individual differences. For a proper approach to individual differences, Stephenson (1953) felt that the individual should be understood completely rather than focusing on their 'bits' (variables, traits and so on). So as to avoid this kind of dissection, Stephenson found a way to use factor analysis to correlate persons as opposed to their bits – instead of a by-variable, a by-person factor analysis.

Very simply, the initial stage in Q often involves generating a set of statements. This can be achieved by consulting what has already been written about the topic ('the literature') and by asking others, including your participants, for their views about the topic in question, maybe from interviewing or focus groups. The participants are asked to sort the statements, based on their likes and dislikes. The completed Q sorts are factor analysed. Factors are revealed based on shared viewpoints which are then interpreted so as to see the world from the perspectives of your participants. The interpreted factors then allow you to engage in further research and/or discussion opportunities if you wish to pursue them.

To realise his ambition, Stephenson needed a metric, a form of measurement that enabled people to be compared and his invention includes three particular features that characterise Q.

1. Data must be gathered in an appropriate form that allows this kind of by-person analysis, namely in the form of the first unusual characteristic of Q, the Q sort. Figure 11.1 shows a typical arrangement for a Q sort where our participant is arranging items according to how much they agree (right-hand side of the grid) or disagree (left-hand side) with them. The Q sort is a method that requires a participant to sort items according to some kind of criterion, such as the degree to which they agree or disagree with, like or dislike an item. Items can be anything that can be sorted but are usually statements written on cards. Items are placed in a position on a grid consisting of columns of different heights, which in total, describe the shape of a normal distribution curve (the outer columns are shorter than the middle columns). It makes no difference where in a column an item is placed, but moving an item to the right or left is determined by how much a participant agrees or disagrees (for instance) with an item. When asking participants to sort items, there is an important distinction between valence and salience. Items are not

Figure 11.1   *Participant engaged in a Q sort using a grid*

simply ranked from right to left in descending order of value to the sorter. Instead, when the Q sort is completed, the items are arranged so that they spread out from the middle column to the left- and right-hand outermost columns with increasing salience. The outer columns thus contain items about which the participant feels most strongly in contrast to the middle column, where 'neutral' items are placed, or those that the participant may not be particularly bothered either way about.

2. The second unusual or characteristic feature is Q factor analysis. This involves Q sorts being compared with each other so that similarities and differences lead to the identification of factors. Each Q factor represents a pattern of sorting which forms the basis of a participant's viewpoint. In Q, a factor represents a particular level of statistical correlation for the assertion to be made that, although the participants providing Q sorts for it differed in certain respects in relation to the way that they sorted the items, their Q sorts were similar enough for them to subscribe to a pattern. This pattern is called a Q factor.

3. A third unusual aspect of Q is the interpretation of the Q factors. Each of the patterns are scrutinised so as to search for descriptions which enable the factors to be expressed. Such expression can be regarded as a viewpoint which articulates the strongest areas of agreement and disagreement when compared with, or relative to, the other viewpoints.

Q AS AN ETHICAL METHODOLOGY

While a researcher's positionality cannot be avoided and in the sense that one is aiming to keep it in check, methodology 'should avoid imposing the researcher's view of the world on the people being researched. This issue has been obscured by the qualitative/quantitative debate with which it has been linked' (Kitzinger, 1984, p. 64). In my research and practice I am keen to go beyond the notion of using method to transfer information from a research participant's head into my own, as if I was emptying a vessel. If I am serious about 'voice', then I need to explore and understand approaches that facilitate co-construction between researcher and researched. Q methodology seems well suited to this, serving as an example of what Ravet (2007b) refers to as an ethical methodology.

Ravet (2007b, p. 338) notes that 'relationships between adults and children carry an implicit and unavoidable power differential'. In my work, I aim to reduce the potential harm stemming from this in a number of ways, as 'the imposition of adult viewpoints upon children is often subtle, implicit and taken for granted' (Ravet, 2007b, p. 337). Ravet (2007a) describes the shift in voice research from information gathering and regarding children as objects to a focus on empowerment with children as subjects, summarising neatly an important trend in this area.

A methodology that contests a one-size-fits-all solution, hears multivocal and marginalised voices

For many professionals working with children and young people (including educational psychologists), a phrase such as 'the voice of the child' trips neatly off the tongue, masking a complexity with which a critical psychology seeks to engage. Some writers contest whether voice can be achieved at all. Alcoff (1991, p. 6), for instance, stating that from a feminist perspective, 'speaking for others is arrogant, vain, unethical and politically illegitimate'. Alcoff asks if it is ever valid to speak for others unlike or less privileged than oneself and under what conditions this might be done, concluding that the researcher needs to ask if their involvement will lead to empowerment. If, as Alcoff argues, the researcher engages in the act of representation and so participates in the construction of subject-position, this focuses on the need to find a methodology which deals with data respectfully and holistically, that avoids breaking down the other into parts more easily digested by the prevailing majority.

James (2007, p. 262) argues that 'giving voice to children is not simply or only about letting children speak' but also about children's perspectives helping us to better understand the social world. She discusses the rhetoric about 'giving voice to children' and problems related to authenticity (translation, interpretation and mediation), the use to which voice is put, a glossing over of multivocality and the nature of young people's participation in research, including as co-researchers.

I believe that Q gives voice to all participants (including the marginalised) so as to challenge a one-size-fits-all solution and remains close to the experiences of the disempowered (Brown, 2006). Factors that are found and interpreted usually relate to a dominant discourse but also include views that are heard less frequently and which are often surprising.

An approach that illuminates a 'first-person perspective': it 'gets' people

One of the biggest 'take-aways' from my research perhaps, for me as a practitioner, is to focus my ambition on 'getting' those that I work with and in particular on nurturing the child's voice, developing a first-person interpretation which 'gets' them, imagining what it might be like to be them. Watts echoes this when he encourages us to try to see the world through the eyes of our participant, 'try to be them' (Watts, 2014). So, the view of the 'first person' is not *my* perspective, but a desire, as far as is possible, to see things from the perspective of my participants – to understand my subject *through their eyes*. This relates directly to my belief in Q as an *ethical* approach, one that hears a range of views, including minority voices, without foregrounding my own. This is important. Methods such as questionnaires with a limited range of questions, where concepts are predetermined, have been criticised (Stainton Rogers, 1991), as the analysis, rather than revealing the social world being investigated, is more likely to tell us something about the researcher who constructed the questionnaire. A similar point is made by Brown, when he considers social science scales and how an observer (or researcher) imposes their will on reality, 'by defining ahead of time, what a response is to mean' (Brown, 1980, p. 3). In contrast, Q puts the focus squarely on the participant's world.

EXAMPLES FROM SHEFFIELD UNIVERSITY

A number of doctoral students at Sheffield have used Q in their work with children and young people, and their approach has illuminated first-person perspectives, viewpoints across a range of topics which can be explored further by accessing the e-theses on the White Rose web page (details are given in the Further Reading and Resources). For example, I worked on a project with young people, where I had engaged them as 'co-researchers' (Hughes, 2012, 2014; and see White Rose e-theses). Generating statements, aiming to represent the 'co-researcher' experience, I developed a set of 59 statements which reflected the perspectives of the young people I was working with and the themes found in the literature. Q-sort data collected from participants were entered into PQMethod (see http://schmolck.userweb.mwn.de/qmethod/) for analysis which led to a solution with a number of the young researcher participants loading on five factors (see Figure 11.2). The analysis revealed that there was enough similarity between the Q sorts to indicate that there were five distinct patterns (factors) or viewpoints and the young people's individual Q sorts that were most closely associated with each of them.

As shown in Figure 11.2, we can see that a participant sorting the items into this particular grid would have agreed with statements 52 and 59 the most, placing them in the extreme right-hand column. Items 9, 13 and 16 were also agreed with but not as much as those items placed in column 5 and so were placed in column 4. On the left-hand side of the grid, we find that this participant disagreed with items 4 and 25 the most, placing them therefore in the column headed '–5'.

The five viewpoints were interpreted from the analysis and the results from this study indicate a number of different viewpoints held by young people, based on their experience of having worked as young researchers. In my work it is clear that the situation is more complex than being able to conclude that young researchers are a 'good thing'.

−5	−4	−3	−2	−1	0	1	2	3	4	5
Most Disagree ←		Disagree					Agree →		Most Agree	
4	11	1	7	6	3	2	26	17	9	52
25	20	14	15	12	8	5	37	31	13	59
	58	18	22	28	10	27	39	36	16	
		19	32	34	21	29	43	42		
		47	41	35	23	30	44	57		
			45	38	24	40	53			
			50	46	33	48	56			
				55	49	51				
					54					

Figure 11.2   *Factor array for an 'idealised' sort for YPF2 (YPF2 'Happy assistants – happy to assist adults in their work')*

I wanted an approach that would reduce complex data, enable me to hear a range of voices, illuminating something of significance related to what being a young researcher means, so as to explore the viewpoints of young people concerning *their* experiences of working as researchers. I attempted to remain open to the diversity of children and young people, individuals with unique experiences, capable negotiators of reality, constructing different realities, living within multiple realities, able to weave stories to create order out of chaos and make sense of their world moment by moment (Stainton Rogers, 1991). An approach in which I attempted to create a 'climate of perturbation', instead of pursuing 'psychology's "wild goose chase" after nomothetic knowledge' (Stainton Rogers, 1997), seemed well suited to my desire to problematise the term 'co-researcher' (Hughes, 2014).

This work attempts to 'stay close' to the young participants, to interpret and represent their views with integrity, to 'get' them, demonstrating that there is not a 'one-size-fits-all' solution. In contrast to adults defining in advance, thinking they have already understood with 'premature knowing' (Stenner, 1998) what children and young people are like and then measuring them against such templates, I have remained curious about what participants might think or feel and enabled their different and sometimes marginalised voices to be heard.

How does Q contribute to a critical educational psychology?

A critical educational psychology perhaps shares some similarities with an art form such as improvisation – something that is crafted over time, honed to (im)perfection. Although a melody might be discernible, what is played differs each time according to context (audience, other players, differing abilities of the musicians, mood, state of mind and so on). In exploring freedom in improvised music (where jazz might be regarded as the highest art form) musicians crawl out on a limb, are placed on the edge, face terrible moments by risking making fools of themselves. Oldfather and West (1994, p. 22) explore qualitative research within a jazz metaphor, creating a 'pathway for making explicit the tacit understandings that enable us to make our ways as researchers without fully orchestrated scores'. Like improvisation, research and critical practice can be risky enterprises and it is affirming to realise that we can, in our performances, deal with the stress of the unknown, using principles and skills to approach each situation as if it was 'the first time', ensuring respect for those with whom we meet (Kamoche, Pina e Cunha & Vieira da Cunha, 2003).

Earlier, I discussed some of my principles in selecting and applying an ethical methodology, in ways that are respectful and engage with understandings and meanings of voice. For me this leans towards a critical psychology. Developing this further, we can also contest the notion of childhood, which is important because the way in which researchers conceive childhood will shape the research in which they engage. Indeed, the extent to which researchers embrace or reject the idea of children as 'different' shapes the nature of their research (Harden et al., 2000, p. 11). Punch (2003) comments that an approach that takes children's views seriously draws attention to children as social actors and power differences between children and adults as opposed to a child's developmental age and stage. I believe that the work described here does this well.

In *Stories of Childhood*, Stainton Rogers and Stainton Rogers (1992) seek a multiplicity of texts, referred to as critical polytextualism (Curt, 1994; Watts, 2002), where any topic of significance has a number of subject positions. There is also overlap with positioning theory (Davies & Harré, 1990; Harré & Moghaddam, 2003) 'which is concerned with revealing the explicit and implicit patterns of reasoning that are realised in the ways that people act towards others' (Harré et al., 2009, p. 5). With positions defined as 'patterns of beliefs in the members of a relatively coherent speech community' (Harré & Moghaddam, 2003, p. 4), the similarity to factors revealed by Q (viewpoints) is striking.

In developing a critical educational psychology curriculum this might include attention to the importance of context, of time, space and place; exploration of the tension between being and becoming, what goes on between rather than within people; an acknowledgement of diversity – multiple ways in which any topic is 'storied into being' where no one way is superior, and exploring how these ways have been constructed and the use to which they are put (see Stainton Rogers et al., 1995). At Sheffield, some of us have employed Q qualitatively and critically from a social-constructionist standpoint in order to further an influential agenda that others before us have fashioned (Stainton Rogers et al., 1995; Curt, 1994) so as to describe different stories that children and young people might tell about a range of topics. We invite you to join the Q!

ACKNOWLEDGEMENT

My thanks to Simon Watts for his comments on an earlier draft of this chapter.

REFERENCES

Alcoff, L. (1991). The problem of speaking for others. *Cultural Critique, 20*, 5–32.

Brown, S. (1980). *Political subjectivity. Applications of Q methodology in political science.* New Haven, CT: Yale University Press.

Brown, S. (2006). A match made in heaven: A marginalized methodology for studying the marginalized. *Quality and Quantity, 40*, 361–382

Curt, B. (1994). *Textuality and tectonics: Troubling social and psychological science.* Buckingham: Open University Press.

Davies, B. & Harré, R. (1990). Positioning: The discursive production of selves. *Journal for the Theory of Social Behaviour, 20*(1), 43–63.

Flynn, G. (2012). *Gone Girl.* New York: Crown.

Harden, J., Scott, S., Backett-Milburn, K. & Jackson, S. (2000). Can't talk, won't talk? Methodological issues in researching children. *Sociological Research Online, 5*(2). Online at http://www.socresonline.org.uk/5/2/harden.html (accessed 29 May 2016).

Harré, R. & Moghaddam, F.M. (2003). *The self and others: Positioning individuals and groups in personal, political, and cultural contexts.* Westport, CN: Praeger.

Harré, R., Moghaddam, F.M., Sabat, S.R., Cairnie, T.P. & Rothbart, D. (2009). Recent advances in positioning theory. *Theory and Psychology, 19*(1), 5–31.

Hughes, M. (2012). Researching behaviour: A Q methodological exploration of the position of the young person as researcher. Unpublished Doctor of Education (Educational Psychology) thesis, Department of Educational Studies, University of Sheffield.

Hughes, M. (2014). What might adults learn from working with young researchers? In J. Westwood, C. Larkins, D. Moxon, Y. Perry & N. Thomas (Eds.), *Participation, citizenship and intergenerational relations in children and young people's lives: Children and adults in conversation* (ch. 14). London: Palgrave Macmillan.

James, A. (2007). Giving voice to children's voices: Practices and problems, pitfalls and potentials. *American Anthropologist, 109*(2), 261–272.

Kamoche, K., Pina e Cunha, M. & Vieira da Cunha, J. (2003). Towards a theory of organizational improvisation: Looking beyond the jazz metaphor. *Journal of Management Studies, 40*(8), 2023–2051.

Kitzinger, C. (1984). The construction of lesbian identities. Unpublished PhD thesis (Psychology), Reading University.

Oldfather, P. & West, J. (1994). Qualitative research as jazz. *Educational Researcher, 23*(8), 22–26.

Punch, S. (2003). Childhoods in the majority world: Miniature adults or tribal children? *Sociology, 37*(2), 277–295

Psychologist, The. (2008). Mixed feelings about mixed methods. *The Psychologist, 21*(6), 481.

Ravet, J. (2007a). Enabling pupil participation in a study of perceptions of disengagement: Methodological matters. *British Journal of Special Education, 34*(4), 234–242.

Ravet, J. (2007b). Making sense of disengagement in the primary classroom: A study of pupil, teacher and parent perceptions. *Research Papers in Education, 22*(3), 333–362.

Stainton Rogers, R. & Stainton Rogers, W. (1992). *Stories of childhood. Shifting concerns of child concern.* London: Harvester Wheatsheaf.

Stainton Rogers, R., Stenner, P., Gleeson, K. & Stainton Rogers, W. (1995). *Social psychology. A critical agenda.* Cambridge: Polity Press.

Stainton Rogers, W. (1991). *Explaining health and illness: An exploration of diversity.* London: Harvester Wheatsheaf.

Stainton Rogers, W. (1997). Q methodology, textuality, and tectonics. *Operant Subjectivity, 21*(1/2), 1–18.

Stenner, P. (1998). Heidegger and the subject: Questioning concerning psychology. *Theory & Psychology, 8*(1), 59–77.

Stephenson, W. (1953). *The study of behaviour: Q technique and its methodology*. Chicago: University of Chicago Press.

Watts, S. (2002). Stories of partnership love: Q methodological investigations. Unpublished PhD thesis, University of East London.

Watts, S. (2014). User skills for qualitative analysis: Perspective, interpretation and the delivery of impact. *Qualitative Research in Psychology, 11*(1), 1–14.

Psychologists Now?

ANTONY WILLIAMS

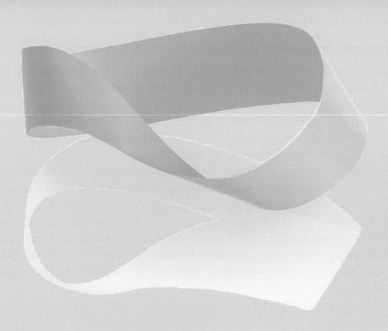

LEARNING OBJECTIVES

After reading this chapter you should be able to:

1. Consider the degree to which psychological language has become the everyday way we talk about others and ourselves.

2. Understand the ways in which the language of psychology can function ideologically.

3. Recognise the implications of psychologisation for how children are understood.

This chapter brings together strands of critical thought that have existed within the professional practice of a number of professions comprising the psy-complex (psychiatry, educational and clinical psychology, social work as well as parts of the juridical and education services). The term psy-complex was first used in the mid-1980s by both David Ingleby (1985) and Nikolas Rose (1985) as they tracked the rising influence of psychological frames of reference on descriptions of the self. This chapter presents a brief analysis of the consequences – the question presented in the title. The overarching aim is to illuminate the work psychological knowledge does in everyday life and how new forms of communication continue to reshape the impact of psychological knowledge through the increasing variety of ways it is disseminated.

In considering the degree to which we are all psychologists now, we will explore how psychological knowledge may induce a glossing over of subjectivity in the way it encourages people to look upon themselves and others from what is understood to be a scientific point of view, as if a psychologist. Over 40 years ago David Ingleby published a chapter in *Reconstructing Social Psychology* titled 'The Job Psychologists Do' (Ingleby, 1974). In this chapter he critically analysed the job of the psychologist. Ingleby suggested that psychology has an important role to play in depoliticising lived distress through the incorporation of social norms into the laws of nature, representing social laws 'as if' laws of nature. Ingleby (1974) proposed that in overlooking such a distinction the social/political (and potentially changeable) relations between people are represented as the natural relations between things, ruled by unchangeable laws. The title of this current chapter seeks to explore this theme over 40 years later by asking, to what degree do we all now think and speak like psychologists and, in so doing, asking in what ways are we overlooking the social, relational dimension of the psychological subject?

THE JOB PSYCHOLOGISTS DO

Definition

Subjectivity: A process of finding yourself becoming a subject over the course of an infinite series of encounters, involving reflexivity and creativity in imaginative transformation of desire and anxiety. (Hollway et al., 1998, p. xvii)

Definition

Psychologisation: The fact of the knowledge of psychology having become central in mediating the presence of the human being with herself, the others and the world. (De Vos, 2013, p. 2)

Ingleby (1974, p. 316) describes the contradiction in the social role of the applied psychologist, explaining 'that he [sic] fails to discover truth because he is paid (in part) to conceal it'. Ingleby links this concealing to personal interests, asking for whom does the psychologist work?

What and whose interests (whose truth) does the psychologist further? The next step of the analysis in unpicking these questions shifts to focus on the knowledge that psychology generates and uses. Drawing on Sartre's (1972) analysis of the technicians of practical knowledge, the argument is that 'the corpus of psychological knowledge is conceptual, that is to say assumed to be universal, but it never serves all mankind. It serves above all certain categories of people belonging to the ruling class and their allies' (Ingleby, 1974, p. 316, quoting Sartre, 1972, p. 608). Ingleby's analysis concludes by highlighting how the various twists and turns entwined into the role of the psychologist produce a person 'employed to restore people's humanity to them without touching on the inhumanity of their situation' (Ingleby, 1974, p. 326). As such Ingleby asks if it is possible to practise a psychology which does something more than reproduce collective illusions? In this challenge to those that use psychological knowledge (which the title of this chapter suggests is now all of us) Ingleby highlights the need to 'lose one's illusions' or to examine our collective and individual 'refusal to apprehend certain disturbing facts of life'. This amounts to a position very similar to that outlined by Burr (1998), which emphasises the inseparable nature of the social, political and the psychological. In line with what can be considered a 'critical' position, Ingelby (1974, p. 327) calls for 'psychologists to try to hold political realities and psychological problems in focus at the same time'.

Ingleby's (1974) analysis of the role of the psychologist sees the psychologist as involved in perpetuating the naturalisation of the symbolic order (see definition 2 of ideology below), as a member of a profession that has a disavowed ideological function, in the first sense outlined by Žižek (Abercrombie et al., 2012, pp. 10–11) below. It was suggested that this is inherent through the psychologist's actions which are at root aimed at maintaining and ensuring the smooth running of a range of social practices and systems that structure society; in the case of educational psychologists, those that form the schooling experience. Through their position in social systems (e.g., educational psychologists in the UK positioned within local authorities or employed directly by a school or chain of schools), educational psychologists are involved in producing the knowledge and concepts that makes such maintenance possible. While there is no value judgement inherent in such an analysis, Ingleby (1974) also offers an analysis of the ideological nature of psychology to suggest certain vested interests, primarily those of the ruling class and their allies (a more contemporary term would be 'the establishment' (see Jones, 2015)), benefit from ideology masquerading as truth.

PSYCHOLOGY AS IDEOLOGY

In asking if we are all psychologists now, this chapter is also seeking to explore the degree to which the language of psychology is no longer solely the expertise of the psychologist as it has become increasingly the everyday language for talking about the self and others. Through considering this change (in the everyday talk about self and others) the suggestion

> **Definition**
>
> **Ideology (1):** As doctrine, a composite of ideas, beliefs, concepts and so on, destined to convince us of its 'truth' yet actually serving some unavowed particular power interest... The blurred (false) notion of reality caused by various 'pathological' interests (fear of death, of natural forces, of power interests etc.).

> **Definition**
>
> **Ideology (2):** As the very notion of an access to reality unbiased by any discursive devices or conjunctions with power. The (mis)perceiving of a discursive formation as an extra dis-cursive fact. Ideology as the 'naturalisation' of the symbolic order – that is, as a perception that reifies the results of discursive procedures into properties of the 'thing itself'.

is that there may be an implicit assumption that talk and language referring to the self, children and childhood has become less ideological as it has become more explicitly based on psychological research and as such more scientific. However, despite psychological language's claims to science, the argument presented here is that psychological language can be considered ideological in two differing but related ways.

The concept of ideology is traditionally used to examine the role of political and religious ideas in social life. In this sense ideologies are:

> sets of interrelated beliefs and attitudes that can provide many different individuals with the same 'lenses' through which to view the world and thereby communicate with each other... Ideologies, in other words, may function as 'pre-packaged' units of interpretation that are useful for regulating interpersonal relationships and navigating social and political life. (Jost, Ledgerwood & Hardin, 2008, p. 5)

To understand the ways in which psychological language is increasing the pre-packaged unit of interpretation two differing definitions of ideology have been presented to help develop an understanding of what this means and why it may matter to the critical educa-tional psychologist.

First, we will begin with an examination of how psychology can act ideologically in the first sense outlined above. In this sense the power interests (described in the definition above) tend to be institutional forms of government, but increasingly can also be seen to be companies that, in a free market psychologised culture, emerge to meet the need illu-minated by the psychological gaze (see China Mills, Chapter 13, for a discussion of this process in relation to attention deficit hyperactivity disorder). This definition tends towards supporting a conceptualisation of ideology as problematic and formative of exploitative power relations.

The second sense of ideology outlined above in some ways confounds the first, but this definition of ideology is vital in helping us to appreciate the inherently ideological potential of language itself. This definition does not suggest that ideology is either good or bad, rather that it is an inherent potential in the process of mistaking a discursive formation (the textual means of describing some thing or phenomena) for the thing in itself (as an extra discursive phenomena). This definition describes a process (reification) in which the (psychological) language used to describe someone might become an assumed property of that person. As such, a young person who has gone through a diagnostic process which has resulted in a diagnosis of attention deficit hyperactivity disorder (ADHD) might come to think of themselves as ADHD – for example, explaining who they are by saying, 'I'm Paul and I find it difficult to concentrate because of my ADHD'. The assumption of what the psychological language means in this sentence gives such language its ideological potential.

There is a defined truth, 'I find it difficult to concentrate', which is rationalised as 'because I am/have ADHD'. This is presented without any recognition of the social context and the set of social relations (family, community, societal) which are formative of both the behaviour and the judgement of what the behaviour means, in this case ADHD.

The second definition of ideology is important in helping us to recognise how ideology often functions (as in the first definition) but importantly also helps us guard against being drawn into a search for the truth. That is, the second definition forces a recognition that any truth is in some way shaped by various social relations which are subject to power. An understandable response to the first definition is to engage in a quest in order to see more clearly, to rid oneself of the blurred vision (an ideologically structured vision) and to return to a clearer and hence more truthful vision of others and ourselves in the world. This in many ways is the hope that psychology offers, the prospect of finding the psychological truth that offers an escape from a troubling truth (or a truth explicitly shaped by various social power relations). This opens the option for a parent, for example, to claim that their child is not 'naughty' or 'bad', rather that they have ADHD. While the first formulation is clearly unhelpful, the suggestion here is that the psychological alternative, while useful in that it avoids the obvious stigma of thinking of oneself or family member as being either naughty or bad, is, in less straightforward ways, still ideological. It is ideological in that:

- This psychological truth may in fact serve opaque power interests (definition 1).
- The psychological perspective is presented as the truth, devoid of an analysis of the socio-relational context which is an inherent dimension of understanding the meaning of this truth claim (definition 2).

This is presented here as a potential problem for the critical educational psychologist in that, while functioning as truth, the psychological explanation acts as a barrier to understanding rather than a facilitator. In absolute terms no particular claim is made in general about the desirability or otherwise of the psychological labelling of a way of being. Rather four related points are made in respect of the rising need for such psychological explanations.

1. That although empirically based, psychological explanations do not offer a truth outside ideology, merely a set of signifiers, that with the human propensity for sense-making may become important reference points for the understanding of self/others.

2. Such diagnoses are used as a way of managing finite resources and as such pursuing such a diagnosis may be a tactic that is employed to gain access to services. The issue here becomes how the tactic is used and whether the person labelled knows it is a tactic or comes to believe it is a life sentence.

3. Is the resource/service one that the person themselves actively desires (with a reasonable understanding of the implications of access) or is it one which they are attempting to resist?

4. Is your participation (or desire to participate) in labelling processes part of your 'responsibility in accord with the best interests of social government' (Billington, 2006, p. 151). If so, how are the particulars of the individual human situation acknowledged within the process of applying psychological knowledge?

FROM PSYCHOLOGY TO PSYCHOLOGISATION

The suggestions here are that psychology acts ideologically; and that problems of living which are actually produced by social interactions are reproduced as 'psychological problems' by psychology. Ingleby (1974) suggests that this is part of the job of the psychologist and is often in the psychologist's best interests, as agents of the state, rather than in the interests of those with whom they work. This is a theme taken up by some in educational psychology in 1978 with the publication of *Reconstructing Educational Psychology* and with clinical psychologists in the 1981 publication *Reconstructing Psychological Practice*. However, this critical analysis gained little purchase in undermining the use of reified psychological concepts in psychology and since the 1970s and 1980s rather the reverse has occurred, with psychological language becoming increasingly the given way in which we think of ourselves and others. As we all become psychologically minded we enter an age of psychologisation. Given this continuing trend, what does the original 1970s critique miss and how has this has led to a psychologised culture in which we are all our own psychologist?

The alienated object of psychological science is the modern capitalist subject or 'How the enunciation of the Other tells you who you are'

The psychological subject is known and comes to know themselves, their children, partners, friends and colleagues through psychological knowledge, which presents as true and innately just. As our second definition of ideology suggests, it is neither necessarily true nor innately just. It is rather 'sets of knowledge', or 'pre-packaged units of interpretation' that are used as a form of governance to manage populations guiding them towards public ends, which, as our first definition of ideology suggests, tend to serve particular interests.

Psychological knowledge, then, is a truth about the person as understood in reference to psychological knowledge about people in general. It is a set of contingent truths of governance that are held in place not by their truth-value but by their allotted role in maintaining current forms of governance.

As psychological knowledge becomes increasingly central in mediating the relations between people it increasingly functions as an unquestionable set of understandings. In the psychologised state, a developing sense of self and others that emerges over time in 'an infinite series of encounters, involving reflexivity and creativity in imaginative transformations of desire and anxiety' (Hollway et al., 1998, p. xvi) is reduced to a quest for 'the psychological facts'; facts which are presented via social media, internet sources, the radio and television discussion. The psychologist in the age of psychologisation becomes an authority figure who merely confirms to the client (and their parent or teacher) a fact already known by those psychologically minded.

The point of recognising psychology as ideological is to recognise not that psychological explanations offer a masking of, or a capacity to stand outside politicised power relations as suggested earlier, rather that psychology as ideology fixes those relations. Psychological knowledge self-confidently offers an escape from the questions of: Who are we? How did we come to be? (It does so through the offer of convincing scientific answers.)

As we all become our own psychologist, what eludes symbolism (and as such can't be thought about) is the desire to know[1], which draws us towards psychological knowledge and, paradoxically, towards the desire to deny. In this the danger is that psychological knowledge is used to avoid rather than recognise the traumatic experience of being.

NOTE

1. This desire to know I would liken to Melanie Klein's notion of the epistemophilic instinct, which she highlighted in her early work: for example, 'Early Stages of the Oedipus Conflict' (1928).

REFERENCES

Abercrombie, N., Adorno, T., Althusser, L. & Barrett, M. (2012). *Mapping ideology*. Ed. S. Žižek. London: Verso Books.

Billington, T. (2006). Working with children: Assessment, representation and intervention. London: Sage.

Burr, V. (1998). Overview: Realism, relativism, social constructionism and discourse. Social constructionism, discourse and realism. In I. Parker (Ed.), *Social constructionism, discourse and realism* (pp. 13–26). London: Sage.

De Vos, J. (2013). *Psychologization and the subject of late modernity*. London: Palgrave Macmillan.

Hollway, W., Venn, C., Walkerdine, V., Henriques, J. & Urwin, C. (1998). *Changing the subject: Psychology, social regulation and subjectivity*. London: Routledge.

Ingleby, D. (1974). The job psychologists do. In N. Armistead (Ed.), *Reconstructing social psychology*. Harmondsworth: Penguin Books.

Ingleby, D. (1985). Professionals as socializers: The 'psy complex'. *Research in Law, Deviance and Social Control, 7*, 79–109.

Jones, O. (2015). *The Establishment: And how they get away with it*. London: Melville House.

Jost, J.T., Ledgerwood, A., & Hardin, C.D. (2008). Shared reality, system justification, and the relational basis of ideological beliefs. *Social and Personality Psychology Compass*, *2*(1), 171–186.

Parker, I. (2007). *Revolution in psychology: Alienation to emancipation*. London: Pluto Press.

Rose, N. (1985). *The psychological complex: Psychology, politics and society in England 1869–1939*. London: Routledge & Kegan Paul.

Sartre, J-.P. (1972). The nature and social function of intellectuals: Interview reprinted. Trans. G. Gross. *Human Context, 4*, 608–618.

Part III Putting Critical Psychological Resources to Work in Educational Psychology

In this section of the book the contributors will consider the notion of what constitutes psychological practice. This concept can be employed in relation to methodologies adopted in research (orientations which guide the ways in which the subject matter of the research is approached) and educational psychology practice (positionalities of the practitioner that s/he adopts in order to work with children, schools and other stakeholders). Contributors draw upon their own critical reflexive practitioner research and professional practice to uncover some of the challenges and possibilities of working with children, drawing on specific methodologies/practitioner orientations/positionalities.

13 Epidemic or Psychiatrisation? Children's Mental Health in a Global Context

CHINA MILLS

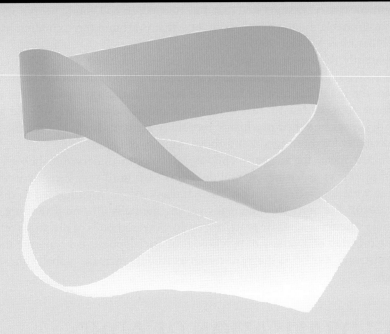

LEARNING OBJECTIVES

After reading this chapter you should be able to:

1. Think critically about whether diagnoses from Western countries, such as attention deficit hyperactivity disorder (ADHD), can or should be applied to children in low- and middle-income countries of the Global South.

2. Critically reflect on attempts to scale up mental health services for children globally.

3. Explore the process by which children's behaviour is increasingly being framed as a concern for psychiatric intervention, including medication, and how this might be read as a process of psychiatrisation.

4. Grasp how the side effects of psychiatrisation, and particularly prescribing psychotropic drugs to children, may be individual, familial, societal, political and economic.

Being labelled both as a 'child' and as 'mentally ill' in a saneist, ableist, adultist world often ain't easy. All these '-ists' and their many '-isms' are ways of trying to explain how society privileges some ways of being (e.g., non-disabled, white, rational, adult and male) and to explore what happens to those who don't 'fit'. Sometimes those children whose behaviour or thinking don't fit are framed as 'problematic' and talked about as being 'mentally ill' – as children whose brain chemicals are 'imbalanced'.

In fact, growing numbers of children are diagnosed with 'mental disorder' and prescribed psychotropic medication: so many that some say this is a modern epidemic (Whitaker, 2010). In the USA, 'mental disorder' is the leading cause of disability in children (Whitaker, 2010). In the UK, in 2004, surveys suggested that 1 in 10 children and young people aged 5–16 suffer from a diagnosable mental health disorder – that is around three children in every class (Green, McGinnity & Meltzer, 2005).

And apparently this 'epidemic' isn't only in richer countries of the West. Children are targeted as a special group for global mental health interventions on the basis that 'mental disorders are the major contributor to disease burden in this age-group' (Patel et al., 2007, p. 1302). Some suggest that 10–20% of children and adolescents are affected annually by psychiatric disorders, and their psychiatric morbidity accounts for five of the top ten leading causes of disability for those aged 5 and above (Murray & Lopez, 1996).

What does it mean for so many children globally to understand themselves and be understood by others as having 'mental disorders'? Up until very recently it was thought that children were unaffected by most 'mental disorder', so what has led to this epidemic (Whitaker, 2010)? Are more children really getting mentally ill? And if they are, then why? Does this reflect better diagnostic practices, or do increased rates of diagnosis reflect a complex coming together of a variety of psychological, social, political, economic and historical factors (Armstrong, 1997)? As diagnoses such as ADHD increase globally, these questions are pertinent.

THE GLOBALISATION OF ADHD

Over the past 40 years, ADHD has been among the most commonly diagnosed psychiatric conditions for children in the USA (Kessler et al., 2006), where 11% of school-age children and nearly 1 in 5 high-school-age boys have been diagnosed – a 16% increase since 2007 and a 41% rise in the past decade (Schwarz & Cohen, 2013). Until recently there has been little evidence about ADHD diagnosis outside the USA; however, growing evidence suggests that ADHD is now diagnosed in various countries across the globe, with an estimated worldwide prevalence of 5.29% (Polanczyk et al., 2007).

Within global mental health literature ADHD is described as 'a neurobiological syndrome' that 'affects individuals…across all cultural contexts' (Flisher et al., 2010, pp. 1, 6). Such claims are used to justify the 'scale-up' in global access to mental health services and to psychotropic drugs, which are scarce in some low- and middle-income countries.

But there are no biological tests for ADHD. This means that diagnoses are made through asking parents and children a series of questions and sometimes observing them. Such questions are based on diagnostic systems, such as the American Psychiatric Association's *Diagnostic and Statistical Manual of Mental Disorders* (DSM), now in its fifth edition, which lists the behaviours typical of ADHD. When assessing prevalence of ADHD across different cultural contexts, shorter checklists of 'symptoms' are used, based on the DSM, such as the Composite International Diagnostic Interview (CIDI) (WHO, 2004) which includes questions about: how often a child loses things, makes careless mistakes, loses concentration, talks more than other people their age, and fidgets when sitting down.

These questions are part of a checklist that can be used by non-professionals as part of surveys that aim to calculate the prevalence of ADHD in a country, and to compare this with other countries.

Using data partly generated from such checklists, can you guess which country is estimated to have the highest rate of ADHD according to data from the Global Burden of Disease Report? (Institute for Health Metrics and Evaluation, 2013)

Iraq.

And where do you think has the highest projected rates of depression (in adults)?

Afghanistan (where it is claimed 1 in 5 people are depressed (Ferrari et al., 2013)).

But these global prevalence rates of ADHD and depression do not reflect the actual number of people diagnosed with these disorders in a country because for many countries these data do not exist. Instead, many studies calculate prevalence based on answers to simple diagnostic check-lists administered within community surveys, or estimate rates based on those in Western countries.

Why might this be problematic?

First, because basing these estimates on data from countries like the USA, where overdiagnosis and overprescribing are major problems, seems likely to generate biased prevalence figures.

Second, there may be many reasons why a child might fidget, not be able to concentrate, or feel sad, and some of these may be the result of living in conditions of poverty or conflict. It can be hard to concentrate if you are hungry, if you live in a conflict zone where bombing or gunfire have kept you awake all night, or if you are responsible for your siblings because your parents have died from HIV/AIDS. These are the realities of many children's lives, with over half of the world's children living in poverty, and millions without access to safe drinking water or basic health care (UNICEF, 2014). Yet diagnostic checklists, especially when administered as part of surveys, do not allow those being interviewed to explain why they struggle to concentrate or feel sad. Feelings of sadness or lack of concentration may therefore be normal responses to conditions of poverty, injustice and oppression, but we would never learn this if we rely solely on the use of checklists (Horwitz & Wakefield, 2006). This might go some way to problematising the claim that Iraq and Afghanistan have high projected prevalence rates of ADHD and depression, making us question how useful it is to understand this kind of distress as 'mental illness'. It seems the answer to this may depend on the degree to which we can connect the often fractured links between political realities, childhood experience and psychological subjectivity (Ingleby, 1974, p. 327). Yet the use of checklists explicitly decontextualises children's distress, treating it as if it happens in a vacuum.

Third, are mental health problems really universal – that is, the same all over the world? Can we apply diagnoses that originate from specific cultures at specific times, such as ADHD, to all peoples, worldwide? What if we did this in the reverse direction? So, for example, we might take Dhat syndrome – a condition found in the Indian subcontinent, in which male patients report fatigue often associated with premature ejaculation and the belief they are passing semen in their urine. We could devise and administer a checklist for diagnosis, then calculate the prevalence of this condition in the UK (Jadhav, 2007). While the prevalence might even be high, such a process would lack any validity because in the UK 'Dhat syndrome' has little meaning to most people. This, for Kleinman (1988), is a form of category fallacy or category error: the application of diagnostic categories in settings where they lack cultural validity. Is this what is happening when children in non-Western countries are diagnosed with ADHD?

Do diagnoses such as ADHD, depression and conduct disorder reflect biological differences that have yet to be found, or might such labels operate as methods of social control for children whose behaviour is deemed 'problematic' or 'threatening'? While such diagnoses can be important for families to get access to the educational and financial support they may need, how might such labels affect children's lives and their understandings of themselves, as well as how adults, professionals and society can respond to children in distress? Furthermore, the globalisation of diagnostic categories may discredit or replace alternative ways of understanding children and distress, such as indigenous or traditional approaches.

Fourth, context also plays a part in whether we understand the effects of medication on children's behaviour as desirable or not. For example, the effects of stimulants may cause a child to concentrate and focus, which may be desirable in a school, but may seem 'abnormal' at home or when a child is playing with friends.

THE SIDE EFFECTS OF PSYCHIATRISATION

The application of medicine and psychiatry to understand increasing numbers of children's experiences is referred to by some as the medicalisation or the psychiatrisation of childhood.

> **Definition**
>
> **Medicalisation:** The way that human problems come to be defined and treated as medical problems.

> **Definition**
>
> **Psychiatrisation:** The way that human problems come to be defined and treated as psychiatric problems, meaning that increasing numbers of experiences come to be seen as 'symptoms' and increasing numbers of people come to be seen as 'mentally ill'.

By this process of psychiatrisation, 'millions of children are no longer regarded as part of the ordinary spectrum…but as people who are qualitatively different from the "normal" population' (Schrag & Divoky, 1981, p. 36).

> ### Reflection point
>
> What does it mean that millions of children are no longer seen as normal? As well as the individual and familial 'side effects' of reliance on psychotropic drugs, what are the social and political 'side effects'?

Skovdal (2012) found the literature on the mental health of HIV-affected children in sub-Saharan Africa focused on pathology and overlooked resilience and local support. This is problematic because classifications and labels ultimately provide the conceptual tools with which children understand themselves, how they negotiate local support within communities, and how others relate to them. If these labels focus on pathology and vulnerability this may render children powerless and increasingly reliant on professional expertise and psychiatric medications.

Focus on 'illness' and pathology may also divert attention from the wider sociopolitical context in which both children, and understandings of what constitutes a 'good childhood', are embedded. For example, Rabaia, Saleh and Giacaman (2014, p. 172) point out that the emphasis on attending to Palestinian children's distress as an 'illness' in need of 'cure' obscures the source of this distress as embedded in the historical, collective and cumulative exposure to 'dispossession, expulsion, occupation, repression and military attacks'.

> ### Reflection point
>
> How might a psychologist react differently to a child they were told was 'mentally ill' than to a child they were told was sad? How would you work with a child you were told has a chemical imbalance compared to a child you were told has recently been through a hard time?

If children's fidgeting, lack of concentration or sadness are understood as being 'symptoms' of 'mental disorders', then arguably one of the implications is that more children globally should have access to medication. But by assuming the 'problem' is inside children's brains, in their faulty brain chemicals, does this divert attention and resources away from pushing for social equality and eradicating poverty?

So, a central danger of psychiatrisation is that, while living in poverty or conflict may lead to psychological distress, correcting only the psychological issues will not necessarily correct the conditions that lead to children's distress in the first place. In fact, it may actually allow such conditions to persist or worsen. Thus, one of the side effects of psychiatrisation is that it may constitute an approach that promotes pills for life's ills.

PSYCHOTROPIC CHILDHOODS: ADHD EXAMINED

Of the 11% of children diagnosed with ADHD in the USA, two-thirds were prescribed psychostimulants (methylphenidate) – the medication given for ADHD, often known by brand names, such as Ritalin (Schwarz & Cohen, 2013). Children as young as 2 years old are increasingly being given psychotropic drugs, and children are increasingly being prescribed more than one psychotropic drug at a time – known as polypharmacy (Zito et al., 2008; Olfson et al., 2002). Thus, while medication may be helpful to some children at certain times, a grave concern is that it dominates mental health care and obscures other options and ways of supporting children.

There is growing evidence that questions the science behind psychiatric diagnoses and the efficacy of many psychotropic drugs. In fact, critical psychiatrist Joanna Moncrieff (2009) points out that there is no evidence that psychiatric disorders are caused by imbalances of chemicals in brains and no evidence that psychotropic drugs work by correcting these imbalances.

Furthermore, these drugs can sometimes be harmful. For example, Sami Timimi (2002) points out that psychostimulants, the drugs prescribed for ADHD, are highly addictive and have no proven long-term benefit for children. In fact, research into the long-term effects of stimulant use in children has found: suppressed growth, tics, sudden cardiac death, dullness, anxiety and psychosis (Breggin, 2002; for a review of the literature, see Whitaker, 2010). Healy (n.d.) points out that:

> The drugs used to treat ADHD are the same [chemically] as speed and cocaine. We react with horror to the idea that our kids would use such drugs, but don't react about drugs such as Ritalin being given to them, by doctors. (Cited in Fowler, 2010, p. 21)

Why do adults worry about children taking 'recreational' drugs but then actively promote use of prescribed drugs for children? And why do doctors prescribe these drugs to children?

Sales of stimulants to treat ADHD more than doubled in the USA, from $4 billion in 2007 to $9 billion in 2012 (Schwarz & Cohen, 2013). Because of the huge financial profits to be gained from persuading doctors to frame more and more of children's behaviour as symptoms of 'mental disorder', some critics say that the pharmaceutical industry is responsible for the huge increase in diagnosis. And it is not only stimulants that are prescribed to children. Despite never having been tested on children, from 1993–2002, prescriptions for neuroleptics (antipsychotics) in the USA for young people increased fivefold, in part due to pharmaceutical company promotion (Crystal et al., 2009). The companies that promoted these drugs in the USA were recently sued for deceptive promotion when harmful side effects of the drugs came to light. However, even where drugs have been tested on children, as with the newer antidepressants, when trials showed an increased risk of suicide among children taking the drug, the company running the trials kept this secret (Healy, 2006). Yet despite the problems we have seen with antidepressants and antipsychotics, both drugs are on the World Health Organization's list of essential medicines for children (WHO, 2011).

Furthermore, despite the lack of evidence about efficacy, many proponents of global mental health – who call for the scale-up of mental health services to low- and middle-income countries – argue that a 'crucial aspect of access to effective treatment for ADHD is access to the psychostimulants and other pharmacological agents' (Flisher et al., 2010, pp. 1, 5). They argue that children in low- and middle-income countries have less or no access to these medications, that this reflects an inequality between children in rich and poor countries and lobby for the inclusion of psychostimulants on the WHO's list of essential medicines.

Reflection point

Thinking about the evidence that shows these drugs can be harmful, should every child have the right to access drugs that have been found to be harmful in the long term? How does potentially harmful or ineffective treatment, like drugs, get redefined as being essential?

A further important and underresearched question centres on how children understand ADHD and the medication they take. On speaking with children with a diagnosis of ADHD, Arora and Mackey (2004) found that many children saw themselves as passive recipients in a process where they had little choice or control; and many children saw medication as a way of controlling their behaviour. Thus, diagnosis and prescriptions of medication may work to reduce a child's sense of agency leading them to internalise 'a potentially lifelong script of disability', which 'exposes children to a plethora of untested, possibly harmful, psychotropic medications' (Timimi & Maitra, 2005, p. 22). In LeFrançois' (2006) research, children in an inpatient unit in the UK felt adults were 'infecting' their bodies forcibly with medications. In Spandler's (1996) work with young people who self-harm, young people wanted adults to recognise and respect different ways of coping and provide safe spaces for children to engage in this. Taking this research seriously, should we advocate for every child to have the right to a psychiatric or psychotropic childhood?

Final reflections

- How do psychotropic drugs bring into being new categories of childhood, and new ways to be a child?
- What does it mean that millions of children now understand themselves through brain chemicals and see medication as a means for them to control their behaviour?
- How can psychologists recognise and alleviate children's distress without pathologising children; without reducing children's agency; and without overlooking that children's lives are embedded within social and economic conditions?

REFERENCES

Armstrong, T. (1997). *The myth of the A.D.D. child: 50 ways to improve your child's behavior and attention span without drugs, labels, or coercion*. New York: Plume.

Arora, T. & Mackey, L. (2004). Talking and listening to children diagnosed with ADHD and taking psychostimulants. In T. Billington & M. Pomerantz (Eds.), *Children at the margins: Supporting children, supporting schools*. Stoke-on-Trent: Trentham Books.

Breggin, P.R. (2002). *The Ritalin fact book. What your doctor won't tell you.* Cambridge: Perseus Books.

Crystal, S., Olfson, M., Huang, C., Pincus, H. & Gerhard, T. (2009). Broadened use of atypical antipsychotics: Safety, effectiveness, and policy challenges. *Health Affairs, 28*, 770–781.

Ferrari, A.J., Charlson, F.J., Norman, R.E., Patten, S.B., Freedman, G., Murray, C.J.L., Vos, T. & Whiteford, H.A. (2013). Burden of depressive disorders by country, sex, age, and year: Findings from the Global Burden of Disease Study 2010. *PLOS Medicine, 10*(11), e1001547. doi:10.1371/journal.pmed.1001547.

Flisher, A.J., Sorsdahl, K., Hatherill, S., & Chehil, S. (2010). Packages of care for attention-deficit hyperactivity disorder in low- and middle-income countries. *PLoS Medicine, 7*(2), 1–7.

Fowler, G. (2010). Turning children into mental patients: ADHD in the UK. *Asylum, 17*(2), n.p.

Green, H., McGinnity, A., Meltzer, H., et al. (2005). *Mental health of children and young people in Great Britain 2004.* London: Palgrave.

Healy, D. (2006). The latest mania: Selling bipolar disorder. *PLoS Medicine, 3*(4), 441–444.

Horwitz, A.V. & Wakefield, J.C. (2006). The epidemic in mental illness: Clinical fact or survey artifact? *Contexts, 5*(1), 19–23.

Ingleby, D. (1974). The psychology of child psychology. In M.P.M. Richards (Ed.), *The integration of a child into a social world.* Cambridge: Cambridge University Press.

Institute for Health Metrics and Evaluation. (2013). *GBD Compare.* University of Washington. Online at http://viz.healthmetricsandevaluation.org/gbd-compare/# (accessed 5 April 2014).

Jadhav, S. (2007). Dhis and dhat: Evidence of semen retention syndrome amongst white Britons. *Anthropology and Medicine, 14*(3), 229–239.

Kessler, R.C., Adler, L., Barkley, R., Biederman, J., Conners, C.K., Demler, O., … & Spencer, T. (2006). The prevalence and correlates of adult ADHD in the United States: Results from the National Comorbidity Survey Replication. *American Journal of Psychiatry, 163*, 716–723.

Kleinman, A. (1988). *Rethinking psychiatry: From cultural category to personal experience.* New York: The Free Press.

LeFrançois, B.A. (2006). 'They will find us and infect our bodies': The views of adolescent inpatients taking psychiatric medication. *Radical Psychology, 5.* Online at http://www.radpsynet.org/journal/vol5/LeFrancois.html (accessed 28 July 2016).

Moncrieff, J. (2009). *A straight talking introduction to psychiatric drugs.* Ross-on-Wye: PCCS Books.

Murray, C.J. & Lopez, A.D. (1996). *The Global Burden of Disease: A comprehensive assessment of mortality and disability from diseases, injuries and risk factors in 1990 and projected to 2020,* Vol. I. Cambridge, MA: Harvard School of Public Health.

Olfson, M., Marcus, S.C., Weissman, M.M. & Jensen, P.S. (2002). National trends in the use of psychotropic medications by children. *Journal of American Child and Adolescent Psychiatry, 41*(5), 514–521.

Patel, V., Flisher, A.J., Hetrick, S. & McGorry, P. (2007). Mental health of young people: A global public-health challenge. *Lancet, 369*, 1302–1313.

Polanczyk, G., de Lima, M.S., Horta, B.L., Biederman, J. & Rohde, L.A. (2007). The worldwide prevalence of ADHD: A systematic review and meta-regression analysis. *American Journal of Psychiatry, 164*, e942–e948.

Rabaia, Y., Saleh, M.F. & Giacaman, R. (2014). Sick or sad? Supporting Palestinian children living in conditions of chronic political violence. *Children and Society, 28*, 172–181.

Schwarz, A. & Cohen, S. (2013). A.D.H.D. seen in 11% of U.S. children as diagnoses rise. *New York Times*, 31 March 2013. Online at http://www.nytimes.com/2013/04/01/health/more-diagnoses-of-hyperactivity-causing-concern.html (accessed 10 July 2013).

Schrag, P. & Divoky, D. (1981). *The myth of the hyperactive child and other means of child control.* Harmondsworth: Penguin.

Skovdal, M. (2012). Pathologising healthy children? A review of the literature exploring the mental health of HIV-affected children in sub-Saharan Africa. *Transcultural Psychiatry, 49*(3–4), 461–491.

Spandler, H. (1996). *Who's hurting who?* Gloucester: Handsell.

Timimi S. (2002). *Pathological child psychiatry and the medicalization of childhood.* Hove: Brunner-Routledge.

Timimi, S. & Maitra, B. (Eds.) (2005). *Critical voices in child and adolescent mental health.* London: Free Association Books.

UNICEF. (2014).*The state of the world's children 2014 in numbers. Every child counts: Revealing disparities, advancing children's rights.* New York: UNICEF.

Whitaker, R. (2010). *Anatomy of an epidemic: Magic bullets, psychiatric drugs, and the astonishing rise of mental illness in America.* New York: Broadway Paperbacks.

WHO. (2004). The World Health Organization Composite International Diagnostic Interview (CIDI). Online at www.hcp.med.harvard.edu/wmhcidi/ (accessed 23 September 2012).

WHO. (2011). *Model list of essential medicines for children* (3rd edn). Geneva: World Health Organization.

Zito, J.M., Safer, D.J., Sai, D., Gardner, J.F., Thomas, D., Coombes, P., Dubowski, M. & Mendez-Lewis, M. (2008). Psychotropic medication patterns among youth in foster care. *Pediatrics, 121*(1), e157–e164.

14 The Teacher's Role in Supporting Student Mental Health and Well-being

HELEN MONKMAN

LEARNING OBJECTIVES

After reading this chapter you should be able to:

1. Understand some of the ways in which teachers construct mental health.

2. Recognise how teachers can position themselves as having a role in supporting student mental health.

3. Understand that through the language they use teachers are active agents in constructing their identity and role in meeting the mental health and well-being needs of students.

Within the context of a reported rise in mental health problems (MacKay, 2007; Child and Adolescent Mental Health Services Review (CAMHS Review), 2008; Department of Health (DoH), 2011), there has been an escalation in government initiatives and guidance documents with the expressed purpose of promoting collaborative work between agencies and enhancing the role of schools in supporting the mental health and well-being of children and young people (National Healthy Schools Programme (DCSF & DoH, 2007); CAMHS Review, 2008; Targeted Mental Health in Schools Project (TaMHS: DCSF, 2008).

With the promotion of collaborative working and the influence of health agencies, medicalised language has gained an impetus within government initiatives and guidance documents. For example, the TaMHS Project (DCSF, 2008, p. 8) recognises the wide range of terminology used but specifically states the importance of using the term 'mental health… since a key aspect is to bring the expertise of medical professionals into school'. Within the TaMHS Project document specific language around pathology is introduced in the section providing descriptions of different areas of mental health need such as 'eating disorders', 'depression' and 'deliberate self-harm' (DCSF, 2008, pp. 35–43). The TaMHS Project even places teachers in the group of practitioners they call 'Generic CAMHS', suggesting that this 'umbrella term' (DCSF, 2008, p. 11) should include all services contributing towards the mental health of children and young people, making it 'everybody's business'.

It could be suggested that the danger of using medicalised language is to introduce discourses around 'illness' and 'pathology' into schools with suggestions that children will require 'therapeutic intervention' or 'treatment'. However, teachers may feel uncomfortable with such a drive and feel themselves in conflict with the 'mental health in schools' priority which is to make issues around mental health 'everybody's business'. Although such initiatives place teachers at the front line in supporting the mental health and well-being needs of young people, the views of teachers regarding the extension of their role have not been fully explored (Kidger et al., 2010).

This chapter gives an overview of a recent study which explored how teachers positioned themselves as having a role and responsibility in meeting the mental health and well-being needs of their students (Monkman, 2013). This research identified and analysed the 'interpretative repertoires' teachers draw on when talking about mental health and well-being. The results provided an insight into how young people are being supported and how teachers may need to be supported themselves when meeting the mental health and well-being needs of the young people in the school.

THE STUDY

Participants were six secondary school teachers from a high school in the north of England, which had been selected to implement the TaMHS Project (DCSF, 2008) – a project funded by the DCSF with the aim of encouraging collaborative work between agencies involved in supporting the mental health of children and young people in schools. The teachers were interviewed to explore narratives of their experience. To protect the teachers' anonymity substitute names have been used when reporting their responses. Transcripts from the interviews were analysed using discourse analysis (see Appendix for an explanation of the symbols used). Three interpretative repertoires were identified; mental health as illness, mental health as well-being, and mental health and behaviour. Each interpretative repertoire was examined to consider how teachers drew on ethical, moral, social and institutional norms to construct a position within their role and responsibility towards the young people in the school.

REPERTOIRE 1: MENTAL HEALTH AS ILLNESS

When constructing mental health as illness the teachers drew on psychiatric discourses using language around the labelling of behaviour as reported in the DSM-5 (American Psychiatric Association, 2012), such as 'schizophrenia' and 'depression'. This is illustrated in the extract below when Sally is asked what mental health means to her:

> Em (.) when I think of mental health I think of things like depression (.) em (1) things like schizophrenia things like (.) em (.) sort of mental illness I don't really (2) think of anything beyond that… (Sally)

   When constructing mental health as illness the teachers positioned themselves as under-confident, disempowered and apprehensive within their role and responsibilities towards the young people, resulting in the view that they need to pass the problem on as illustrated in the extract from Bev below:

> You know like at my old school there was a boy who was self-harming so I just referred him straight away…yeh so I referred him straight away because that's <u>totally</u> out of my remit (.) and in a way I I wouldn't want that responsibility I wouldn't <u>want</u> training on how to deal with self-harm because actually I (.) <u>don't</u> know that I could cope with it or deal with it (.) so you know I think that's kind of a separate job. (Bev)

Question: What impact has the introduction of psychiatric language in policy had on the teachers' view of their role to support mental health?

Reflection point

It could be suggested that the introduction of psychiatric language in policy (TaMHS: DCSF, 2008) produces discourses around pathology which results in teachers feeling de-skilled and helpless such that they need to pass the problem on. Perhaps mental health as illness is a repertoire drawn on by teachers from which they can totally distance themselves, such that it 'dulls reflection' (Crowe, 2000), encouraging them to stop thinking and to stop ask-ing questions. Do the teachers draw on the mental health as illness repertoire when they do not feel they can cope with a situation and the level of responsibility involved? So, by drawing on this repertoire, does it alienate and disempower teachers, absolving them from responsibility and encouraging passivity and passing on to 'specialists'? Alternatively, does the language empower the teachers to act appropriately by referring the young people to 'specialists' (allowing them access to interventions that they would otherwise go without), thus maintaining their responsibility towards the young people?

REPERTOIRE 2: MENTAL HEALTH AS WELL-BEING

In contrast, when the teachers drew on the repertoire of mental health as well-being they positioned themselves as having a positive role and responsibility in supporting the young people, using language around empowerment, emotions, positive support and control. They related this to developing a positive relationship with their students and part of what they did as teachers anyway within their role and responsibility to educate.

Keith indicates the importance of having a positive relationship with the students, suggesting that the relationship is 'essential'. When asked 'Why do you think that is?', he responds:

> because I think kids respond er to people that they know (.) certainly…from my point of view if I know a kid and I know what makes them tick and what they enjoy (.) what they don't like what they're good at and what they're perhaps not so good at you can (.) angle things towards them so that (1) they do better and enjoy themselves more and feel more comfortable. (Keith)

Question: Why do teachers see themselves as having a positive role when drawing on the repertoire of mental health as well-being?

Reflection point

It may be that teachers view their role as supporting students' mental health as well-being as this is implicit to the practice of teaching in order to support learning (Hargreaves, 1998), such that it is 'part and parcel of teaching' (Kidger et al., 2010), or as Mike in the present study puts it: 'that's what we as teachers do anyway…that's common practice'. Could it be that schools often fail to see the relevance of mental health with their concern for learning when they link it to the pathologising discourse? However, when they link it to language around well-being they see their role as linked to learning. This was evident in the study as, when teachers constructed themselves as having a role, they drew on the mental health as well-being repertoire.

REPERTOIRE 3: MENTAL HEALTH AND BEHAVIOUR

Within their narratives the teachers relayed experiences of supporting specific students who they felt had issues around mental health, drawing on descriptions of the student's behaviour when talking about the positive support they had given them. The narratives tended to be lengthy, uninterrupted, confidently delivered and with some sense of positive feeling and responsibility towards the young person. Through their talk teachers positioned themselves as caring, confident and wanting to help. However, on occasions the teachers 'slipped' into the pathological discourse and in doing this their talk became less confident as they constructed a sense of pessimism, disassociating them from responsibility towards supporting the young person – rather abruptly in some cases.

> **Question:** Why, when drawing on the language of behaviour, do teachers feel more confident about meeting the mental health needs of young people without additional specialist support?

> **Reflection point**
>
> It was interesting that when the teachers described the work they did to support the students through descriptions of the student's behaviour and their own behaviour towards the students, it was frequently associated with critical reflection on the terminology used: 'I mean whether that's a mental health issue or whether that's just quiet or extremely quiet' (Keith). So, by rejecting the pathologising discourses and supporting the normalising language of behaviour, the process often led to them changing their view and recognising that they did have a role. This critical reflection on the discourses used when talking about their practice enabled teachers to reflect on the initial construction of their role and reverse them (Mitchell, 2009). This process could be seen as a form of framing effect whereby different features of an issue are made more accessible when talking about attitudes and when making judgements (Sibley, Liu & Kirkwood, 2006).
>
> By focusing on the normalising discourse, or language of behaviour, teachers created a position where they did have a role. By drawing on the language of behaviour it encouraged the opening up of questions, thought and talk to be proactive in finding solutions.

CONTROL AND RESPONSIBILITY

When talking about mental health and well-being the teachers drew on the concept of control, both in terms of the young people's self-control and responsibilities and the teachers' control and responsibilities in relation to this.

'cause your emotional well-being is how you feel isn't it (mmm) (3) you've perhaps got more control perhaps over your emotional well-being to an extent (.) there's maybe more you can do about that whereas mental health is (.) you know can be chemical imbalances as well can't it? (Bev)

Baker and Newnes (2005) suggest that the dominant medical discourse and the DSM-IV (American Psychiatric Association, 1994) have implications for the discourse of responsibility. They suggest that the DSM creates a version of mentally ill people as not able to control their behaviour and therefore not being responsible. This idea could have an effect on the teachers' confidence in their ability to support; because the young person is not in control they, as teachers, do not feel in control and therefore they do not feel that they have the responsibility, as it is the responsibility of 'specialists'.

Question: Does teacher talk around the concept of control structure their identity in relation to their role and responsibilities?

Reflection point

Teachers see their role as educators so they are comfortable with the concepts of thought and cognition within their role and responsibility to educate. Their talk around well-being, linked to emotions, would suggest a degree of confidence about these concepts – the link to learning and their role and responsibilities as teachers to support this. They can work with the rational and are beginning to relate to the emotions. However, where they see the transition from the rational and emotional linked to health, into ill-heath, physiological factors and 'chemical imbalances' (Bev), which are out of the young person's control, they themselves feel they do not have control and they disengage from responsibility. This hierarchy of control and responsibility is illustrated in Figure 14.1.

DILEMMAS AND TENSIONS

Each teacher produced a variety of contradictory repertoires creating tensions and dilemmas within their talk. One such dilemma was the tension between mental health as illness, and passing the problem and responsibility on, and mental health as well-being with the responsibility to support. The teachers slipped from one repertoire to the other to position themselves in two contrasting ways; as helpless and out of their depth, or being there to support. This is illustrated when Sally talks about a boy who was 'very very very depressed'. She switches from a position of disempowerment and uncertainty – 'I felt a little bit out of my depth...I didn't know how to respond' – to the ethical and moral position of being supportive – 'actually you're probably the best person to keep your eye on them to see how

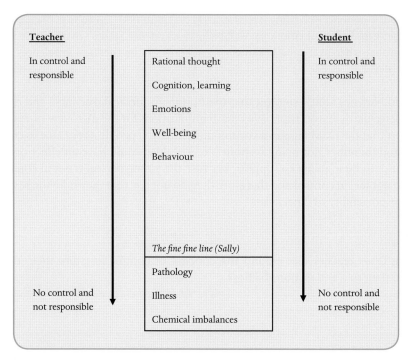

Figure 14.1   *The hierarchy of control and responsibility*

they're feeling; to ask them, you know, what you can do to help them'. The drive within education to support well-being and learning, drawing on teachers' moral responsibility, is complicated by the pathologising discourse, which creates uncertainty about responsibility. This perhaps demands an ethical response from teachers as they grapple with thoughts and feelings related to who is the right person to support young people going through difficult times.

The other dilemma evident in the teachers' talk was their role to support well-being and their role to 'get results'. The dominant government agenda to raise standards may lead to the competing discourses around emotional support and raising standards,

Todd (2003) suggests that teachers are faced with ethical and moral conflicts which stem from their dual responsibility to the individual and to the institution. The existence of such tensions and dilemmas are evident in the teachers' talk. As they grappled with how to negotiate this tension they slip from one priority to the other within the same conversation, either to position themselves as having a role and responsibility in supporting the mental health and well-being of the young people, or in the role to educate and 'get results'.

Question: How do these oppositional constructions impact on policy and practice?

Reflection point

These oppositional constructions of mental health and well-being and raising standards have important implications for policy and practice in the 'everybody's business' agenda and in the agenda promoting education services and CAMHS working collaboratively as promoted by the TaMHS Project. In the study reviewed here (Monkman, 2013), the competing discourses were often used to either explain or defend a position of lack of, or low level of, involvement or responsibility. For example, Keith does this when he defends his position of not 'dealing wi' wi' kids with mental health problems' by stating that 'that's not what we're here to do as professionals … I think we're here to educate'. If a person believes that they are not able to contribute towards a particular activity, in this case supporting mental health difficulties, they may be less likely to take part in collaborative initiatives around that activity (Mitchell, 2009). Mitchell suggests that when roles are constructed based on oppositional discourses this could create resistance to the adoption of new roles and practices.

LISTENING TO THE TEACHERS

The study highlights that teachers are active agents in constructing their identity and role in meeting the mental health and well-being needs of students. Through the discursive practices they use and the interpretative repertoires they tap into, they construct an identity that they want to be heard, and from that identity they construct a role for themselves. The interviews allowed the teachers time and space to tell their story and enabled them to explore their thoughts and feelings about how young people are supported. This allowed them to think through issues, in a less restrictive way, providing them with the space for critical reflection, thus allowing them to form and re-form experiences, to construct and reconstruct their role so as to enhance the sense that they can act appropriately to support the students.

Question: What implications does this have for the role of the educational psychologist?

Reflection point

As educational psychologists, we need to recognise the power of teacher narratives to 'render events socially visible and typically establish expectations for future events' (Gergen, 1973, p. 248). How teachers construct mental health, through their discussions with us, will determine what they expect of us. In our role we need to listen to their story and support them in the process of critical reflection to help them understand their role in supporting the students. This raises the question as to whether teachers are offered space and time, away from the pressures of the classroom, to gather their thoughts and reflect. Hargreaves (2000) comments on the worrying neglect of the emotional dimension of teaching in the world of increasing educational reform.

IMPLICATIONS FOR PRACTICE

This chapter suggests that the language drawn on by teachers, when talking about mental health and well-being, is powerful in positioning them within their role of supporting young people in schools. This has implications for practice as outlined below:

Policy makers

- Care needs to be taken by policy makers when considering the language introduced into schools through policy initiatives and projects around mental health and well-being, so as not to draw on discourses that disempower and disengage teachers from a role to support.

- Policy and research focuses on the need to train teachers in skills to support the mental health needs of children (TaMHS: DCSF, 2008; CAMHS Review, 2008; Finney, 2009; Bostock, Kitt & Kitt, 2011). Careful consideration needs to be given to which mental health and well-being discourses are drawn upon when training teachers. This is important as overly psychiatric language may distance teachers from their role and responsibilities to support.

Supporting professionals

- Within their supporting role, professionals need to be able to think about their professional identity within the context of education. They need to consider the language they use around mental health and well-being when supporting schools. They need to look at how they can collaborate with schools and teachers in a meaningful way to support students rather than seeing their support either as an addition to the system or as a means of taking the responsibility away from the schools or teachers.

Schools and teachers

- There needs to be greater clarity about the teachers' role and responsibilities in supporting students' mental health and well-being, so as to raise their confidence and make them realise that they are not expected to take on the role of therapists and implement specialist interventions. Rather they are key in developing relationships and strategies within their classroom, so as to support the students and have the confidence to draw on outside agencies to support them in this role.

THE ROLE OF THE EDUCATIONAL PSYCHOLOGIST

It needs to be recognised that those that draw upon critical psychological resources are themselves a key resource when it comes to supporting teachers and schools in meeting the mental health and well-being needs of children and young people. Indeed educational psychologists are the professionals, outside school staff, who are most embedded in school systems and have an

THE TEACHER'S ROLE   155

understanding and expertise in child development, mental health interventions, education and school systems. They are a profession that straddles the world of education and psychology. As such, critical educational psychologists and others that draw upon critical psychological resources, might prove to be helpful interpreters of discourses relating to mental health and well-being.

Final reflections

- What interpretative repertoires will you draw upon when you work to support children and young people with social, emotional and mental health needs?
- Are you colluding with or rejecting psychiatric discourse?
- How does this have an impact on how the children and young people you work with are supported?

REFERENCES

American Psychiatric Association. (1994). *Diagnostic and Statistical Manual of Mental Disorders* (DSM-IV). Washington, DC: American Psychiatric Association.

American Psychiatric Association. (2012). *Diagnostic and Statistical Manual of Mental Disorders* (DSM-5). Washington, DC: American Psychiatric Association.

Baker, E. & Newnes, C. (2005). The discourse of responsibility. In C. Newnes & N. Radcliffe (Eds.), *Making and breaking children's lives*. Wyastone Leys: PCCS Books.

Bostock, A.J., Kitt, R. & Kitt, C. (2011). Why wait until qualified? The benefits and experiences of undergoing mental health awareness training for PGCE students. *Pastoral Care in Education*, 29(2), 103–115.

CAMHS Review. (2008). Children and young people in mind: The final report of the national CAMHS Review. Online at http://webarchive.nationalarchives.gov.uk/20081230004520/publications.dcsf.gov.uk/eorderingdownload/camhs-review.pdf (accessed 14 June 2016).

Crowe, M. (2000). Constructing normality: A discourse analysis of the DSM-IV. *Journal of Psychiatric and Mental Health Nursing*, 7, 69–77

Department for Children, Schools and Families (DCSF). (2008). Targeted Mental Health in Schools Project. Using the evidence to inform your approach: A practical guide for headteachers and commissioners. Online at http://webarchive.nationalarchives.gov.uk/20130401151715/https://www.education.gov.uk/publications/eorderingdownload/00784-2008bkt-en.pdf (accessed 14 June 2016).

Department for Children, Schools and Families (DCSF) & Department of Health (DoH). (2007). Guidance for schools on developing emotional health and well-being. Online at http://www.healthyschools.london.gov.uk/sites/default/files/EHWB.pdf (accessed 14 June 2016)

Department of Health (DoH). (2011). *No health without mental health*. London: DH Publications.

Finney, D. (2009). The road to self-efficacy: A discussion of generic training in mental health competencies for educational professionals. *Pastoral Care in Education*, 27(1), 21–28.

Gergen, K.J. (1973). Social psychology as history. Cited in C. Willig. (2001). *Introducing qualitative research in psychology*. Philadelphia: Open University Press.

Hargreaves, A. (1998). The emotional politics of teaching and teacher development: With implications for educational leadership. *International Journal of Leadership in Education*, 1(4), 315–336.

Hargreaves, A. (2000). Mixed emotions: Teachers' perceptions of their interactions with students. *Teaching and Teacher Education*, 16, 811–826.

Jefferson, G. (1984). Transcript notation. Cited in K. Pomerantz (2008). Analysing and interpreting spoken discourse: Educational psychologists as reflexive practitioners. *Educational & Child Psychology*, 25(1), 5–16.

Kidger, J., Gunnell, D., Biddle, L., Campbell, R. & Donovan, J. (2010). Part and parcel of teaching? Secondary school staff's views on supporting student emotional health and well-being. *British Educational Research Journal*, 36(6), 919–935.

Mackay, T. (2007). Educational psychology: The fall and rise of therapy. *Educational & Child Psychology*, 24(2), 125–139.

Mitchell, P.F. (2009). A discourse analysis on how service providers in non-medical primary health and social care services understand their roles in mental health care. *Social Science & Medicine*, 68, 1213–1220.

Monkman, H. (2013). The teacher's role in supporting student mental health and wellbeing – A discursive case study. Unpublished research thesis submitted in part requirement for the Doctor of Education, Department of Educational Studies, University of Sheffield.

Sibley, C.G., Liu, J.H. & Kirkwood, S. (2006). Towards a social representations theory of attitude change: The effect of message framing on general and specific attitudes towards equality and entitlement. *New Zealand Journal of Psychology*, 35(1), 3–13. Cited in P.F. Mitchell (2009), A discourse analysis on how service providers in non-medical primary health and social care services understand their roles in mental health care. *Social Science & Medicine*, 68, 1213–1220.

Todd, S. (2003). A fine risk to be run? The ambiguity of eros and teacher responsibility. *Studies in Philosophy and Education*, 22, 31–44.

APPENDIX

The method of transcription used when transcribing the interviews included aspects of Jefferson's (1984) transcription as indicated below:

(.) pause less than one second

(1) pause approximately one second, and so on

[ ] utterances overlap

= at the end of speech signals that it has been interrupted, and at the beginning signals that it has recommenced.

Underlined added emphasis

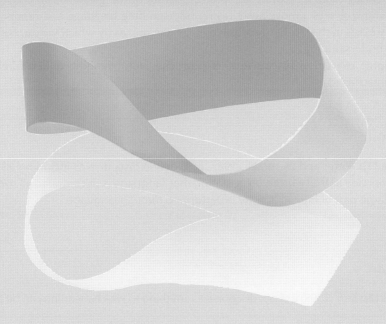

LEARNING OBJECTIVES

After reading this chapter you should be able to:

1. Become familiar with some critical perspectives on discourses around difficult behaviour in schools.

2. Understand the basic principles of restorative justice.

3. Develop an awareness of how making links between different discourses can assist practitioners in introducing preferred ways of thinking.

INTRODUCTION

As outlined earlier (Tim Corcoran, Chapter 2), within ontological (social) constructionism a focus on language sees a move away from understanding language as a representation of what already exists in the world towards language as a means by which we can construct our ontological understanding.

This chapter recognises discourse as a powerful factor in how difficult behaviour in schools is constructed.

> **Definition**
>
> **Discourse (1):** Potter and Wetherell (1987, p. 9) define discourse as including all forms of spoken language and all written texts, stating that 'language is so central to all social activities…'; a large part of human activity is performed *through* language.

> **Definition**
>
> **Discourse (2):** Burr (2003) defines discourse as anything to which meaning can be attached.

I will take a critical look at dominant discourses on difficult behaviour and outline the need to consider how we might develop alternative discourses based on restorative justice (RJ) in order to 'open new paths to action' (Gergen, 2009, p. 81). I will consider how making links and highlighting commonalities between discourses can assist in constructing alternative discourses (McNamee & Gergen, 1999), such as RJ.

DOMINANT DISCOURSES ON DIFFICULT BEHAVIOUR

Behaviourism

Behaviourism and social learning has predominated within behaviour management and continues to be influential in education today (Morrison & Vaandering, 2012; Shaughnessy, 2012). Two frameworks – the antedecent–behaviour–consequence framework (Bull & Solity, 1987; Cameron, 1998) and assertive discipline model (Cameron, 1998; Canter & Canter, 1992) – have been developed within education in particular.

The influence of these models is clear in behaviour management texts, government documentation and general advice on behaviour management (e.g., Shaughnessy, 2012; DfE,

2010; Cowley, 2003). Cowley (2003) outlines the basics of behaviour management as being definite, aware, calm and consistent, providing structure and being positive. Sir Alan Steer as part of his government review summarised what works for schools as follows:

> Consistent experience of good teaching promotes good behaviour. But schools also need to have positive strategies for managing pupil behaviour that helps pupils understand their school's expectations, underpinned by a clear range of rewards and sanctions, which are applied fairly and consistently by all staff. It is also vital to teach pupils how to behave – good behaviour has to be learnt – so schools must adopt procedures and practices that help pupils learn how to behave. Good behaviour has to be modelled by all staff all of the time in their interaction with pupils. (DfES, 2005, p. 10)

Data from the author's own doctoral study (Harold & Corcoran, 2013; Harold, 2012) indicated that behaviourism was dominant within the high school which participated in the study, where there was a proliferation of discussion and vocabulary around consistency, clarity and expectations as well as a stated desire to achieve these ideals.

While the principles of behaviourism per se have come in for some critique – it can be perceived as a 'quick fix' (Shaughnessy, 2012), lacking the capacity to acknowledge the complexities of life, focusing too heavily on control and fragment behaviour (Cameron, 1998) – it is the rigidity with which such models are often executed which has received the greatest criticism, including a focus on punishment and its application within discourses of zero tolerance.

Reflection point

What are your own experiences of behaviourist discourses in education?

Zero tolerance

A discourse of zero tolerance (ZT) draws heavily on principles of reinforcement and modelling and is characterised by hierarchies of rewards and sanctions, usually culminating in exclusion. The American Psychological Association Zero Tolerance Task Force (APA, 2008, p. 852) define a discourse of ZT as 'a philosophy or policy that mandates the application of predetermined consequences, most often severe and punitive in nature, that are intended to be applied regardless of the gravity of behaviour, mitigating circumstances, or situational context'. ZT includes the presumption that the removal of students from the classroom will deter others.

There are indications that a discourse of ZT is increasingly dominant within schools, particularly within the USA (APA, 2008; Schoonover, 2008), but to an increasing extent within the UK. Parsons (1999) reports that Britain is dominated by an authoritative and punitive orientation and Clough et al. (2005) argue that Britain is experiencing an era characterised by ZT, while McCluskey et al. (2011) conclude that one of the biggest challenges to alternative approaches is the 'default' setting of punishment. The policy document of the school participating in the author's study (Harold & Corcoran, 2013; Harold, 2012) provides an example of the hierarchical use of sanctions (see extract 1 below).

Extract 1

iii. Consequences

When addressing undesired behaviour, staff <u>should</u> apply the following consequences:

- C1: Polite warning
- C2: Second warning
- C3: 10–20 minutes detention
- C4: Removal to other classroom and/or 30 minute detention
- C5: 'On-Call' + 45 minute detention

Reflection point

What longer term outcomes may be achieved for pupil behaviour using this approach?

Concerns

The use of sanctions and exclusion are repeatedly reported to be ineffective in changing student behaviour (APA, 2008; Galvin, 1999). Concerns have also been raised about the impact that ZT approaches have on minority groups (APA, 2008; MacGillivary, Medal & Drakey, 2008; Sullivan, 2008); their failure to address causal factors (Stinchcomb, Bazemore & Reistenberg, 2006) and to meet underlying needs (Mahaffey & Newton, 2008); the inflexibility of such approaches and a 'one-size-fits-all' attitude (APA, 2008; MacGillivary et al., 2008; Galvin, 1999); their capacity to alienate (Morrison, 2007); the negative impact on the community and on crime (Thorsborne & Vinegrad, 2008); and the inconsistency of such approaches with adolescent development (APA, 2008).

> Policy and practice which seek to exclude those very students who are in greatest need of social support and an education simply relocate the problem in time and place and may exacerbate it. (Cameron & Thorsborne, 2001, p. 189)

A ZT discourse draws heavily on the need for a socially constructed standard against which all students can be judged, which may not be equally accessible to all children from all ethnic backgrounds (Vavrus & Cole, 2002). The Restorative Practices Development Team (RPDT, 2003) believe that punitive discourses use totalising, deficit and internalising language, which can lead only to the conclusion that fault lies with the individual. This risks presenting a fixed or static view of an individual and implies objectivity to our understanding of children akin to that which has developed around the topic of intelligence (see Tim Corcoran, Chapter 2). In doing so it fails to recognise the socially constructed nature of both the behaviours being condemned, the systems developed in response to these behaviours and the role of the school in those behaviours (Shaughnessy, 2012); engaging Corcoran's notion of first nature psychology and the presumption that knowledge represents the natural state of human beings.

It has been argued that it is schools' needs and not those of the students which have influenced the predominance of some discourses over others, including schools' need to regulate time, activity, speech and body; and that schools frequently commit 'fundamental attribution error' in presuming that the causation of difficult behaviour lies outside of them and within someone else (Thomas, 2005).

> The organisation of schools requires rules and paradoxically obedience to rules also implies the possibility for disobedience. (Lloyd Bennett, 2005, p. 13)

O'Brien and Miller (2005) analysed the conversation between an educational psychologist and school staff about a pupil's behaviour. Their analysis indicated a tendency for school staff to employ a range of discursive techniques to maintain a within-child explanation and undermine alternative discourses.

However, it would be inappropriate to suggest that the dominance of these discourses is absolute or without alternative. A range of discourses are simultaneously available to us within education (Shaugnessy, 2012), including the 'whole child', emotional learning (Morrison & Vaandering, 2012), cognitive psychology and the concept of 'need'; as well as an enduring recognition of the importance of relationships.

> At the end of the day it is not the drawings, discipline, encouragement, even 'rewards' that see changes in behaviour…it is the quality of the ongoing relationship between teacher and student. (Rogers, 2005, p. 258)

However, many of these approaches fail to fully give up a deficit or within-child understanding (Miller & Todd, 2002) and there are concerns that such approaches represent a polarisation of discipline and pastoral approaches (RPDT, 2003). This would seem to indicate that engagement with additional discourses may be required to adequately address these concerns.

Reflection point

What factors may be contributing to the maintenance of a within-child or individualistic understanding of behaviour? (Consider Chapter 2 on ontological constructionism or Chapter 5 on psychoanalysis.)

RESTORATIVE JUSTICE

Restorative justice (RJ) is a traditional approach (Liebmann, 2007) for addressing conflict or wrongdoing; it focuses on repairing harm and the relationships which may have been damaged. It is characterised by the coming together of the 'wrongdoer' and those affected by the situation in a circle to discuss what has happened and to consider who needs to take accountability, what can be done to put right the wrong and how the needs of the different individuals can be met. It asks the key questions: Who has been hurt? What are their needs? Whose obligations are these? (Zehr, 2002). The definition of RJ is not necessarily universal and, as its popularity has increased, its name has been given to an increasingly varied number of practices (Miller & Blackler, 2000). As such RJ might best be understood not as a particular approach but as a philosophy or way of thinking about conflict.

While the theory of reintegrative shaming (Braithwaite, 1989) has been the most influential theory to date to describe the mechanisms at work within RJ, Corcoran (2014) has offered an alternative lens through which to view RJ, namely social constructionism and Shotter's (1995) 'joint action'. Shotter (1995) describes how when you are 'in it' you feel ethically and morally interlinked – you have a position or place – which is consistent with the involvement of all interested and affected parties within an RJ circle.

Both language and relationships are key aspects within a discourse of RJ. Morris and Young (2000) highlight how within the criminal justice system RJ allows for the voice of 'victims' to be heard, while the RPDT (2003) argue that it is through discourse that individuals come to understand certain actions as just or unjust (see also Cvetkovich & Earle's 'discursive justice', 1994). They believe that RJ can challenge the 'spoiled identities' assigned to people through discourse (RPDT, 2003) and that RJ demands a change of language from one that places fault within individuals to one which recognises collective responsibility.

As such, RJ can also be considered alongside McNamee and Gergen's (1999) work on 'relational responsibility'. Their discontent with the individualistic nature of Western thinking, including its ineffectiveness in resolving conflict and argument, is replaced with the notion of relational responsibility. Relational responsibility is described as an individual participating in an open-ended process of exploration via conversation through which relationships can be altered. Burkitt (1999) describes this as a 'generative dance' – a continual and regulated improvisation where individuals are constantly repositioning themselves. The opportunity for dialogue within RJ practices and the emphasis on valuing a range of perspectives provides the potential for such a dance to occur.

BRIDGING BETWEEN DISCOURSES

Many authors recognise the challenge of changing culture and/or discourses (Roland et al., 2012; Morrison, 2007; Hopkins, 2004), especially in relation to RJ. A common theme is the need to win the 'hearts and minds' of school staff, Blood and Thorsborne (2005, p. 18) stating that 'the implementation of restorative practices risks the fate of many other well intentioned programs unless we understand what it takes to change the hearts and minds of our school communities'.

Morrison (2007) describes the need for 'professional bridging' in the initial stages of introducing RJ. The notion of bridging between two or more positions/discourses is addressed by Gergen (2009) and McNamee and Gergen (1999, p. 19) in their descriptions of how common realities or 'orientating practices' can form the basis of constructing alternative or adapted discourses around which some agreement can be formed. McNamee and Gergen (1999) suggest the need to extend and modify existing discourses, locating traditions where relationships are already central, and energising these alternative discourses. Energising might be understood here as encouraging 're-awareness' of the discourses that people share but which have been forgotten or hidden by more dominant discourses.

This approach could be taken to identify points of agreement between RJ and other more dominant discourses. The social discipline window offered by Wachtel and McCold (2001, p. 117) (see Figure 15.1) presents a model which places the discourse of RJ within continuums of both control and support.

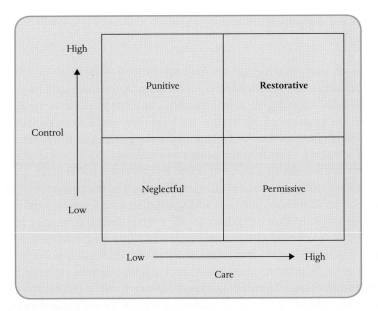

Figure 15.1   *Wachtel and McCold's social discipline window*

Source: Wachtel and McCold (2001, p. 117). Reproduced with permission of Cambridge University Press.

This potentially places RJ as acceptable to those currently concerned with discipline but encourages a shift to allow pastoral approaches and relationships to be more centrally embedded. Like behaviourism, RJ has a focus on consequences and a 'systems discourse'. However, RJ is different in its focus on collective responsibility and on how the behaviour impacts others; and rather than applying specific rules inflexibly it applies general principles in context. This highlights the potential to take a dominant discourse and 'rework' it into something alternative yet familiar. The Restorative Justice Consortium (2010) have used 'bridging' in their briefing to Michael Gove (former Secretary for State for Education) by presenting RJ as 'effective discipline'. McNamee and Gergen (1999, p. 19) describe this as 'conversational moves [which] may broaden and deepen our forms of discourse and enrich the range of reasonable actions in such a way that cultural participants are more fully (or less lethally) coordinated'.

However, a note of caution is required to avoid the potential for RJ's more unique principles of social engagement and social responsibility (Morrison & Vaandering, 2012) to be corrupted. Wheeldon (2009) warns of the risk of co-option of RJ into traditional approaches, highlighting the need to ensure that it does not become a process individuals 'have to' do and that it does not provide a different language for achieving social control. This is an important consideration in light of McCluskey et al.'s (2011) findings that the need for authority and control within schools can support a default 'punishment' position (Vaandering, 2013) and Shaughnessy's (2012) assertion that the power dynamics in schools are often underestimated in discussions about behaviour.

This would suggest the importance of embedding RJ within critical theories of psychology as outlined within previous chapters, including critical psychology and social constructionism; and so ensuring that principles of collectivism, relationships and the importance of language remain non-negotiable.

CONCLUSIONS

The dominance of particular discourses around difficult behaviour in schools is readily present across literature and practice and consideration of the assumptions and implications inherent within them should give pause for thought. This is relevant to educational psychologists given the position of authority and 'expertise' implicit in the role of (signifier) 'psychologist'. Words both spoken and written have the power and the potential to reinforce certain ways of speaking as well as the power to challenge this. That traditions should be discarded and replaced is not an argument posed by this chapter. We have, as Gergen (2009) reminds us, a responsibility to consider the pitfalls as well as the promises of our traditions. RJ is not offered as an alternative but as an additional discourse to use in how we engage with schools in discussion of difficult behaviour. It offers the potential to engage schools in thinking about collective or relational responsibility and to allow for multiple voices to be heard; as well as to critique alternative discourses, their relevance for our schools and the pupils with whom we work. Billington summarises much of this when he reflects that educational psychologists should change from being expert 'knowers' to 'interpreters' or 'experts not necessarily in answers but in the range of questions we can formulate and interpretations we can access' (Billington, 1995, p. 37).

REFERENCES

American Psychological Association Zero Tolerance Task Force (APA). (2008). Are zero tolerance policies effective in the schools? *American Psychologist, 63*(9), 852–862.

Billington, T. (1995). Discourse analysis: Acknowledging interpretation in everyday practice. *Educational Psychology in Practice, 11*(3), 36–45.

Blood, P. & Thorsborne, M. (2005). Overcoming resistance to whole-school uptake of restorative practices. Online at http://www.thorsborne.com.au/ (accessed 12 June 2009).

Braithwaite, J. (1989). *Crime, shame and reintegration.* New York: Cambridge UniversityPress.

Bull, S.L. & Solity, J.E. (1987). *Classroom management: Principles to practice.* London: Routledge.

Burkitt, I. (1999). Relational moves and generative dances. In S. McNamee & K. Gergen (Eds.), *Relational responsibility: Resources for sustainable dialogue* (pp. 71–79). Thousand Oaks, CA: Sage.

Burr, V. (2003). *Social constructionism* (2nd edn). Hove and New York: Routledge.

Cameron, L. & Thorsborne, M. (2001). Restorative justice and school discipline: Mutually exclusive. In H. Strang & J. Braithwaite (Eds.), *Restorative justice and civil society* (pp. 180–194). Cambridge: Cambridge University Press.

Cameron, R.J. (1998). School discipline in the UK: Promoting classroom behaviour which encourages effective teaching and learning. *Educational & Child Psychology, 15*(3), 40–55.

Canter, L. & Canter, M. (1992). *Assertive discipline: Positive discipline for today's classrooms.* Santa Monica: Lee Carter Associates.

Clough, P., Garner, P., Pardeck, J. & Yeun, F. (2005). Themes and dimensions of EBD: A conceptual overview. In P. Clough, P. Garner & F. Yeun (Eds.), *Handbook of emotional and behavioural difficulties* (pp. 3–19). London: Sage.

Corcoran, T. (2014). Doing restorative practices justice: Questioning the psychology of affect theory. In G.S. Goodman (Ed.), *Educational psychology reader: The art and science of how people learn* (pp. 598–610). New York: Peter Lang.

Cowley, S. (2003). Getting the buggers to behave. London: Continuum.

Cvetkovich, G. & Earle, T.C. (1994). The construction of justice: A case study of public participation in land management. *Journal of Social Issues, 50*(3), 161–178.

Department for Education (DfE). (2010). *The importance of teaching: The Schools White Paper 2010.* Norwich: The Stationery Office.

Department for Education and Skills (DfES). (2005). *The report of the practitioners' group on school behaviour and discipline,* Chair: Sir Alan Steer. Nottingham: DfES.

Galvin, P. (1999). *Behaviour and discipline in schools: Practical, positive and creative strategies for the classroom.* London: David Fulton.

Gergen, K.J. (2009). *An invitation to social constructionism* (2nd edn). London: Sage.

Harold, V. (2012). Discourses on behaviour: Is there room for restorative justice in a secondary school? Unpublished doctoral thesis, University of Sheffield.

Harold, V. & Corcoran, T. (2013). Discourses on behaviour: A role for restorative justice? *The International Journal on School Disaffection, 10*(2), 45–62.

Hopkins, B. (2004). *Just schools: A whole school approach to restorative justice.* London: Jessica Kingsley.

Liebmann, M. (2007). *Restorative justice: How it works.* London: Jessica Kingsley.

Lloyd Bennett, P.L. (2005). A broad conceptual framework for the development and management of young people's behavioural difficulties. *Educational & Child Psychology, 22*(3), 6–16.

MacGillivary, H., Medal, M. & Drakey, C. (2008). Zero tolerance policies: A precarious balance between school safety and educational opportunity for all. In K.G. Welner & W.C. Chi (Eds.), *Current issues in educational policy and the law* (pp. 191–127). Charlotte, NC: Information Age.

Mahaffey, H. & Newton, C. (2008). *Restorative solutions: Making it work.* Inclusive Solutions UK.

McCluskey, G., Kane, J., Lloyd, G., Stead, J., Riddell, S. & Weedon, E. (2011). 'Teachers are afraid we are stealing their strength': A risk society and restorative approaches in school. *British Journal of Educational Studies, 59*(2), 105–119.

McNamee, S. & Gergen, K.J. (1999). *Relational responsibility: Resources for sustainable dialogue.* Thousand Oaks, CA: Sage.

Miller, A. & Todd, Z. (2002). Educational psychology and difficult behaviour in schools: Conceptual and methodological challenges for an evidence based profession. *Educational & Child Psychology, 17*(3), 82–95.

Miller, S. & Blackler, J. (2000). Restorative justice: Retribution, confession and shame. In H. Strang & J. Braithwaite (Eds.), *Restorative justice: Philosophy to practice* (pp. 77–91). Aldershot: Dartmoor Publishing.

Morris, A. & Young, W. (2000). Reforming criminal justice: The potential of restorative justice. In H. Strang & J. Braithwaite (Eds.), *Restorative justice: Philosophy to practice* (pp. 11–31). Aldershot: Dartmoor Publishing.

Morrison, B. (2007). *Restoring safe school communities: A whole school response to bullying, violence and alienation.* Sydney: The Federation Press.

Morrison, B.E. & Vaandering, D. (2012). Restorative justice: Pedagogy, praxis, and discipline. *Journal of School Violence, 11*(2), 138–155.

O'Brien, L. & Miller, A. (2005). Challenging behaviour: Analysing teacher language in a school-based consultation within the discursive action model. *Educational & Child Psychology*, 22(1), 61–73.

Parsons, C. (1999). *Education, exclusion and citizenship*. London: Routledge.

Potter, J. & Wetherell, M. (1987). *Discourse and social psychology: Beyond attitudes and behaviour*. London: Sage.

Restorative Justice Consortium. (2010). Briefing to Michael Gove, Secretary of State for Education – Restorative justice in schools. Unpublished letter.

Restorative Practices Development Team (RPDT). (2003). *Restorative practices for schools: a resource*. Online at http://www.waikato.ac.nz/__data/assets/pdf_file/0018/240903/Restorative_Practices_for_Schools_A_Resource-1.pdf (accessed 14 June 2016).

Rogers, B. (2005). Teaching pupils with emotional behavioural disorders. In P. Clough, P. Garner & F. Yeun (Eds.), *Handbook of emotional and behavioural difficulties* (pp. 245–259). London: Sage.

Roland, K., Rideout, G., Salinitri, G. & Frey, M.P. (2012). Development and use of a restorative justice ideology instrument: Assessing beliefs. *Contemporary Justice Review*, 15(4), 435–447.

Schoonover, B.J. (2008). Zero tolerance policies in Florida school districts. *Dissertation Abstracts International Section A: Humanities and Social Sciences*, 68(9A), 3693.

Shaughnessy, J. (2012). The challenge for English schools in responding to current debates on behaviour and violence. *Pastoral Care in Education*, 30(2), 87–97.

Shotter, J. (1995). In conversation: Joint action, shared intentionality and ethics. *Theory and Psychology*, 5(1), 49–73.

Stinchcomb, J.B., Bazemore, G. & Reistenberg, N. (2006). Beyond zero tolerance: Restoring justice in secondary schools. *Youth Violence and Juvenile Justice*, 4, 123–146.

Sullivan, E.L. (2008). The critical policy analysis: The impact of zero tolerance on out-of-school suspensions and expulsions of students of colour in the state of Texas by gender and school level. *Dissertation Abstracts International Section A: Humanities and Social Sciences*, 68, 3719.

Thomas, G. (2005). What do we mean by EBD? In P. Clough, P. Garner & F. Yeun (Eds.), *Handbook of emotional and behavioural difficulties* (pp. 59–82). London: Sage.

Thorsborne, M. & Vinegrad, D. (2008). *Restorative practices and bullying*. Milton Keynes: Speechmark.

Vaandering, D. (2013). Implementing restorative justice practice in schools: What pedagogy reveals. *Journal of Peace Education*, 11(1), 64–80.

Vavrus, F. & Cole, K. (2002). 'I didn't do nothin'': The discursive construction of school suspension. *The Urban Review*, 34(2) 87–111.

Wachtel, T. & McCold, P. (2001). Restorative justice in everyday life. In H. Strang & J. Braithwaite (Eds.), *Restorative justice and civil society* (pp.114–129). Cambridge: Cambridge University Press.

Wheeldon, J. (2009). Finding common ground: Restorative justice and its theoretical construction(s). *Contemporary Justice Review*, 12(1), 91–100.

Zehr, H. (2002). *The little book of restorative justice*. Intercourse, PA: Good Books.

Psychology: Empowering Islamic Perspectives of Muslim Parents

SAMANA SAXTON

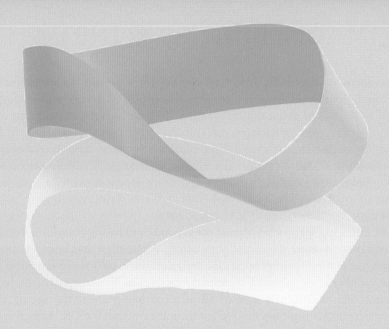

LEARNING OBJECTIVES

After reading this chapter you should be able to:

1. Understand the importance of faith for many Muslim parents in understanding their child's special educational needs.

2. Reflect on how culturally sensitive educational psychology is as a profession in meeting the needs of Muslim families.

This chapter explores the relevance of mainstream Western psychologies for some Muslim families living in the UK. The importance of faith and how it can have an impact on belief systems and the decision-making process of Muslim parents of children with SEN (special educational needs) will be discussed. A context of Islam is provided with an emphasis on disability and emotional well-being through an Islamic faith-based perspective. The aim of this chapter, however, is not to provide a definitive 'Muslim' view; the hope is to go beyond providing an introduction to Islam. The views of some Muslim mothers of children with SEN will be shared in regards to their faith and the impact it has on their understanding of their children's disabilities. All the mothers had worked with an educational psychology service, as well as a number of other professionals within health care and children's services. All names used within this chapter have been anonymised to ensure confidentiality.

MUSLIM COMMUNITIES IN THE UK

Religion can form an important aspect of identity for a person on an individual, family, community and global level. Muslims are a diverse group of people and assumptions cannot be made in regards to geographical location, linguistics, levels of religious observance, acculturation, socio-economic background, cultural identity and political beliefs. The impact of faith is an important area of exploration, particularly given some recent perceptions of Muslim communities. Due to numerous events, such as 9/11, the London, Madrid and Mumbai bombings, the Woolwich murder and more recent terrorist attrocities, Muslims have become more visible, which has resulted in a greater scrutiny of Islamic belief systems and lifestyle patterns (Weatherhead & Daiches, 2010).

The 2011 Census highlights that Islam is the second largest religion within the UK, with 2.7 million Muslims comprising 5% of the population. While there has been a national decline in individuals associating themselves with a religion, since 2001 there has been an increase of 2% in the number of people who identify themselves as Muslims, particularly among the younger generation, with nearly 50% of all Muslims being under the age of 25. Muslims also represent the most ethnically diverse communities within the UK, with over half of the Muslim population being born outside of the UK. Muslims, however, have the highest levels of unemployment of all faith groups in the UK (Office for National Statistics, 2011).

LIMITATIONS OF EDUCATIONAL PSYCHOLOGY

Research shows that parents of disabled children from some Muslim communities experience difficulties in accessing services for their children (Raghavan & Waseem, 2007). While there is an obvious dedication to social justice within educational psychology, there has been little recent discussion, publication and research on issues relating to race and faith. Given the current political climate within the UK, with an increased scrutiny on immigration, multiculturalism and terrorism, and the impact this has on life for minority communities within the UK, there is a strong need to focus on how as a profession educational psychology meets the needs of ethnic minority families. By not discussing such issues there is a danger of marginalising minority communities even further. A failure to have an open and current narrative about race, faith and culture can lead to institutionalised racism becoming invisible and therefore discriminatory practices become more likely to go unchallenged (Inayat, 2005). Therefore there needs to be a greater recognition of the diverse population within which we work as educational psychologists, if we are to adhere to our commitment to social justice.

Reflection points

- Can we encompass faith and spirituality into our work as educational psychologists?
- How confident are we as practitioners in talking about religion?

COMMONALITY AND DIVERSITY AMONG MUSLIM COMMUNITIES

While a variety of theological perspectives and lifestyles exists, Thompson (1997, p. 5) points out that 'religion is a total experience, not just a set of propositions'. As a professional it is important to understand the religious experiences of others in relation to disability to allow for appropriate interventions. Miles (1995, p. 51) highlights that 'to devise suitable resources, one should study people's cultures and their concepts of disability, in order to communicate appropriately'.

Although there are broad variations of beliefs, practices and lifestyle patterns among Muslims, a key commonality is a belief in one God – 'Allah' – and associated belief systems regarding morality and mental health that are unique and distinctive from other faith groups (Rajabi-Ardeshiri, 2009). The notion of *ummah* can also hold tremendous significance for Muslims. *Ummah* refers to a group of individuals who, despite differences, share in the fundamental principles of Islam and therefore have a connection with the faith (Rajabi-Ardeshiri, 2009).

ISLAMIC CONCEPT OF DISABILITY

The Qur'an is the source of divine revelation or scripture for Muslims and is believed to have been revealed to the Prophet Muhammad. The Qur'an is perceived as Allah's direct personal account to humankind and for many Muslims is the true word of God (Asad, 1980). On examination of the Qur'an, Bazna and Hatab (2005) conclude that the term 'disability' is not found in the conventional sense. Instead there is an emphasis on the disadvantage that is created by society and on individuals who may not possess social, economic or physical attributes that society may value at a certain time and place. The Qur'an portrays physical disabilities as being 'morally neutral', as the Qur'an states that 'every person is potentially perfect so long as they work on developing their innate and individual qualities to the limit of individual differentiation' (Bazna & Hatab, 2005, p. 25). Physical conditions are perceived as a part of the human condition that exists as a part of life. The Qur'an highlights a Muslim obligation to stand up for the rights of those that are disadvantaged in society, as well as to actively seek to improve their conditions (Bazna & Hatab, 2005).

Inner heart/emotional pain

Islam also provides teachings that offer psychological insight and guidance for reflection for Muslims. The Qur'an teaches that the human mind comprises of four aspects that influence thinking and subsequent behaviour: The *ruh* (soul), *nafs* (ego), *qalb* (spiritual heart) and *fitra* (divine potential), all believed to be located within the heart (Inayat, 2005). Following the teachings of Islam and succeeding in overcoming negative and non-Islamic leanings allows a Muslim to become closer to purity. It is an incongruent heart, or an imbalance of the four elements, that can lead to emotional pain and mental unrest. An unstable soul is one that is believed to have become distant from Allah, and therefore the ultimate cause of the pain and difficulties for an individual (Inayat, 2005).

For many Muslims, if the causes of their difficulties are ultimately linked to their distance in a relationship with Allah, then solutions to any difficulties will incorporate the need to re-establish this connection. Therefore help-seeking behaviours and interventions for many Muslim parents may not solely lead to the expertise of educational or healthcare professionals, but also religious leaders who can provide faith-based guidance (Weatherhead & Daiches, 2010). Many Muslims may also generate their own solutions based on their own understanding of Islam and their own personal relationship with Allah. This can include fasting, going on pilgrimage, returning to regular prayer, giving money to charity, increasing recitations of the Qur'an and repentance.

It should not be surprising that Islamic beliefs could hold more significance than psychological perspectives for some Muslim families. In fact the relevance of 'Western' psychology for individuals with a strong faith base has been questioned. Skinner (2010) refutes the notion that since the beginning of 'modern' psychology, an understanding of mental health has continued to develop, leading to an enhanced current understanding of the needs of Muslim clients. Instead, Skinner argues that Western psychology fails to recognise religious and spiritual beliefs, and that a 'dangerous unconscious assumption' exists that psychological perspectives and interventions are universal.

In contrast, the need to engage with the underlying belief system of an individual would be more effective, allowing for culturally appropriate support. The need to reflect on what may be appropriate for different populations is essential, as well as recognising the impact that culture and faith have upon the work that we engage in.

Reflection points

- As educational psychologists, do we actively promote to families that as professionals we are interested in the influence of their faith and culture?
- How can interpreters be used effectively within a consultation between parents, school staff and an educational psychologist?

IS A PSYCHOLOGICAL OFFER UNIVERSAL?

Islam, like many faiths, provides a framework for life for those that wish to adhere to the religion. Islam can influence thinking around all aspects of life, including the nature of 'family', emotional well-being and disability. There is also a conceptualisation within Islam that all suffering in life, including illness, occurs in accordance to the will of Allah (Hussain, 2001).

For example, take this mother's belief in Allah as a supreme being and controller of destiny when discussing their child's needs:

> I've got faith in him up there, you know. If he's put me in that situation then he's going to get me out of the situation.

The belief in her child's disability as part of Allah's plan seemed to allow for an acceptance of difficulties but also reassurance:

> I just believe that it's a test from Allah, and he loves us and loves my daughters. I just think it's a test, a very hard one, but I think it's going to be one that we'll get through. Insha'Allah.

One mother even likened her child's disability to the pilgrimage of Hajj, one of the five pillars of Islam and thus a central aspect of the faith:

> Bringing up our children and raising them is our Hajj. It's from Allah to see how you cope.

Allah is seen as the primary cause of the child's disability, and such religious beliefs are integral to the mothers in understanding and accepting their children's needs through an important aspect of their identity. Faith is an important coping mechanism for these mothers and understanding this can provide a crucial insight into how their child's needs are perceived and managed as a family.

When discussing faith-based interventions, some mothers expressed a belief that visiting places of pilgrimage would have an impact on their physical and mental health. This mother defined a 'durbar' as a place where individuals of religious significance were buried and a belief that attendance and prayer at the location would have a positive effect on her emotional well-being:

> They're places where we go for peace of mind and the places where religious people have been buried. People just go there and basically pray in front of them just for health and happiness and peace. That's one of the reasons why I want to go.

To embark upon such a pilgrimage was also believed by a mother to have the ability to have a positive impact on her child's disability, leading to feelings of hope for positive change.

> They have special places like durbars, you go round there and pray in Pakistan. It might help her, but I think if we don't try it, we'll never know really.

These religious perspectives and approaches encourage feelings of emotional calm, clarity and hope, which are essential for these mothers in being able to accept and respond to their children's needs. The potential to further support these feelings as a professional is tremendous.

Holding a religious perspective does not necessarily mean a parent may not want to engage with professionals. Take this mother who previously stated a strong belief in Allah as a controller of destiny and an acceptance of her daughter's Down syndrome as part of Allah's plan for her. While holding this belief, this mother also holds value in recommendations provided by the professionals that she has been working with. The professional advice for this mother may then fall under an overarching religious perspective. However, for her husband, the two perspectives seem to exist in isolation, resulting in the professional view being rejected.

> My husband doesn't believe in going to see professionals as he prefers to go and pray. He goes to the mosque instead, that is his way of trying to help Amina. I go and see the psychologist who can give some hands-on strategies to help her to stop self-harming.

The father's rejection of professional advice in favour of a religious perspective indicates the need for professionals to be aware of alternative perspectives and to examine how culturally sensitive their practice is. Professional advice appears irrelevant for the father as it does not incorporate his Islamic beliefs.

> My husband's views were don't take her to these appointments; get out the prayer mat instead and pray to Allah. The doctors can't help, speech and language won't help.

This father appears to be seeking a reconnection with Allah to support him during a time of difficulty. Holding a religious explanation of his child's disability, and a perception of professional support as irrelevant and difficult to engage with, leads to solely faith-based help-seeking behaviours.

Prayer for many Muslims plays an integral role in re-establishing a balance in the inner heart, and becoming closer to Allah, as well as being a significant coping mechanism (Hussain, 2001). The ability to appreciate such views as a professional would allow for more effective and culturally sensitive interventions to occur. However, for the mother, prayer alongside professional advice is seen as essential in supporting her daughter.

An unequal access to services may contribute to the perception of professional support as irrelevant. The mother on this occasion was a British-born Muslim who was proficient in the English language. Her husband in contrast was born in Pakistan and, having recently moved to the UK, had a limited command of the English language.

LANGUAGE

Ineffective communication patterns can exist between professionals and families who are not confident in the use of English, which is a crucial factor in the needs of many families not being met effectively by service providers (Fazil et al., 2002). Another mother acknowledges that this is a significant barrier for her husband in understanding professional views during meetings:

> And it isn't that he doesn't want to go to these meetings, it's just that his English isn't up to scratch because you've got to understand the nitty gritty of it. Possibly if it was in Punjabi and they were explaining it then maybe he'd go. When I go to all the meetings it is all English-speaking people and a lot of times they use abbreviations and jargon which he wouldn't understand.

The reliability and inconsistent use of interpreters has been questioned, although there is little published literature in this area (Tribe & Raval, 2002). Individuals who are unable to speak English have the right to access information and it is the duty of the services involved to ensure this. However, in reality interpreters are often used inappropriately, with bilingual family members being relied on and services having a lack of resources and allocated training (Tribe & Raval, 2002).

This again is an area that has been given little consideration within educational psychology, particularly the impact language barriers can have on educational psychologists' interventions, such as consultation. As educational psychologists our conversations with families and staff can often involve a high level of emotional content and vocabulary that may not be easily translated into other languages, such as the term 'statutory assessment'. One mother when reflecting on her experiences, acknowledges that being proficient in English may have been a significant factor in the support that has been made available to her son:

> I think for parents who haven't been brought up here it could be quite scary for them; the confidence might not be there. Luckily I have got enough education so if I really needed something I know where to turn to.

A lack of appropriate support for parents who are unable to speak English can also lead to some parents being depended on to relay information to partners who are not proficient in English. The parent with the better spoken English is more likely to be the parent who has the most contact with the service provider (Fazil et al., 2002). Assumptions can also be made that the parent who is more proficient in English will relay information to the parent for whom English is limited. This can lead to significant power imbalance as well as difficulties in the decision-making process. This, along with failure to recognise alternative perspectives, can further compound difficulties when attempting to work with some Muslim parents.

CHAPTER SUMMARY

This chapter has highlighted the importance of faith in the lives of Muslim families. Associating educational and psychological issues alongside faith-based perspectives may be a challenge to many professionals. As reflective practitioners, we are aware that our own cultural, political, social and ideological understandings can influence our work. However, working within a religious paradigm may be difficult, even surprising, for some professionals, especially if the beliefs expressed are contrary to their own personal values and for those who do not consciously think in religious terms (Miles, 1995). There is also a danger that such alternative perspectives may be perceived as 'Eastern fatalism, outdated and barbaric' (Miles, 1995, p. 50). This holds great significance for working with the Muslim population within the UK, particularly considering over 50% were born outside of Britain.

There has been criticism regarding the ability of mental health practitioners to work effectively with Muslim families due to the scarce availability of effective training to deal with faith-based perspectives (Bywaters et al., 2003). This has been argued to result in a lack of availability of culturally competent practitioners, leading to a failure to respond to the unique needs of some Muslim individuals (Ahmed & Amer, 2012).

There are huge benefits that can be achieved by demonstrating to Muslim parents that there is a respect for their faith and an understanding of how Islam shapes not only their view of their child's needs but also their daily lives. As practitioners, we should aim to generate a holistic view, allowing parents to make sense of their children and their family within a perspective that is meaningful to them (Weatherhead & Daiches, 2010). This approach will also encourage parents to realise their own inner strength and resourcefulness, and it is essential as practitioners that we do not fail to recognise this potential. A failure to do so also leads to the danger of imposing values and belief systems onto parents from non-Western traditions (Hussain, 2001). As a profession, educational psychology must value the diversity of the communities within which it works. A starting point is demonstrating that we recognise and respect the impact of faith and show an openness to learning about how it might affect any solutions a family may seek.

REFERENCES

Ahmed, S. & Amer, S. (2012). *Counselling Muslims: Handbook of mental health issues and interventions.* London: Routledge.

Asad, M. (1980). *Message of the Qur'an.* Lahore: Maktaba Jawahar Ul Uloom.

Bazna, M.S. & Hatab, T.A. (2005). Disability in the Qur'an: The Islamic alternative to defining, viewing and relating to disability. *Journal of Religion, Disability & Health, 9*(1), 5–27.

Bywaters, P., Ali, Z., Fazil, Q., Wallace, L.M. & Singh, G. (2003). Attitudes towards disability amongst Pakistani and Bangladeshi parents of disabled children in the UK: Considerations for service providers and the disability movement. *Health and Social Care in the Community, 11*(6), 502–509.

Fazil, Q., Bywaters, P., Ali, Z., Wallace, L. & Singh, G. (2002). Disadvantage and discrimination compounded: The experience of Pakistani and Bangladeshi parents of disabled children in the UK. *Disability & Society, 17*(3), 237–253.

Hussain, A. (2001). Islamic beliefs and mental health. *Mental Health Nursing, 21*(2), 6–9.

Inayat, Q. (2005). The Islamic concept of the self. *Counselling Psychology Review, 20*(3), 2–10.

Miles, M. (1995). Disability in an Eastern religious context: Historical perspectives. *Disability & Society, 10*(1), 49–69.

Office for National Statistics. (2011). *Full story: What does the Census tell us about religion in 2011?* Online at http://www.ons.gov.uk/ons/dcp171776_310454.pdf (accessed 25 July 2013).

Raghavan, R. & Waseem, F. (2007). Services for young people with learning disabilities and mental health needs from South Asian communities. *Advances in Mental Health and Learning Disabilities, 1*, 27–31.

Rajabi-Ardeshiri, M. (2009). Belonging through difference: Children's experiences of informal religious education among the Muslim minority in the UK. Unpublished thesis, University of Sheffield.

Skinner, R. (2010). An Islamic approach to psychology and mental health. *Mental Health, Religion & Culture, 13*(6), 547–551.

Thompson, M. (1997). *Philosophy of religion.* Illinois: Contemporary Publishing.

Tribe, R. & Raval, H. (2002). *Working with interpreters in mental health.* Hove: Brunner-Routledge.

Weatherhead, S. & Daiches, A. (2010). Muslim views on mental health and psychotherapy. *Psychology and Psychotherapy: Theory, Research and Practice, 83*, 75–89.

17 Gender, Non-normativity and Young Women who Have Been Excluded

DAWN BRADLEY

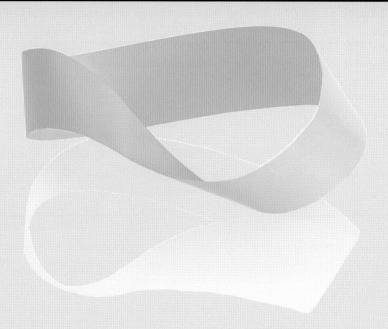

LEARNING OBJECTIVES

After reading this chapter you should be able to:

1. Understand how non-conformity to gendered norms can lead to experiences of exclusion.

2. Understand how gendered norms can be produced and reproduced.

3. Identify the importance of identifying your own ontological position in relation to constructions of 'being' female.

This chapter critically explores, from a feminist perspective, the subjective experiences of young women who have been excluded from mainstream school and draws attention to how schools as institutions can operate and maintain systems that are both patriarchal and oppressive. Existing cultural and social abstractions of 'being a woman' essentialise young women, thus reducing the self and positioning young women as something other. When young women do not conform to social constructions of gender, they may be excluded and punished. This is a concern within education for young women who do not conform to social abstractions of what it is to 'be' a young woman.

Simone de Beauvoir's (1997 [1949]) theory of the lived body is explicitly called upon to theorise the subjective self and how women experience the world existentially through the corporeal living body. Experiences of gendered violence and gendered exclusion are discussed against a number of interrelating factors ranging from the intrapersonal to the interpersonal and from policy to practice. This chapter concludes with outlining how educational psychologists can critically orient themselves to subvert, resist and disrupt forms of subjugation and oppression which uphold and perpetuate patriarchal gender orders and dominant forms of masculinity within educational settings.

GENDER, SYSTEMS AND STRUCTURES

Think back over the past few weeks and consider in how many different ways you and others have been positioned according to your gender. Were you consciously aware and, if so, did you challenge the assumptions that may have sought to define you according to your sex? If you didn't, have you thought about why that may be?

Experience has taught me that young women who are struggling are largely hidden from society's view. As an educational psychologist, the ratio of boys to girls I work with is somewhere in the region of 20:1. As practitioners we should ask: Why is there such a difference? Research shows that girls do struggle with a variety of concerns, yet why are schools not recognising this fact? It would seem girls tend to struggle silently in the background (Cruddas & Haddock, 2003; Besser & Blatt, 2007); young women appear to endure (an arguably female gendered performative). However, when young women adopt and express themselves through masculine behaviours, each risks becoming visible. In behaving in gender non-normative ways girls and young women become visible to their peers (Ewing Lee & Troop-Gordan, 2011), to schools' senior management teams, to disciplinary procedures and to internal and external agencies.

The engendering of young women within school structures pervades and perpetuates gender orders at a systemic level; this in turn establishes and upholds structural norms. Gendered structures provide privileges for some, while limiting the options of others; and such structures are inherently oppressive. Gender should therefore be viewed as an oppressive structured attribute. When schools operate according to patriarchal systems, violence is institutionalised through the vehicles of governmental policy that at a macro level propagates discipline, force and control (*The Importance of Teaching*: DfE, 2010). At an organisational level, the projects and desires of young women can be limited by virtue of their sex, additionally perpetuating gender orders through language and discourse, which writes and shapes policy and legislation governing our schools.

Through systemic inertia and lack of challenge, hegemonic masculinities are fed. It has to be acknowledged schools as institutions have the means of bringing power relations into being and, where power exists, choice and freedom do not. At a macro level, power relations have been progressively governmentalised, rationalised, centralised and elaborated under the auspices of, or in the forms of, state institutions. The exertion of power at a structural level needs to be challenged where it limits individual freedoms to a state of compliance and conformity. This is of significance when considering the affect that the imposition of power might have on an individual and their experiences of the self as they move within governmentalised structures and systems – education being one.

If structures attribute identity, this has wide-ranging implications for subjective experiences of being. To be her self, a young woman has to overcome the structure which imposes power over her. This self can be limited by the policing of individualisation set against the gender order, maintaining the body as object against the frame of what systems, society and historical and political context dictate what it is to 'be' a young woman. Systems and structures which police physical bodies and expressions of individuality are therefore oppressive and complicit in the production and reproduction of gendered norms.

SUBJECTIVE BEING AND THE LIVED BODY

Moi (2001) argued that feminist perspectives don't always encapsulate elements of subjectivity, thus theories, which seek to define a person by either sex or gender, are both limiting and objectifying. Further, she suggested the sex/gender debate can be better addressed through invoking the work of Simone de Beauvoir's (1997 [1949]) existential view of being in the world as experienced through the lived body. Within her analysis, Iris Marion Young (2002) retains the importance of understanding gender not as a living body subjectively, but as living body that is gendered by sociocultural and institutional structures with implications for both power and control over the living body. De Beauvoir's theory of the living body encapsulates how a person may make sense of their identity without reducing the subjective self and unique experiences to either sex or gender. As a theoretical frame this could be applied to deconstruct and reconceptualise experiences of the subjective self beyond sex and gender and which potentially has wider implications than are discussed in this chapter.

As highlighted by Young, difficulties arise when considering how the norms and conventions of sex and gender are constructed discursively. Language use and discourse have the ability to shape expectations of how a particular body should act and respond in relation to the words, rules and discursive norms of a given sociocultural context. Language writes our legislation and guides our thoughts that are then projected onto the bodies of others along with expectations of what a particular body should or should not do as it materially exists within the world (Butler, 2011). In this regard, I argue gender is literally written on the body. Experiences, both positive and negative can then become embodied as young women move within the structures and systems of schools. The existential phenomenology of the account of the living body removes the difficulties in theorising the irreducible social structures of gender when seeking to explore a young woman's lived experiences. De Beauvoir describes the living body as the body through which we experience the world in differing sociocultural contexts. It is the body in situ. These situations give rise to the facticity of existence. Facticity explains the concept that a woman always experiences her physical body in relation to a given environment. Facticity is therefore both limitation and freedom. We can not chose where we are born, the sociocultural and historical context in which we live or are educated within, the geographical location of the world in which we are raised, or the sex we are born as. When we move within the world, we are situated within it's facticity and experience the facticity of the world and people through our own physical bodies as embodied human beings in situation.

Human beings, for Sartre (2003) and de Beauvoir, seek meaning through actions, through their projects; therefore, being is both progressive and emergent but is only experienced through the living body. The living body is relevant as the body is distinctive, but similar and different to others and is determinate in the context of sociocultural behaviours and also in relation to the expectations of others. This theory states that there is no choice in how others respond to the living body, but there is choice in how the person, in experiencing the world as an embodied human being, responds to others (Young, 2002). For de Beauvoir the body is situation and by virtue of being born female, this is a limiting factor in and of itself. This then has implications for schools, which have the power to control and contain the facticity of a young woman's experiences of herself as an embodied human being.

STACEY'S EXPERIENCE

An example of this would be Stacey, a young woman I had the pleasure of knowing in my role as an educational psychologist (EP). Stacey shared with me that she perceived male peers and men more generally had greater freedoms and more autonomy than she did. In response to this, Stacey abandoned and challenged gendered norms, perhaps identifying that to be free to be her self, to be noticed, to be seen and heard, that she had to adopt male traits and interests. Stacey explained:

> I love guns. At Cadettes, I'm the best shooter in [county anonymised] and I'm supposed to wear glasses but I don't wear them (giggles). It's quite weird, 'cause without me glasses it's supposed to stop me but I can see right on the spot.

Stacey 'loves guns', which she perceived as a male weapon. Stacey saw her self as the 'best shooter' which for me suggested a drawing of parallels between men and women. I felt that in disclosing this aspect of her self Stacey was expressing that she was just as good as any man, better in fact because she is the *best*. Even though Stacey was supposed to wear glasses she did not and would not be restrained by the limitations of her sight or physical body which is female. Her body would not 'stop' her, she could 'see right on the spot'. Stacey's vision was clear and I had the sense that it was not just the shooting range which Stacey was referring to, but that Stacey had explicitly recognised for her self the gender order which she seemed to purposefully challenge.

Stacey also spoke about wanting to join the army, a traditionally male dominated career:

> [I can do] anything, apart from a tank 'cause I'm a female. Females can't be in tanks, which is stupid really. When they told me I was like that…(exasperated gestures). But that's the thing I wanted to do, get in a tank. At least drive it down the street or something. They just said that you're not allowed to and being on the front line, I was like that…(sighs)…what can we do?

I asked Stacey, 'What can you do?' She replied:

> We can still do quite a lot and the things I wanted was like front line and stuff, but I can't. I was like that, that's just sexist.

Stacey felt that she could do *anything*. To restrict her opportunities as a woman based on her sex she saw as *sexist*. She could still 'do quite a lot', but was not privy to the same opportunities as men. She couldn't be a soldier on the front line, asking me as a woman, 'what can we do?' – explicitly recognising her sex potentially excluded her from reaching her dreams (projects and desires). In wanting to drive the tank, Stacey was shouting to be noticed, she wanted to 'at least drive it down the street or something'. A woman in a huge machine made for men, made for soldiers that she was in control of, that she was driving with the entire street to see her do it, and in so doing challenging the facticity of her situation. My interpretation was that Stacey wanted not only for her self but also for her sex to be recognised and not to be excluded by virtue of her physical being which was her own female body:

> I asked Stacey, 'What are you trying to express?' She answered, 'That girls can do the same things as boys just sometimes in a different format.'

'That girls can do the same things as boys' and the 'different format' that she referred to was the imposition of societal norms and expectations as to what it was Stacey should be doing, rather than what she believed she could actually do. Stacey couldn't change her sex and as such challenged her self and others to recognise the limitations of being. The situation of Stacey's being and the facticity of her existence was continually challenged by Stacey as she sought to define her self through ontological freedoms in reaching for her projects and desires.

ONTOLOGICAL CONCERNS OF THE BODY

The 'body object' simply defined is the body that is known by the other. The other observes the living body, can praise or criticise it, seek to exert power over it and, in so doing, make the person aware of their own body as a material, biological thing (Finlay & Langdridge, 2006). In viewing the body as object, we can make others so aware of the material existence of their physical being; they can also view their own lived body as body object. This can be achieved by positioning with mechanisms of patriarchal control seeking to diminish female bodies as sites to be controlled, regulated and contained. Thus subjective embodied existence can be repositioned to one of self-surveillance and self-policing through discursive gendered performances (Butler, 2010) or something that one does rather than what one is (Ussher, 2006). While human beings are conscious of the world through their bodies, they are also made conscious of their bodies by the world and others who gaze upon it (Merleau-Ponty in Moran, 2000). This then transforms a living body to body object, a bodily self-consciousness.

My experiences of working with three amazing school-excluded young women served to highlight the consequences of non-conformity to social abstractions of what it is to 'be a woman'. In the IPA research undertaken, I explored the phenomenon of exclusion from a subjective female perspective (Bradley, 2012). The dominant experiences for the three young women were of violence and aggression, not being heard and a constant comparison of the self to others as each sought to understand why they were positioned as something 'other' by adults and peers alike. From this research, what can be said with certainty was that there was a distinct dynamic of power central to each experience. Each young woman spoke of oppression brought to bear by both male and female peers and also from teachers when gendered performatives were abandoned by each in pursuit of being the self. In order to be liberated from this oppression, each of the young women had to overcome the oppressed–oppressor dichotomy which they could not do because it was rooted in the school's systems arising from a gender order.

VOICE, CONTROL AND SILENCING

The relational aggression from female peers experienced by all three young women echoes the research of Osler (2010) who identifies relational aggression as a way in which girls exert more covert and social forms of exclusion to gain dominance over others. In considering the phenomenology of female voice (Fisher, 2010) and the normalising of girls fighting I argue that within this there is further gendering of female norms. Women are often viewed as more talkative, emotional and vocal in emotional expression and more verbally orientated than men. Within this is an interplay of nature and biology; the voice being of the body and the body being physical. Patriarchy advocates that men are more reasoned and logical whereas women can be viewed as of Mother Nature, of voice and, therefore, inessential when compared to men, as voice tends to be gendered to women.

> Not that this means that voices necessarily possess intrinsically masculine or feminine qualities, but that vocal gendering is the product of a complex interplay among anatomical differences, socialisation into culturally prescribed gender roles and contrasting possibilities for expression for men and women in a given society. (Fisher, 2010, p. 88)

This has implications for self-expression and intentionality, which have broader implications for agency, selfhood and power. In the absence of the voice and freedom to create and express the self there exists silence and silencing practices. There is a sad irony in the fact that each young woman was expected to talk through their difficulties, a gendered performative, yet when they asked to speak the staff they spoke to neither listened nor helped. In losing the voice, there is an absence of the self, a detachment of the self intersubjectively from others. When young women, in seeking help from adults are compromised and silenced, expression of the self is denied.

It is through the voice that we contact and make meaning between and within relationships. This was a clear area of need for each young woman who was asking to be heard and to engage in dialogue that would help each make sense of her experiences (Bradley, 2012). Ultimately, each young woman silenced her own voice, refusing to speak rather than be ignored. In the absence of the voice, there is also the absence of relationships and arguably, an absence from the self. The self is then limited in situ. Withdrawal from others denies the possibility of accessing potentially transformative relationships (Michel & Wortham, 2002). The lack of voice can inhibit social interactions with peers; this has implications for the capacity to learn in the social groupings of the classroom. Rejected young people are far less likely to engage verbally with peers (Parault, Davis & Pellegrini, 2007) and due to teaching methods are less likely to be included within a learning experience.

> **Reflection points**
>
> - In a single-sex school, could patriarchy exist?
> - Does matriarchy exist in schools?
> - Could young women in a single-sex school experience the same forms of oppression, relational aggression and forms of exclusion as discussed within this chapter?
> - Could young men, as well as young women, be excluded and marginalised by patriarchal systems and structures?
> - How is the theory of the 'lived body' useful in theorising embodied subjectivity, beyond the scope of sex and gender?

CONCLUSIONS

Implications for EPs are to take seriously and explicitly ask questions about young women who are at risk of exclusion. If practitioners engage with this, there is the opportunity to halt disciplinary proceedings, or to at least hold schools accountable by offering due process and advocacy within disciplinary proceedings. It is too common in my own experience that young people are excluded without my ever having known them until they arrive at a pupil referral unit, and which is often my first experience of them.

The implications for practice are, therefore, complicated but at the very least suggest the need for practitioners to raise awareness of the seriousness of both girls' experiences and accounts of bullying, school truanting, absenteeism and the way in which school staff speak of girls, which can occur when young women resist the facticity of their situations and resist the control of the systems within which they move. Individuals and systems have the power to either empower or oppress. Practitioners also need to question seriously what opportunities and arenas schools provide that really allow girls the freedom to explore, create and be themselves. When young women withdraw from school, professionals need to think of and challenge schools which allow absenteeism, and, in so doing, condone this form of social withdrawal.

REFERENCES

Besser, A. & Blatt, S. (2007). Identity consolidation and internalising and externalising problem behaviours in early adolescence. *Psychoanalytic Psychology, 24*(1), 126–129.

Bradley, D. (2012). 'Who do you think you are?' How do excluded female adolescents make sense of their identities and what are the implications for school experience? Unpublished doctoral thesis, University of Sheffield.

Butler, J. (2010). *Gender trouble: Feminism and the subversion of identity.* London: Routledge.

Butler, J. (2011). *Bodies that matter: On the discursive limits of 'sex'.* London: Routledge.

Cruddas, L. & Haddock, L. (2003). *Girls' voices: Supporting girls' learning and emotional development.* Stoke-on-Trent: Trentham.

De Beauvoir, S. (1997 [1949]). *The second sex*. London: Vintage Classics.

Department for Education (DfE). (2010). *The importance of teaching*. London: The Stationery Office. Online at http://www.official-documents.gov.uk/ (accessed 10 January 2011).

Ewing Lee, A. & Troop-Gordon, W. (2011). Peer socialization of masculinity and femininity: Differential effects of overt and relational forms of peer victimisation. *British Journal of Developmental Psychology, 29*, 197–213.

Finlay, L. & Langdridge, D. (2006). Embodiment. In W. Hollway, H. Lucey & A. Phoenix (Eds.), *Social psychology matters*. Maidenhead and Milton Keynes: The Open University.

Fisher, L. (2010). Feminist phenomenological voices. *Continental Philosophical Review, 43*, 83–95.

Michel, A. & Wortham, S. (2002). Clearing away the self. *Theory & Psychology, 12*(5), 625–650.

Moi, T. (2001). *What is a woman?: And other essays*, Oxford: Oxford University Press.

Moran, D. (2000). *Introduction to phenomenology*. London: Routledge.

Osler, A. (2010). Girls and exclusion: Why are we overlooking the experiences of half the school population? In D. Weekes-Bernard (Ed.), *Did they get it right? A re-examination of school exclusions and race equality*. London: Runnymede Trust.

Parault, S.J., Davis, H.A. & Pellegrini, A.D. (2007). The social contexts of bullying and victimization. *Journal of Early Adolescence, 27*(2), 145–174.

Sartre, J.P. (2003). *Being and nothingness*. Oxford: Routledge.

Ussher, J.M. (2006). *Managing the monstrous feminine: Regulating the reproductive body*. Hove: Routledge.

Young, I.M. (2002). Lived body vs. gender: Reflections on social structure and subjectivity. *Psychology of Women Quarterly, 15*(4), 410–428.

Psychology Practice

SAHAJA DAVIS

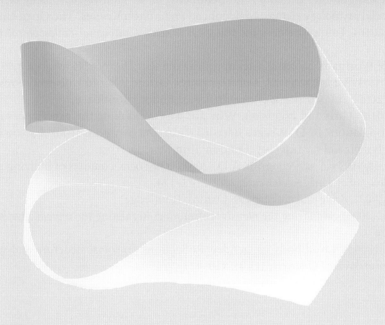

LEARNING OBJECTIVES

After reading this chapter you should be able to:

1. Understand the concept of mindfulness from different theoretical positions.

2. Appreciate the potential for mindfulness to effect educational psychology practice.

3. Explore an experiential encounter with mindfulness through specific practices.

A RADICAL APPROACH TO CONTINUING PROFESSIONAL DEVELOPMENT

Much of the effort I put into my daily work activities and continuing professional development is focused on treading a path towards embodying and exemplifying where I position myself as an educational psychologist. Fundamentally my aim is to have greater flexibility with regard to the narratives that arise within and around me, to be more receptive, and for my actions to be driven by my values. For me mindfulness has played a central role in this journey. Mindfulness has enabled me to release some of my mental preoccupations and self-serving agendas, to be freer to truly attend, respond sensitively and manifest my values. As such, mindfulness has offered me a radical approach to continuing professional development and improving my educational psychology practice, with a focus on ontological transformation as opposed to the accumulation of specific knowledge and skills. In a sense, I believe I have become a better educational psychologist more through what I have learnt to let go of than what I have learnt or acquired.

Reflection points

- What might you personally carry into consultation that inhibits your ability to really listen?
- What might be occupying you when you are with a child that clouds your ability to fully be with them and see them?
- What happens at those times when you are less burdened and preoccupied and you are more free and present?

In this chapter I share some of my concerns with how mindfulness has manifested in North America and Europe, offering what I feel is a more nuanced and useful understanding. Through my own personal path of understanding and practising mindfulness I have received teachings from different cultural traditions including Indian, Burmese, Thai, Tibetan and Japanese. Within these different traditions, while there is a clear thread of concordance, the understanding and methods of practising mindfulness reveal themselves quite differently. As such it would be expected that mindfulness in North America and Europe would have a distinctive manifestation. Subsequently I explore mindfulness through the lenses of narrative psychology and critical theory providing insight into what mindfulness is and the way it can be applied to educational psychology practice. Finally I offer some practical exercises an individual might wish to experiment with to taste the state of mindfulness.

WHAT IS MINDFULNESS?

A state as opposed to a pill

Unfortunately, in much of the available research literature, mindfulness is often understood as yet another 'quick fix' offered to children and adults to make them better. It is suggested that mindfulness can make children more able to concentrate (Franco et al., 2011), behave better (Mendelson et al., 2010), more able to relate to others (Beauchemin, Hutchins & Patterson, 2008), as well as increasing their psychological well-being (Huppert & Johnson, 2010), changing the neurological structure of the brain (Tang et al., 2012) and, most importantly, increasing their academic achievement (Beauchemin, Hutchins & Patterson, 2008). Teachers are also said to benefit, with reduced absenteeism, a decrease in stress-related illness and more effective classroom management (Gold et al., 2010). The commodification of mindfulness into a package that can be administered has led to a burgeoning interest in the field from research and professional communities dominated by the free-market economies. Like many professional activities, mindfulness has become a product, which can be tested, delivered, bought, sold and promoted. Yet, I suggest, by viewing mindfulness as a 'state' as opposed to an 'approach' (e.g., 'mindfulness-based approaches'), a thicker and more authentic narrative is created.

Mindfulness is commonly understood by the approaches used, for example, wilfully directing one's attention or attempting to employ a non-judgemental attitude. Probably the most referred-to definition of mindfulness is by its main proponent John Kabat-Zinn (1994, p. 4) who describes mindfulness as 'paying attention in a particular way: on purpose, in the present moment, and non-judgmentally'. The approaches mentioned here may for certain people at certain times be helpful in facilitating a state of mindfulness but they are not mindfulness itself; that is, they are not necessary or exclusive to mindfulness. In my experience as a mindfulness teacher some of these approaches when adopted by certain individuals at certain times, can in fact impede a mindful state. Facilitating a state of mindfulness is more akin to learning the art of coaxing the mind into a particular way of being as opposed to a set methodology.

Mindfulness as a way of being

Mindfulness as a state refers to our experience of our sense of self in relationship to other phenomena. From the social-constructionist stance of the sense of self as fluid and malleable, mindfulness might be said to be an attempt at renarrating our experience in relation to self and other; what is seen as objective and subjective; and what is considered as being experienced from the inside of oneself and outside of oneself. Mindfulness does not attempt to alter or change the objects that arise in consciousness but suggests a manipulation of our sense of self in relationship to the phenomena.

Mindfulness offers a practical approach moving towards what can be seen as preferred ontological positions (see Tim Corcoran, Chapter 2). To explain the ontological shift that mindfulness specifically refers to, it may help to divide our experience into events and the context in which these events take place. Events in this respect include all aspects and layers of conscious experience, whether regarded as internal or external, including visual experience, sounds, tactile sensation, thoughts, feelings and bodily sensations. In a mindful state the *self* who is receiving or witnessing these events is not defined by the characteristics of the event. Take the example of sadness: in a typically non-mindful state one may regard *oneself* as sad, as in 'I am sad'. This may result in further associated self-identifying thoughts such as 'I am defective' or 'I am wrong'. Alternatively, from a mindful state, the '*I*' witnesses the thoughts and feelings as in '*I am* watching the sensations of sadness and the thoughts which surround these sensations. *I am the witness*, these thoughts and feelings are passing events.' Therefore in the non-mindful state the '*I*' is the contents of given experience; in the mindful state the '*I*' is the witness of given experience.

The practice of mindfulness involves actively cultivating identification with the background or space in which events manifest as opposed to the things in themselves. A common approach to facilitate this shift is for the practitioner to notice the impermanent and fleeting nature of experience. Within a meditative attitude the individual might spend 20 minutes observing directly the transmogrification of sensations and feelings, and witness thoughts coming and going. Through this process of direct observation there is a recognition based on experience that there is nothing endurable for the self to identify with. Another approach is to visualise oneself as a boundless physical space. Sounds, sensations, thoughts and feelings are experienced as arising out of and disappearing into this space described by Hayes et al. as 'self as context' (Hayes, Strosahl & Wilson, 2011, p. 112). Mindful practitioners often describe this shift from identifying with events to the context in which the events arise as an experience of freedom or emancipation. It is important to note that the mindful state does not foster a position of non-action or passivity in response to experience but provides a space within activity to reflect. Neither does mindfulness encourage a distancing from, nor dampening of, experience.

Fundamentally, it is this shift in the ontological experience of self and phenomena that best describe what mindfulness is, as opposed to the practices or approaches that may facilitate this shift. Mindfulness understood in this way most closely resembles the translation of the Pali terms *smṛti*, *sarati* and *sam-pajanna*, from which mindfulness originally derived, and I suggest is a richer more subtle understanding of the concept. This understanding offers greater possibilities and opportunities for creativity with regards to the practice of mindfulness as well as preventing its reification into a commodity. Due to the ontological nature of change that mindfulness encourages, mindfulness is best understood experientially. Below are three exercises that the reader might wish to try to facilitate this state.

Exercise 1: Sensations

As you sit here reading these words, notice where the sensations are most dominant in your body; perhaps around your temples or in the base of your back. Once you have finished reading this paragraph, spend a few minutes focusing intently on these sensations. Looking at them in more detail, notice whether they are moving or still, sharp, soft, light or hard. Try to give these sensations shape and colour.

Notice the sounds around you and for a few more minutes explore what similarities you can find between the sensations in your body and the sounds outside of your body. This may include textures, movements and imagined colours. Try not to think this exercise; allow it to help you feel closer and more intimate with your experience.

Exercise 2: The breath

Try to find a place and time where you will not be disturbed for 15 minutes. Sitting in an upright, comfortable posture close your eyes and bring your attention to the sensation of your breath. It is very likely that your attention will repeatedly drift off to other aspects of your experience or get lost in thoughts. When this happens simply gently bring your attention back to the breath. As you do so, explore the visceral experience of the full range of sensations in your body that make up your experience of breathing.

Exercise 3: Letting go

First visualise being in a tug of war with yourself on one side and your mental activity on the other, in your imagination pull as hard as you can for around 20 seconds, then imagine letting go of the rope. Now spend 15 minutes watching your mind engage in various mental activities such as thinking about what you should be doing later. The moment you notice the engagement imagine letting go of the rope. As you do so you may experience a sense of release and perhaps relief until the next engagement, which once noticed similarly let it go.

NARRATIVE APPROACH TO MINDFULNESS

Narrative psychology offer us an excellent approach to make sense of and explore our and others' relationship to experience. Through the narrative lens we are able to be receptive to stories that emerge within and around us with interest and flexibility. The very act of reframing words from 'truths' to 'narratives' in itself creates the opportunity to listen to diverse voices with equal attention to their significance. Through a release from truth claims that describing words as narratives achieves, there is a potential for the redistribution of power and influence that voices may have. A narrative approach offers the possibility of humility to one's own narratives and the opportunity to give weight to otherwise marginalised voices. As described by Penny Fogg in Chapter 3, 'What use is a story? Narrative, in practice', the narrative lens 'allows us to question our own "truths" and engage in the truth of others'.

While the narrative approach in itself can help the practitioner have a more flexible relationship to many narratives, simply as an idea it is not sufficient as a means to emancipation from more tightly held stories. It can be very challenging to gain release from deeply held ideas about our professional role or rigid beliefs about health and education. It is far easier to release from narratives we are less personally invested. Which narratives we have a looser or tighter grip on will very much depend on our own personal, social and cultural context. I suggest that mindfulness offers a practical means of carrying out the cognitively and emotional demanding work of becoming less identified with our own tightly held narratives and our reactions to the narratives of others.

Through the practice of suspending our 'natural attitude' of grasping and rejecting the thoughts that make up our stories and our responses to stories, one can work at a form of emancipation that makes the embodiment of narrative approaches more possible. Within a daily mindfulness practice one is attempting to witness one's relationship to thoughts and therefore narratives, watching the play of events within the mind. Through this witnessing and with the use of analogies such as 'letting go' the practitioner is able to practise releasing from one's identification with narratives.

FREEING FROM OPPRESSIVE DISCOURSES AND MANIFESTING VALUES

The aim of critical theory as a tool for emancipation has been a central feature of my positioning as a practitioner and academic helping focus my intention and action. By emancipation in this context I am referring to the act of being liberated from or set free from something that is confining, restrictive or even oppressive. Importantly for me critical theory provides an understanding of the ideological nature of what I am emancipating from and a reasoning or value base behind my practice as a facilitator of social transformation.

Mindfulness has provided me with the means to develop both the normative and reflective aspects of a critical practitioner. There is a clarity that can be developed through mindfulness by gaining some independence from what is in the field of experience and at the same time mindfulness helps retain the intimacy required for a moral or ethical intent.

Within critical theory the notion of 'critical consciousness' refers to the development of a state of awareness in which the individual is able to emancipate from prevailing oppressive discourses (Freire, 1970). The application of critical consciousness applies equally to the practitioner as it does to those they engage with. Being in the role of educational psychologist, I am in a powerful position as a propagator of both oppressive and emancipatory discourses – therefore my own ability to develop critical consciousness is vital.

While it is important that reflection occurs in the public social domain, I suggest that mindfulness offers an effective tool in becoming more aware of the circumstances that restrict freedom. Within critical theory might the mindfulness concept of 'fusion' be seen as expressing the processes of consenting to immersing ourselves in the 'common sense' ideologies that pervade our social environment? Through the ongoing systematic development of being mindful of our own thoughts and beliefs as they manifest in the present moment, the individual can became more aware of the social and political conditions that restrict and facilitate freedom. With regard to observing a child, the immediate internal and external voices directed at helping the child change their behaviour might be watched with some detachment, allowing for critical reflection. This reflection may lead to challenging commonsense notions, including demands from the cultural, political and social context of the classroom.

One instance of this I remember was when I was asked to help to develop strategies that would enable a year 1 child to sit on the carpet for longer periods of time without fidgeting, distracting others and 'making silly noises'. As I was observing the child I could see these behaviours manifest. I found my mind travelling along the teacher's story of the issue and potential solutions. Perhaps driven by a desire to be useful my thoughts drifted to sticker charts, sand timers and peer support. I observed my thoughts filtering and influencing my watching of this child. Through this process I became aware of this child attempting to express themselves within a confining, highly controlled environment. This attempt of expression was not in itself wrong, bad or in need of fixing. It was a consequence of the demands of the situation, which were in themselves shaped by wider cultural and political influences. This led to explorations with the teacher about the needs of this child and how they could be best met through adapting the classroom environment. It was my practice of mindfulness that enabled me to release from my tendency of being directed by habitual self-referential thoughts that were focused on my need to be of use to the needs of the teacher. In that release I felt more able to see the wider context and redirect my attention to the needs of the child.

Within critical theory the importance of action being informed by values or moral imperatives is central (Prilleltensky, Peirson & Nelson, 1997). I have often found it a significant personal challenge to express my values within the complex social and psychological dynamics of my work environment. Nevertheless, I have found the practice of mindfulness provides me with a greater ability to let go of my emotional imperatives, allowing me to pay attention to what has more lasting value. One example of this effect of mindfulness was during my delivery of training to adults and, ironically, it was during a mindfulness training session I gave to an educational psychology service. When I asked for a response from the attendees after some group work I noticed myself losing contact with the lived experience of being present with the attendees. At the time I was particularly anxious. Unfortunately I felt my immediate reaction to one individual's answer to my question characterised by a lack of attention, nodding at the right times while my thoughts were drawn to other concerns such as the timing of the session and whether the training was being well received. Through the practice of mindfulness I have found myself watching my anxiety, letting go of these extraneous agendas and placing greater value on the attendees' responses. Consequently, I found myself being more present and genuinely receptive. I have found that mindfulness has helped me in a range of similar situations. It has helped me practise as a critical psychologist through the development of critical consciousness, thereby being more able to pay attention to my values.

CONCLUSION

In my experience I have found that mindfulness has offered me a means to embody and manifest those positions that I align myself to as an educational psychologist and academic. Continuous daily effort to be mindful has supported a personal and professional lifelong journey to be more present, receptive, flexible and value driven. While there is a body of peer-reviewed literature covering a range of studies that support the use of mindfulness by the practitioner, I feel the premise that this research is based on, with regard to its understanding of mindfulness, is limited. This chapter has attempted to offer an invitation for practitioners to examine the notion of mindfulness through a different epistemological lens. There is plenty of literature available to those who wish to explore this area further; however, I would suggest that it is only through an experiential understanding that one can really comprehend and utilise mindfulness.

REFERENCES

Beauchemin, J., Hutchins, T.L. & Patterson, F. (2008). Mindfulness meditation may lessen anxiety, promote social skills, and improve academic performance among adolescents with learning disabilities. *Complementary Health Practice Review*, 13(1), 34–45.

Ferrari, M. & Potworowski, G. (Eds.) (2008). *Teaching for wisdom: Cross-cultural perspectives on fostering wisdom*. New York: Springer.

Franco, C., Mañas, I., Cangas, A.J. & Gallego, J. (2011). Exploring the effects of a mindfulness program for students of secondary school. *International Journal of Knowledge Society Research (IJKSR)*, *2*(1), 14–28.

Freire, P. (1970). Cultural action and conscientization. *Harvard Educational Review*, *40*(3), 452–477.

Gold, E., Smith, A., Hopper, I., Herne, D., Tansey, G. & Hulland, C. (2010). Mindfulness-based stress reduction (MBSR) for primary school teachers. *Journal of Child and Family Studies*, *19*(2), 184–189.

Hayes, S.C., Strosahl, K.D. & Wilson, K.G. (2011). *Acceptance and commitment therapy: The process and practice of mindful change*. New York: Guilford Press.

Huppert, F.A. & Johnson, D.M. (2010). A controlled trial of mindfulness training in schools: The importance of practice for an impact on well-being. *The Journal of Positive Psychology*, *5*(4), 264–274.

Kabat-Zinn, J. (1994). *Wherever you go, there you are: Mindfulness meditation in everyday life*. New York: Hyperion Books.

Mendelson, T., Greenberg, M.T., Dariotis, J.K., Gould, L.F., Rhoades, B.L. & Leaf, P.J. (2010). Feasibility and preliminary outcomes of a school-based mindfulness intervention for urban youth. *Journal of Abnormal Child Psychology*, *38*(7), 985–994.

Prilleltensky, I., Peirson, L. & Nelson, G. (1997). The application of community psychology values and guiding concepts to school consultation. *Journal of Educational and Psychological Consultation*, *8*(2),153–173.

Tang, Y.Y., Yang, L., Leve, L.D. & Harold, G.T. (2012). Improving executive function and its neurobiological mechanisms through a mindfulness-based intervention: Advances within the field of developmental neuroscience. *Child Development Perspectives*, *6*(4), 361–366.

19 Some Reflections on Educational Psychology Practice

MAJID KHOSHKHOO

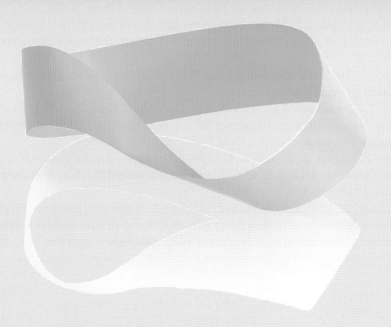

LEARNING OBJECTIVES

After reading this chapter you should be able to:

1. Understand of the role of educational psychologists.

2. Recognise the importance of strengthening communities as support networks.

3. Identify the important role that individuals play in creating supportive structures.

This chapter is a personal reflection on some of my experiences working as an educational psychologist (EP). I specifically link this chapter with my own research, where I examined the subjective experiences of two people and the positive impact social support structures had on their ability to adapt to their changing circumstances. The focus will be on critically looking at the important role of individuals and communities in providing and maintaining these support structures.

> ### Reflection points
>
> * What settings are you immersed in?
> * How, and to what degree, do those settings within which you live your life promote social justice?

Action should lead and research should follow. Becoming immersed in settings that have a social justice orientation will provide us with a base to do research that appreciates and contributes to the goals of such settings (Prilleltensky & Nelson, 2009).

My research focused on two personal accounts of the impact of social support structures. Therein I saw links between these support structures and personal adaptability to various life challenges. For the purpose of this chapter, social support structures refer to the quality of individual and group support and the feeling of being valued. The concept of 'adaptability' has been used regularly and in varied disciplines. Here I focus on a narrow definition of psychological adaptability as the acquisition of new psychological skills and capacities, and development through learning and appropriate experiences. Some may challenge the construct of adaptability, perceiving it to be internal whereas social support structures might be regarded as external. However, I argue that adaptability and social support structures are not mutually exclusive. In order for internal mechanisms to adapt to a changing world, external sources are needed to play a facilitative role.

Educational psychologists at any time can be dealing with children who are subjected to abuse, crime, poverty, maltreatment, long-term illnesses within family, war, diseases, violence, sexual and/or emotional abuse. Under such circumstances children who are able to adapt and somehow manage such adversities are said to be 'resilient'. Please note that by using the term 'adapt' I am not suggesting children should somehow accept these situations but instead my notion of adaptability refers to how a person or child uses all resources available to them to address their circumstances. Ungar (2004), for example, uses a constructionist model where individuals define sources of resilience that suit their needs depending on the interactive nature of different influencing variables. In different situations, coping strategies may require different strategies; different children may exhibit different characteristics; and different cultures may promote different outcomes.

In effect I am arguing for moving away from 'survivor' vs. 'victim' mentality, instead advocating participation in collective action to combat obstacles to emotional well-being through community support. For this purpose, I employ ideas inspired by community and critical psychology where emphases are placed on collective, personal and relational values (e.g., Duckett, Sixsmith & Kagan, 2008; Kagan & Burton, 2001; Kagan et al., 2006; Nelson & Prilleltensky, 2005a; Prilleltensky & Nelson, 2009).

> **Reflection point**
>
> Practice note – As an educational psychologist I use strategies firmly placed within 'personal construct psychology' (PCP) to ascertain a young person's and/or family's own perspectives. PCP suggests that we each have unique, personal theories of life based on our own experiences. As such, our behaviour reflects our theories. Can you see how this acknowledgement helps me to understand how core beliefs and values may be affecting what is going on in any given circumstance?

CRITICAL ISSUES

Educational psychology as a professional practice can be challenged for placing greater focus on internalised properties (i.e., psychometric results or psychopathology) rather than looking at external or social aspects of life. Traditional individualistic psychological approaches negate the importance and influence of external support structures and contrast sharply with ideas coming from community and critical psychology (e.g., Duckett et al., 2008; Kagan & Burton, 2001; Kagan et al., 2006; Nelson & Prilleltensky, 2005a; Prilleltensky & Nelson, 2009). These authors stress participation in collective action to combat obstacles to emotional well-being and emphasise 'a value-laden field of action and research' (Nelson & Prilleltensky, 2005b, p. 45). Nelson and Prilleltensky (2005b) identified three types of values at the heart of community psychology, these being: (1) collective values, (2) personal values and (3) relational values. The interaction between these values aid personal, social and emotional well-being (Khoshkhoo, 2011). My own style as an EP has always been to look for the part of the system that can build strength. For example, in my work not only do I like working with children directly but also I prefer close liaison with learning mentors, teachers and parents. I feel by working with different groups we can strengthen the whole system and in turn that should have some direct positive impact. Now you can imagine how frustrating this can become when the support structures themselves are going through continual crisis (Annan, 2005).

Addressing social justice through educational psychology services can be regarded as too iconoclastic by wider sections of society due to expectations of who we are, what we do and what we should be doing. At moments like these, Burton and colleagues' definition of community psychology provides a basis for my own views of what critical educational psychology should be about:

> Community psychology offers a framework for working with those marginalized by the social system that leads to self-aware social change with an emphasis on value-based participatory work and the forging of alliances. It is a way of working that is pragmatic and reflexive, whilst not wedded to any particular orthodoxy of method. As such, community psychology is one alternative to the dominant individualistic psychology typically taught and practiced in the higher income countries. It is community psychology because it emphasizes a level of analysis and intervention other than the individual and their immediate interpersonal context. It is community psychology because it is nevertheless concerned with how people

feel, think, experience, and act as they work together, resisting oppression and struggling to create a better world. (Burton et al., 2007, p. 219)

As a reflective practitioner I continually question my own personal, collective and relational values and how they position me within the work I do or aspire to do. I sometimes use simple drawing for myself in order to understand what is going on and where I sit in all of these. What does it mean to be in that family or be that child? I question myself about values that I bring to it? What are my motivations? I try to pay attention to my own feelings generated by a particular case. As part of that I reflect on how did I challenge social injustice? How did I challenge false notions which were bandied about in meetings? I also try to address these concerns by using peer supervision. It is often useful listening to perspectives of others who are not directly involved with an individual case. This should hopefully lead to reviewing my own practice.

WHAT ARE EDUCATIONAL PSYCHOLOGISTS DREAMING ABOUT?

The title of this section at first may sound a bit strange. It is a reference to Michel Foucault's (1978) writing on the Iranian revolution. While writing this chapter, Foucault's article, with its discussion of idealistic viewing, has been a vital reference point for me. The term 'idealism' is not used pejoratively or sarcastically. Rather, I genuinely believe holding on to idealism is an important aspect of being an effective educational psychologist. It is for this reason that I feel as an EP (at least for myself) I need to explicate the set of ideals that are the basis of my belief system. In my own research I highlighted the importance of strong external structures that can act as scaffolding in the overall development of personal identity and how these are constructed and interact with wider society. For example, in practical sense as an EP, when working with schools, the approach I use includes working with the whole school to create a supportive climate to address what they would regard as 'difficult behaviour' and thereby not focus on individual interventions. This is one of those messages that needs continued renewal.

> **Reflection point**
>
> Inside out or outside in? How does a child's inner experiences connect to what is going on in their external life?

Most EPs, if not all, emphasise the importance of family and social relations. However, distant influences such as economic factors, cultural issues and general ideology may become barriers to addressing those important proximal influences. The role of the EP has traditionally exhibited a strong emphasis on the examination and analysis of internal characteristics. This at times negates the importance of external structures and participation in collective action to combat obstacles to emotional well-being. Bronfenbrenner's (1979) ecological system model has highlighted the interaction between different system layers and their importance in the overall support for children. It is for this reason EPs should critically evaluate distant factors by challenging not only those structures with which we engage frequently and automatically (i.e., the intrapsychic) but also challenging ourselves and our profession creatively and honestly. Critical introspection should renew the way that we can engage with a wider range of discourses, including those outside of psychology. This can be done by getting involved with assessment of community needs and becoming active in community groups and focusing on local community concerns through direct involvement. For example, a few years ago, along with 'looked-after children' (LAC) social workers, we organised a series of workshops for foster carers and adoptive parents on attachment issues and to discuss the management of children's behaviour. This was organised at a convenient time for attendees and involved starting meetings at 7pm and ending at 9pm at the local library, where we hired a room. This empowered those present to have an avenue to explore their own experiences, build on their existing understanding of attachment issues and support others in their understanding. The group evolved to become more like self-help support. This also taught me about how others see educational psychologists' role, where previously most of them thought it involved something akin to just doing counselling without educational aspects. As well as attachment, a lot of other issues came up. For example, I was able to explain issues relating to SEN such as procedures and processes. Through feedback, it was highlighted that foster carers and adoptive parents were better empowered to work closer with schools and other settings they came across and take part in partnership work with schools and settings.

WILL I STILL BE NEEDED TOMORROW?

As I have argued above, EPs come to their work with diverse experience. It is therefore not a unified profession and nor should it be. Invariably this has an impact on how we respond to individuals, how we listen to their subjective way of describing what is going on for them and how we engage with their stories. There are always different possible responses to these 'stories' requiring continual reflection on decision-making processes related to what is the 'right' way forward. Recent changes in funding for children presenting with special educational needs in the UK has meant more delegated money going directly to schools. In effect this has meant schools deciding whether they want to buy EP services or not and to what level and extent. This has meant not only that EPs have to establish their own way of working but also negotiating with 'their business partners' (the schools) about what type of role they want. This in effect has meant some EPs have had to work to schools' agendas, which at times may not be about collectivism but about how an individual child can 'change for the better'. The EPs' response to these changes has varied between those who have agonised about the profession and its future and those who have 'confidently' accepted the changes and have worked within them.

Warr (1987) has highlighted a model for mental health using what he refers to as the 'vitamin model'. Although this model is primarily related to workplace, and its reference to 'vitamin' can inherently link it to a medical model, the features he has highlighted are relevant and applicable to most environments and situations. The nine features of environment – opportunity for control, opportunity for skill use, externally generated goals, variety, environmental clarity, availability of money, physical security, opportunity for interpersonal contact, and valued social position – are suggested to affect the mental health of a person in the same way that vitamins affect physical health. This model emphasises the overall quality of the environment as being very important for mental health. I would argue the role of EPs has to, to some extent, influence and strengthen these environmental factors.

I wrote the following in my concluding chapter to my thesis:

> In reality we are slaves to other people's expectations of who we are and what we can do and our role as 'experts'. This reminds me of an episode retold by the writer George Orwell about when he was a police officer in the colonial police force in Burma. He describes his feelings about having to shoot an elephant against his own wishes but it was a course of action he was expected to take by the crowd following him:

> 'Here was I, the white man with his gun, standing in front of the unarmed native crowd – seemingly the leading actor of the piece; but in reality I was only an absurd puppet pushed to and fro by the will of those yellow faces behind. I perceived in this moment that when the white man turns tyrant it is his own freedom that he destroys. He becomes a sort of hollow, posing dummy, the conventionalised figure of a sahib. For it is the condition of his rule that he shall spend his life in trying to impress the "natives" and so in every crisis he has got to do what the "natives" expect of him. He wears a mask and his face grows to fit it.' (Orwell, 1979, p. 269)

What I think this means for EPs is always having to consider working differently. This would take seriously our own responsibilities – that is, not merely to critique but to propose new forms of practice. We must emphasise the important role of others and communities. Studies such as those by Werner (1989) have found that the students who overcame what the research calls 'devastated backgrounds' tend to have one thing in common – a caring adult outside of the family who is 'on their side'. So it is important that EPs should harness and strengthen the role of community and community structures. And, yes, we can work differently. It should be part of our responsibilities to create systems which do not merely obey political or economic imperatives but which are responsive to the needs of the communities we serve.

CHAPTER SUMMARY

In this chapter I have critically reflected on my own work as an EP. I believe the profession need not work at a distance from the communities it purports to serve. Yet, progress will be limited if EPs solely focus on children in classrooms and schools. Consultation with community and actively being part of community support networks (e.g., joining management committees, visibly being active in locality work, being part of regular consultation/solution focus approaches to resolving issues within community, and so on), to support the community's own capacity to support children, should be at heart of our work. The overarching factor for me as a practitioner psychologist has always been the notion of reflexivity. I believe the ability to critically reflect on my own practice and beliefs, and when necessary to challenge some of historically situated explicit and implicit assumptions, provides opportunities for practitioners to sharpen and develop their own thought processes. This hopefully should aid us becoming effective and socially conscious educational psychologists. At times this may involve use of alternative psychological, philosophical and political frameworks for practice. This inevitably may provoke some critical dialogue, within our EP community and with others. Nevertheless, we can work differently because as a profession we have opportunities to choose different ways of working.

I will end this chapter by revisiting what I wrote in my thesis about narrowing boundaries between insider experience and outsider knowledge. I feel this is as real for me now as it has always been:

> Perhaps by employing insider experience combined with outsider knowledge we might be able to do away with the loaded responsibility of the 'expert' label and instead we may free our energies to contribute effectively to work and the application of psychology. However this has to be a genuine dynamic relationship, which means that sometimes we have to be brave and let go of safe practices and try something different. We must also allow service users to change their own perception of what to expect as well as changing our own perception of what we can offer. This may sound clear looking at it from afar but, similar to most stories, the closer we get to the story, the foggier it all looks. But having a philosophy and idealism is a good start. (Khoshkhoo, 2011, p. 180)

REFERENCES

Annan, M. (2005). Observations on a service review: Time to move on? *Educational Psychology in Practice*, 21(4), 261–272.

Bronfenbrenner, U. (1979). *The ecology of human development: Experiments by nature and design.* Cambridge, MA: Harvard University Press.

Burton, M., Boyle, S., Harris, C. & Kagan, C. (2007). *Community psychology in Britain. International community psychology: History and theories.* New York: Kluwer Academic.

Duckett, P., Sixsmith, J. & Kagan, C. (2008). Researching pupil wellbeing in UK secondary schools: Community psychology and the politics of research. *Childhood*, 15(1), 89–106.

Foucault, M. (1978). What are the Iranians dreaming about? Trans. K. De Bruin & K. Anderson. In J. Afary & K. Anderson (Eds.) (2005), *Foucault and the Iranian revolution: Gender and the seductions of Islam* (pp. 203–209). Chicago: University of Chicago Press.

Kagan, C. & Burton, M. (2001). Critical community psychology praxis for the 21st century. Paper presented at the British Psychological Society Centennial Conference, Glasgow, March 2001. Online at http://www.compsy.org.uk/GLASGOX5.pdf (accessed 4 August 2016).

Kagan, C., Lawthom, R., Duckett, P. & Burton, M. (2006). Doing community psychology with disabled people. In D. Goodley & R. Lawthom (Eds.), *Disability and psychology: Critical introductions and reflections.* Basingstoke: Palgrave Macmillan.

Khoshkhoo, M. (2011). Beyond and through adversity: Two personal accounts of the impact of social support structures on adaptability. Unpublished EdD (Educational Psychology) thesis, University of Sheffield.

Nelson, G. & Prilleltensky, I. (Eds.) (2005a). *Community psychology: In pursuit of liberation and wellbeing.* New York: Palgrave.

Nelson, G. & Prilleltensky, I. (2005b). Values for community psychology. In G. Nelson & I. Prilleltensky (Eds.), *Community psychology: In pursuit of liberation and wellbeing* (pp. 47–69). New York: Palgrave.

Orwell, G. (1979). *The collected essays, journalism and letters of George Orwell. Vol. 1: An age like this, 1920–1940.* Harmondsworth: Penguin Books.

Prilleltensky, I. & Nelson, G. (2009). Community psychology: Advancing social justice. In D. Fox, I. Prilleltensky & S. Austin (Eds.), *Critical psychology: An Introduction* (pp. 126–143). London: Sage.

Ungar, M. (2004). *Nurturing hidden resilience in troubled youth.* Toronto: University of Toronto Press.

Warr, P. (1987). *Work, unemployment, and mental health.* Oxford: Clarendon Press.

Werner, E.E. (1989). Children of the Garden Island. *Scientific American*, 210, 106–111.

20 Finding Attunement and Promoting Positive Attachments

Kathryn Pomerantz

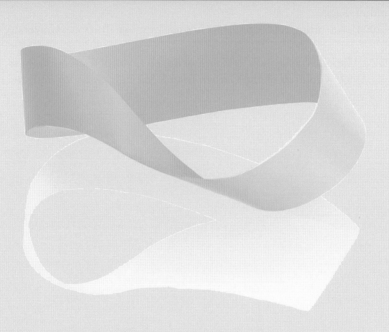

LEARNING OBJECTIVES

After reading this chapter you should be able to:

1. Understand the concept of attachment and its importance in helping adults relate to children in educational and care settings.

2. Demonstrate a basic understanding of the principles and aims of VIG.

3. Consider how VIG can be used to find attunement and promote positive attachments.

4. Develop ideas to begin critically questioning the use of attachment theory in professional practice.

This chapter asks critical questions of attachment theory and considers what is needed to develop positive attachments with children[1] in practice. It explores the topic via the author's experiences of using video interaction guidance (VIG) intervention.

Increased interest in attachment theory over the past decade has led to a rise in interventions to help parents and carers, in particular, develop a more attuned response to their children. Theorising around the development of secure attachments in young children with their caregivers has been available for nearly half a century (Bowlby, 1969). Based on early attachment literature (informed by evolutionary psychology), infants were said to have an innate need to develop a secure base to a key attachment figure in order to keep themselves safe from potential threat. In having that secure base infants can then move away for short periods to explore the world and learn. Child psychologists such as Trevarthen (1980) highlight the importance of intersubjectivity – that is, people are predisposed to collaborate socially and we come to know ourselves through that relatedness. Practitioners such as Bomber (2007) have highlighted the importance of staff working in schools understanding the important role they can play in developing secure attachments with children and young people when these haven't occurred naturally in the home setting. However, texts such as these, while useful in practical terms to those working in educational settings, fall short of helping adults working with children to reflect on the importance of intersubjectivity. The quality of this interaction is paramount and relies on attunement, defined as 'a harmonious and responsive relationship where both partners…play an active role' (Kennedy, 2011, p. 23).

An intervention such as VIG, which takes its theoretical basis from the work of Trevarthen and is based on the principles of promoting attuned interactions between adult and child (Biemans, 1990), offers a promising and powerful way of helping adults find attunement and develop positive attachments with children. Although devised initially to support work with parent–infant dyads, this intervention is now being used by educational psychologists (EPs) and other professionals to support staff working in educational settings as well as with parents and carers to develop the interactions they have with children. The use of VIG is also grounded in ontological constructionism (see Tim Corcoran, Chapter 2). It enables the adults involved to engage in determining how communication and interaction constitutes 'who' they are and 'how' they parent, care, teach and so on. The VIG process is powerfully reflexive for both the professional guider and the client (e.g., parent, carer, teacher) in helping the client and VIG guider recognise the dependence and interrelatedness between the self and the 'other' (see Dan Goodley, Chapter 4).

EXAMPLES FROM EDUCATIONAL PSYCHOLOGY PRACTICE

A few years ago when working as an EP with children permanently excluded from school I noticed there were often different attachment experiences within the same family. For example, one 13-year-old, Ryan, seemed to have an insecure and ambivalent relationship with his mother, being close and desperate for attention one minute and controlling and rejecting the next. However, watching Ryan's mother with her other children I generally observed them to present with a secure attachment pattern. This led me to question the way attachment theory fails to account for variability, suggesting that in *each* developing relationship between child and primary carer there may be certain situational factors that mitigate against optimal conditions for developing an attuned interaction:

> [attachment] fails to engage with the specificity and variability of caregiving and…in its attempts to identify optimal conditions for development it homogenises (treats as the same) normality and pathologises (treats as difference) deviance. (Burman, 2008, p. 139)

This insight inspired me to seek training in VIG as I initially wanted to be able to help the primary carers of children who had become permanently excluded from school to develop attuned interactions with their children. This later led me to develop the use of VIG with key adults in school settings. Three case examples of using VIG are explored below, with more focus given to case two, to allow the reader to gain a basic understanding of VIG in practice.

Lily and Ben

Ben is 9 years old and profoundly deaf. He lives with his mum, Lily, his stepdad, older sister and brother. He attends a facility for hearing impaired children in a mainstream school. In both settings Ben is challenging, but more so at home where he sets fires and threatens his mother with knives. Taking a developmental history is a very useful way of starting work with a parent that avoids lapsing into judgements and quick formulations. For example, on first meeting Lily I discovered that Ben was attached to an incubator for the first 6 months of his life, being unable to breathe or swallow independently. Ben witnessed domestic violence between his parents when he was younger. Lily began to recognise through our conversation that she had been frightened to hold Ben when he was in the first few months of life and spent little time interacting with him as she was fearful he would die. When he was out of hospital her attention was given to Ben's father, trying to keep herself and Ben safe with little opportunity to relax and enjoy interacting with him during his early childhood. Lily felt that all her interactions with Ben were negative; she contrasted this with the positive attachments she felt she had with her two older children.

Early in the VIG process the guider (myself in this case) supports the client (the mother, Lily in this case) to identify a helping question. For Lily she wanted to improve her relationship with Ben. The focus was on taking short films of Lily and Ben at home engaged in activities of their choosing, learning to isolate very short clips and still images to help Lily notice the principles of attuned interaction and guidance she was demonstrating and the effect of this on Ben. These principles included:

- being attentive (e.g., enjoying watching the other and wondering what the other is doing, thinking or feeling),
- encouraging initiatives (e.g., naming positively what you see),
- receiving initiatives (e.g., returning eye contact, smiling, nodding in response),

- developing attuned interactions (e.g., giving and taking short turns),
- guiding (e.g., building on the other's response) and
- deepening the discussion (e.g., reaching new shared understandings). (Kennedy, 2011, p. 28)

To progress this work I took three films of Lily and Ben, which involved reading books and newspapers together and making chocolate cakes. Within the VIG process the guider films the activity, then micro-analyses the film, taking prepared film clips and stills back to the client to engage in a shared review. This review focuses on recognising the contact principles of attuned interaction as described above and the impact this has on the child. The process is strengths-based. What became apparent for Lily in watching herself in the still pictures and clips was the warmth of her body in relation to Ben, the physical closeness between them, how she received this when Ben sought it, and her skills in using British sign language to turn-take with him and have fun. I observed much laughter when filming these activities and during the shared review of film three Lily turned to me and said: 'We really do love each other!'

Sally and Charlie

Sally is a grandmother who has taken her four grandchildren into kinship care. This followed the breakdown of her daughter's relationship with the children's father who had gone to prison for drug dealing and the daughter's inability and lack of interest in continuing to care for the children. When I met Sally she was experiencing difficulty with Charlie, the oldest, aged 10. Charlie had become very withdrawn, controlling and defiant. She had reportedly been told to keep many of her experiences with her father secret yet Sally was desperate for Charlie to open up and talk to her more. This work was commissioned by social care, to help Sally relate to Charlie and offer her the care she required.

In my discussion with clinical psychologists, VIG can at times be used as a directed intervention by the courts to help mothers and children develop attachments to avoid children going into the care system. I have seen powerful, successful examples of VIG being used in this way. However, in my work with Sally I felt that she needed to come to the work without feeling it was imposed. As such in my early discussion with Sally time was spent building rapport, acknowledging her commitment to her grandchildren and starting the work with her own 'helping question'. In Sally's case, through VIG, she wanted 'for Charlie to open up and talk more'.

Sally was a very 'jolly' person with a great sense of humour who laughed and talked a lot, often asking Charlie multiple questions to cajole her into engaging in activities and conversation. Through the VIG process and my attempts to 'guide' her she began to notice that Charlie was beginning to take turns in interactions and would sometimes initiate these. This was often by making a quiet sound or through gesture. In reviewing the selected film clips with me Sally was able to notice that when she paused to watch Charlie, these initiatives occurred more frequently. We moved on to Sally realising the importance of being attentive to these initiatives and receiving them by repeating a sound or gesture made by Charlie or by commenting on what she was doing. Kennedy (2011) notes that this is an essential aspect of developing attuned interaction and has impact for the child in that he or she feels loved, recognised and validated. This experience of intersubjectivity is crucial to enable mediated learning, for the child to learn and grow.

TARGET, MONITORING AND EVALUATION IN VIG

Target, monitoring and evaluation (TME) as developed by Dunsmuir et al. (2009) is a helpful tool to use during VIG to move from the helping question to constructing emerging targets for the client. Two key targets that emerged for Sally are detailed below and show her 'beginning' to shift from focusing exclusively on Charlie to realising her own need to develop skills in the attuned interaction. The impact of this is evident on Charlie's progress below. (The measurement scale used was: Not present 1 2 3 4 5 6 7 8 9 10 Always present.)

Target 1

- For Charlie to like herself better.
- For Sally to have fun and be playful with Charlie, be close to her, use touch, look towards her, smile and show/tell her how she feels being with her.

Baseline (3–4) established during the first VIG shared review:

Charlie can get really angry and likes to be in control. She can also be withdrawn and doesn't always smile much.

Level achieved (5–6), established after the fourth and final shared review:

Charlie enjoys having fun with Sally when they have time together and she can be playful back. Sometimes she lets Sally lead and she will follow and sometimes she takes the lead (they reverse roles).

Target 2

- For Charlie to open up more.
- For Sally to watch Charlie, pause, wait for her to have a turn, notice what she does and then respond.

Baseline (3–4) established during the first VIG shared review:

Charlie tends to be guarded, makes limited eye contact and avoids talking.

Level achieved (5–6), established after the fourth and final shared review:

> Charlie is opening up more, especially in areas of interest to her. She often shows this non-verbally, for example by smiling, shoulders back, looking towards/at Sally, open posture, looking more relaxed.

A future plan for the client is developed at the end of the process and at that point Sally was able to fully recognise her skills in being physically close, making eye contact, being attentive and listening to what Charlie says and does, listening and giving her a chance to speak, and the impact of this on Charlie. Sally identified her continued need to be aware of stepping back more and using shorter turns.

This work involved four films and shared reviews (typical of the length of a VIG intervention) using activities: planting bedding plants in the garden, doing each others' hair and playing board games. When I came to create some still images to leave with Sally at our closure meeting I noticed that towards the end of each activity I could identify a still image that showed Charlie giving Sally full eye contact and smiling. Charlie was clearly enjoying interacting with her grandmother. Trevarthen (2011, p. 212) notes that '…mothers and infants need fun. They enjoy testing the limits of one another's "attunement", making the harmonies hilarious.' This experience of enjoying interacting with the parent or carer stands out from my VIG work as being a significant aim in supporting the development of positive attachments with children and key adults where secure attachments have not effectively developed in the early years.

Kay and Anna

Anna is a 12-year-old girl attending a mainstream school. She has a diagnosis of attention deficit hyperactivity disorder (ADHD) and autism. Anna has experienced rejection from her father and has a strained relationship with her mother and stepfather. Anna is very demanding of staff attention, challenging in class and around the school site and overtly self-harms on a daily basis. She is in danger of permanent exclusion. Kay is the key worker for Anna and has time with her each day to remind her of her targets in school, process incidents, to work on social skills and support her in some lessons.

Kay's VIG targets involved:

- For me to stay calm myself, use a calm voice and give Anna time.
- For Anna and I to have a more equal relationship, with more balance and cooperation in the interaction.

One of the learning experiences for Kay and me that came out of the shared reviews was a recognition of the importance of the way in which Kay showed containment in her body and the effect of this on Anna at times when she became more agitated during an activity. The caregiver (Kay in this example) can remain attuned to the care seeker's

(Anna's) affective state and essentially regulates her own arousal levels (McCluskey, 2005). What is also important here is that through the containing experience the child learns, 'through the other' that it is possible to regulate one's own emotional state (Frosh, 2012). At first Kay sought to take equal turns in conversing with Anna, which was challenging because Anna frequently became very agitated and took long conversational turns. However, through VIG we discovered that at these times Kay had a tendency to show calm by remaining quite still and holding her hands in her arms as if embracing them. At one point I had commented on this to Kay and compared this to a young mother holding her baby. In effect Kay was giving Anna the experience of having her destructive impulses contained by a significant other, and in doing so had gained her trust. Frosh (2002) notes that containment occurs consciously in psychoanalysis on the part of the analyst and is an essential part of the therapeutic process. VIG had enabled Kay to discover the power of remaining still (and containing) at these times and receiving Anna's initiatives non-verbally by punctuating her speech, taking a turn using gesture, to bring Anna back to the original task. The effect was far more than keeping Anna on task (a key objective of a teaching assistant in the classroom) but reflects the intersubjective experience, core to the attuned interaction where the impact on the child is that their initiative has been received and understood (Kennedy, 2011).

We began over time to recognise that Anna was able to show the benefits of experiencing containment (see Tony Williams, Chapter 5); at times when she was not agitated she could mirror the stillness she saw in Kay and take shorter turns in conversation, especially when she was engaged in a conversation about a happy experience at home or in school. Instead of giving Anna time each morning to talk about any problems, Kay began to find opportunities to talk to Anna about happy experiences at the start of each day, which had the effect of helping to regulate Anna's emotional state prior to entering class.

VIGNETTE REFLECTIONS

The reader will have noticed that all the case studies relate to my work with female adults; to date I have not had the opportunity to use VIG in working with fathers or male teachers/teaching assistants. Returning to the work of Burman (2008) highlighted earlier in this chapter, I am reminded of her critique of attachment theory and the dilemmas that this poses for policy and practice. As practitioners we are cautioned to consider 'the ambiguous status of attachment theory as a hybrid model between psychoanalysis, social psychology and sociobiology' (Burman, 2008, p. 149). There is also a tendency in more recent years to use attachment theory as the basis for practitioners' work in scrutinising, measuring and seeking to develop what Miens (1999) refers to as 'maternal mindedness'. As practitioners, then, we may fall into the trap of uncritically drawing on both generalist and gendered concepts of attachment, advocating for interventions such as VIG which draw heavily on a multiparadigmatic theory base which Burman reminds us has an ambiguous status. We are also reminded that attachment theory is only one aspect of the parent–child relationship and yet it is one that tends to focus on realist notions of what constitutes this relationship, reinforcing the Westernised and gendered nature of attunement. In recognising this tension I do not jettison an intervention such as VIG but seek to use the technique cautiously, being careful not to make generalist assumptions by keeping in mind the context and variability of the relationships I encounter in my practice.

CONCLUSION

> Within any relationship, we also become somebody…our participation in relational processes leaves us with the potentials to be the other, to be a certain kind of self, and a form of self/other choreography. From these three sources, we emerge with enormous possibilities for being. (Gergen, 2008, p. 447)

As an EP I have seen many benefits of using VIG with parents and carers. Among other benefits VIG is able to highlight the dependence and interrelatedness between the self and the 'other' and in doing so enhance attunement and promote positive attachments. There is, however, work to be done in encouraging school staff to consider VIG for use as an intervention in developing positive attachments in school settings. This is a challenge for EPs in the light of the changing culture of traded educational psychology service delivery in which EPs in many local authorities are now required to market and sell their professional skills (e.g., the delivery of training and interventions). Luxmoore (2006, p. 75) notes that 'the very idea of attachment is denigrated in most secondary school classrooms'. The tradition of 'attaching' (in the literal sense) teaching assistants to children with additional social, emotional and behavioural needs in school settings is highly costly to the public purse. And yet this practice seems to rely on old-fashioned notions of the attachment system relying on the physical proximity of an attachment figure in providing a secure base for the child. VIG offers the chance to recognise and promote ways of having attuned interactions with children that are crucial to the development of attachment relationships, much of which relies on understanding the importance of recognising and promoting non-verbal aspects of attuned interactions. Finding attunement and developing positive attachments needs to be a conscious effort on the part of carers and educators working with children whose attachment needs were not met in infancy. In a way that is reciprocal and collaborative: 'the *combined function* of care seeking and caregiving is the maintenance of the survival of the care seeker' (Heard, Lake & McCluskey, 2009, p. 226; emphasis added). We cannot assume that attuned interactions happen naturally between any parent, carer, teacher, or teaching assistant and a child. The challenge for EPs is to build up an evidence base for this type of relational work, so that such an intervention can be fully exploited in both home and school settings to help troubled children to be more peaceful selves.

NOTE

1. I will use the term 'children' throughout in reference to those children and young people who struggle to remain in school settings or in their natural home environments due to their traumatic life experiences and presenting challenging behaviours that interrupt their care and educational trajectory. The children and adults referred to in the following vignettes are anonymised.

REFERENCES

Biemans. H. (1990). Video home training: Theory, method and organization of SPIN. In J. Kool (Ed.), *International seminar for innovative institutions*. Ryswijk: Ministry of Welfare, Health and Culture.

Bomber, L. M. (2007). *Inside I'm hurting: Practical strategies for supporting children with attachment difficulties in schools*. London: Worth Publishing.

Bowlby, J. (1969). *Attachment and loss. Vol. 1: Attachment*. New York: Basic Books.

Burman, E. (2008). *Deconstructing developmental psychology* (2nd edn). Hove: Routledge.

Dunsmuir, S., Brown, E., Iyadurai, S. & Monsen, J. (2009). Evidence-based practice and evaluation: From insight to impact. *Educational Psychology in Practice, 25*(1), 53–70.

Frosh, S. (2002). *Key concepts in psychoanalysis*. New York: New York University Press.

Frosh, S. (2012). *A brief introduction to psychoanalytic theory*. Basingstoke: Palgrave Macmillan.

Gergen, K.J. (2008). Therapeutic challenges of multi-being. *Journal of Family Therapy, 30*, 333–348.

Heard, D., Lake, B. & McCluskey, U. (2009). *Attachment therapy with adolescents and adults: Therapy and practice post Bowlby*. London: Karnac Books.

Kennedy, H. (2011). What is video interaction guidance (VIG)? In H. Kennedy, M. Landor & L. Todd (Eds.), *Video-interaction guidance: A relationship-based intervention to promote attunement, empathy and well-being*. London: Jessica Kingsley.

Luxmoore, N. (2006). *Working with anger and young people*. London: Jessica Kingsley.

Meins, E. (1999). Sensitivity, security and internal working models: Bridging the transmission gap. *Attachment and Human Development, 1*, 325–342.

McCluskey, U. (2005). *To be met as a person*. London: Karnac Books.

Trevarthen, C. (1980). The foundations of intersubjectivity: Development of interpersonal and cooperative understanding in infants. In D.R. Olsen (Ed.), *The social foundation of language and thought: Essays in honor of Jerome Bruner*. New York: Norton.

Trevarthen, C. (2011). Confirming companionship in interests, intentions and emotions. In H. Kennedy, M. Landor & L. Todd (Eds.), *Video-interaction guidance: A relationship-based intervention to promote attunement, empathy and well-being*. London: Jessica Kingsley.

Change: The Relevance of Performance Art in Educational Psychology

NICK HAMMOND

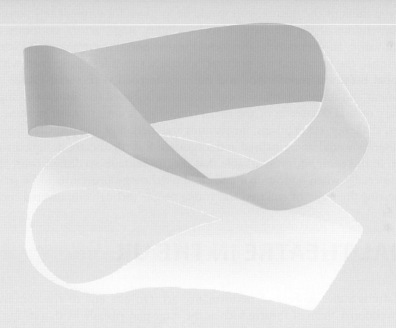

LEARNING OBJECTIVES

After reading this chapter you should be able to:

1. Begin to explore what is meant by social theatre and the variants that make up social theatre.

2. Consider the theoretical and practical relevance of social theatre approaches to psychologists working *with* children and young people.

3. Explore how these ideas are supported by recent evidence from the fields of drama, arts and health and link to a political agenda relevant to the work of educational psychologists.

The performing arts[1] are radically underrepresented in the British educational psychology literature. Examples from practice are often under the radar and discretely carved out by those practitioners who have insight into the value such methods offer. This is perhaps a rather peculiar position when we consider that performance art, such as theatre, is laden with psychological insight and more so when we consider the 'actor' as an embodiment of psychology – behaving, moving, communicating, thinking and reflecting – an argument I have made elsewhere (Hammond, 2015a). Let us extend this premise and consider the 'actor' as engaging in performance as a means of initiating political change and debate in a safe, empowered and liberated way; the actor as a person and the person as a body which is used as a vehicle for social and political action in the post-conventionalist sense described by Dan Goodley in Chapter 4. This can be a powerful force for creating sustainable and transformative personal and community change.

When you think of the theatre, you would be forgiven for immediately considering traditional conventions of the mainstream such as lights, stage, actors, costumes and so on. There is, however, an alternative – the social theatre. Social theatre operates within a triad of the personal, the social and the political. Social theatre is less concerned with adhering to traditional theatrical conventions and more concerned with social justice, liberation, empowerment and transformation. Social theatre is designed to stimulate change through commentary on and discussion of the social condition. It aims to raise awareness of pertinent issues, challenge assumptions, inequalities and inequities and provide a voice to those who are disempowered, marginalised and forgotten. It is the theatre designed with people, for people. In this sense, it is remarkable that theatre remains so distant from applied psychology, especially when educational and child psychology proclaims to be so concerned with advocating the views of children and young people through empowered contributions.

SOCIAL THEATRE IN THE UK

Social theatre is a diverse field of performance art. On one end of the continuum is the more 'conventional' form of theatre such as the stage play (usually with a strong sociopolitical focus). Social theatre writers and directors have had notable impact in the mainstream theatre bringing pertinent issues to the fore of public attention. For example, in the late 1980s, Harold Pinter wrote a short play which held a mirror up to oppressive regimes and as a protest to violated human rights in Eastern Europe of the time. *Mountain Language*, a very short, one-act play tells the story of oppressed voice, restricted movement and conflict. Another example can be seen in the play *4:48 Psychosis* by British playwright Sarah Kane, which depicts clinical depression. Through the medium of theatre Kane, having experienced depression herself, portrays a remarkably haunting account of mental illness. Both Pinter and Kane's work can broadly be considered social in the sense they are concerned with personal plights of real people, the society in which those people live and the political undertones which both support the maintenance and manifestation of the subject matters. Both plays are concerned with the human condition and provide material which stimulates debate and, hopefully, action in the real world.

At the other end of the continuum, theatre is used for development purposes, where the focus is on working with groups and communities around issues which are pertinent to them. These socialist theatre movements favour moving out of traditional spaces and away from customary conventions of the theatre too. These companies often, though not exclusively, work with people without specific actor training. This type of theatre also engages audiences beyond passive observation and makes them integral to the process. Both Boal's Forum Theatre and Brecht's Epic Theatre are examples of social theatre which aim at engaging audiences as critical and active participants. Both approaches vary in specifics while simultaneously addressing the personal, social and political condition.

There is an even further reaching form of socialist theatre, with which some of the above mentioned will also be familiar, namely theatre made by communities for the community. Joan Littlewood, perhaps most famed for her work on the satirical musical *Oh! What a Lovely War*, was a remarkable theatre maker. Her endeavours were intrinsically concerned with providing artistic opportunities for communities to explore their own lives and find their own solutions through theatre arts. The most infamous example was the *Fun Palace*, which encompassed many of these ideas (Nicholson, 2005). Although the *Fun Palace* never came to fruition due to the all too familiar lack of funding and local government support, Littlewood's influence remains far reaching both in traditional and applied theatre practices.

> ### Reflection point
>
> What is the potential of linking social theatre to the psychologist's work with children and young people?

To some readers the combination of theatre and psychology may appear unusual. Many may question training needs and some may be reluctant to trust or be confident in managing the arts process which can be open-ended and vague. These issues are discussed in more detail elsewhere alongside discussion for overcoming such barriers (see Hammond, 2013, 2015a). There will be others, of course, for whom the relevance and appeal of theatre to the psychologist will already be apparent, and even a small number of educational psychologists who may already be using such approaches. We will now explore some of the reasons why social theatre is relevant and why not using such approaches is a great loss to the children, young people and the systems in which we work.

Slade (2001) highlights the ongoing significance of play for children and argues that education must be concerned with both aesthetic experience and academic endeavour to constructively contribute to holistic development. As Slade discusses in his seminal text *Child Play*, drama has an important contribution to make. This argument is not new to psychology; Vygotsky recognised the importance of play on the development of self, offering a means of social communication through symbolic representation. It is through play, including embodied forms such as drama and dance, that we can discover and rediscover, define and redefine role, share and re-script stories. When we lose play, we fundamentally lose what it is to be a human. When we lose embodied play, we lose a central faculty in what it is to experience holistic development.

The children who are afforded the opportunity to engage in embodied play will share symbols through their creation of character, story and plot. The adults privileged to experience this special shared space between the child and the art are afforded the opportunity to co-construct meaning, supporting children to communicate their inner wishes without the necessity of lavish articulation through word or other complex forms of communication (Praglin, 2006). In this space co-creation affords new possibilities, imagined ways forward (Praglin, 2006), and to this extent provides a more tangible possibility orientated and person-centred approach to hearing and advocating on behalf of children and young people, sentiments reflected elsewhere (Billington, 2002) and which become more pertinent in the new SEN guidance (DfE, 2015).

Reflection point

How are children's needs constructed in the settings you work and how do these constructions influence intervention? To what extent do children have a genuine choice in working methods? And how much are current methods of assessment of a child's needs, eliciting and sharing views really fit for purpose if we consider the child as our primary client?

ALICE IN NO-MAN'S LAND

Alice is described by her teachers as disruptive and rude. She refuses to settle in class, ignoring instruction and disengaging with her lessons. At break time Alice is described as outlandish, sometimes absconding from the school grounds and getting into fights, disrespectful to staff and volatile with peers. The initial hypotheses of some of the adults working with Alice was that her behaviour is resembling that of a young person with ADHD, ODD or conduct disorder. Initially observing Alice's behaviour and then working with her and the adults charged with supporting her directly it occurred to me that perhaps the issue was not so much within Alice, but around her, or more specifically in the interactions with and the perceptions of others. Perhaps then, our starting point is in supporting Alice to 'be' and optimising her environment so she can 'become' close to the other (i.e., teachers, parents and peers).

There are three pertinent issues in Alice's case. The first relates to how others make sense of Alice's behaviour. It has been discussed earlier how our constructions of who we are and how we are is related to how we understand the world and how others understand us. In Alice's case, much like Tim Corcoran's story of Kevin (see Chapter 2), adults had begun to theorise that her behaviour had a pathological cause. These socially constructed labels act to make sense of what appears to be bizarre or unexplainable behaviour and in some cases as a political tool to access additional support. However, such labels often place the difficulties within-child and, by doing so, simultaneously legitimise the behaviour and relinquishes the social responsibility of others to help the child to *be* in their environment.

This brings us to the second point of how Alice might learn to *be* in her space. The way one (inter)acts with the world is governed by how one comes to learn about their world, customs and rules. We must learn about ourselves and others, the roles we play and how we adapt to new roles within our world appropriately. We must learn to *be* in spaces and with the other.

A wedding achieves meaning precisely because it has been performed a million times before; and its performance 'cites' those million other weddings. The bride, the priest, the members of the congregation all really only know how to play their part in this performance because they have been to weddings before. They 'cite' earlier behaviour. Someone who has never been to a wedding before is likely to be somewhat puzzled by the proceedings, and, having nothing themselves to cite, may only manage to behave appropriately by observing others who have that experience. (Leach, 2008, p. 4)

Early citations and semiotics can often be seen in a child's symbolic role play (Leach, 2008) through experimentation with character, props and costume with reference to their environment, significant others or from films and television. Citation is one way we begin to understand our world and learn how to *be* in every space or context that we come into contact with.

Earlier, through the story of Kurt, Dan Goodley (Chapter 4) showed how the body can be used for self-empowerment and political purpose. Alice's behaviour, like Kurt, is then making a profound statement. She is noticed and seen as having a body, an autonomous role and purpose beyond the deficits perceived by others. She is also making an attempt to *become* and connect with the other and, to a point, is successful. This brings us to the third point: Alice's behaviour is not only a reflection of her limitations to *be* in a space but also to *become* or connect with the other.

Consider for a moment a time when you have arrived in a new space (a restaurant, a festival, a party and so on) and were not sure how to be because it fell outside your usual point of reference – you had no previous experience to 'cite'. How do you feel when you are unable to fluently understand the rules of that space or the role that you or others are supposed to play? Perhaps you feel apprehensive, self-conscious or intimidated. Now you must become part of and connect with the other (new people and those who are accustomed to the space). It's not difficult to see how learning to *be* is important to fulfilling our social desire to *become* and as a result Alice's behaviour has meaning and purpose, though simultaneously it could further marginalise her. Griffiths et al. (2006) suggest that arts-based approaches can support children to be in multiple spaces through active engagement and re-engagement and thus socially and educationally including children and helping them to become and connect with the other. Drama provides a unique opportunity to promote inclusion and community cohesion.

> **Reflection point**
>
> How might you use drama-based techniques to support Alice and the adults who work with her?

Social theatre approaches hold a mirror up to pertinent issues within a community and encourages everyone to look in the same direction. Forum Theatre is a good example of an interactive dramatic method. This method was developed by Augusto Boal (2003) as a way of sharing stories of oppressive experiences and co-constructing solutions to the challenges faced by the protagonist in the performance. Forum Theatre skilfully works with people to help them learn how to *be* in a co-constructed space and, perhaps more importantly for Alice and the adults around her, help them to become connected with the other (i.e., Alice with her community and Alice's community with her). A detailed explanation of the Forum Theatre process can be found elsewhere (Hammond, 2013, 2015a).

This connection can help stimulate suggestions, comments and, most importantly, action. The actions in the play, in many cases created by children in the school or other setting, belong to the children but also the audience who may act, react and reflect on what they see while bringing their own values, judgements, views, perceptions, desires, wishes and worries to the space. Forum Theatre explicitly attempts to magnify the political and social circumstances at hand, allowing Alice and others to use their bodies constructively and collectively to share, reflect and problem solve.

SILENT ECHOES

Some years ago I was working with a group of young actors touring a Forum Theatre project to young people. The play had been devised through workshops with these actors based on their experiences of life transitions. The play centred on four main characters: Imogen, Megan, Daniel and Harry. All of them were friends sharing rented accommodation, but Megan and Harry were dating. The play told the story of how the relationship between Megan and Harry was put under strain by the living arrangements until eventually they split and, some months later, Harry began to date Imogen. Many of the 'spect-actors' (the name given to the audience in Forum Theatre) offered ideas about the key issues in the play ranging from the living arrangements to Harry and Imogen's disrespect for Megan. Some commented on Daniel's predicament of being caught in the middle. Many of the themes were reoccurring but during one session a spect-actor said 'perhaps Megan wants to hurt herself when she is alone' and 'Megan probably doesn't want to eat anymore because she feels fat', presumably so she could 'compete' with Imogen for Harry's affections.

For this young spect-actor, self-harm and body image were real themes, despite there being no indication of these issues implied in the play or through discussion. There was something about the play which resonated personally with this participant. Through the play spect-actors are able to connect with others and reflect together on pertinent issues; they can explore their sense of self in the post-conventionalist sense, collectively and safely. The problem to be solved is 'out there' in the space being co-constructed and reconstructed among the spect-actors, the problem is tangible yet malleable, spontaneous yet non-threatening. There is space to learn how to *be* and *become*. While extremely fruitful, we must remain mindful that drama naturally facilitates the sharing of one's own story which requires sufficient management and after care (see Hammond, 2015a).

Drama as a means of supporting human development, psychological well-being and of intervening at times of difficulty is not new. Educational psychology in the UK has not been without its pioneers in this area, though many of whom I am aware using the dramatic form in their work often do so under the radar and have scarcely published on the topic.

The point to make here is that drama is already being used in modern educational psychology practice in the UK. These approaches are not out of reach of most educational psychologists, but many may feel they need permission to legitimise their work among more traditional practice. There is, thankfully, an increasing bank of robust studies emerging from educational psychologists and others developing these ways of working (e.g., Brewer, 2012; Murphy, 2009, 2011), contributed not least by former doctoral trainees who arrive with diverse experiences of working with children and young people in non-educational settings. These different experiences have no doubt led to psychologists being more prepared to discuss work which has historically been at the fringes of the profession.

EVIDENCE AND POLITICAL AGENDA

Relevance for educational psychologists using drama

Incorporating drama into educational psychology practice offers some unique challenges. The first relates to personal anxiety of having to be able to 'perform', though with social theatre this is not a necessary prerequisite skill; it is far more important to be a competent facilitator of group processes and be comfortable with spontaneity, ambiguity and child-driven process. The second relates to a negatively skewed perception of the research base for drama and thus the legitimate use of drama by psychologists.

A recent longitudinal cross-cultural study by the Drama Improves Lisbon Key Competences in Education (DICE) Consortium found that educational theatre and drama supported the development of communication, interpersonal and social skills and enhanced learning outcomes (DICE, 2010). The study, which took place over 2 years with nearly 5000 young people used a robust mixed methods design. Those young people engaged in drama activities developed more confidence in reading, task initiation, problem solving and communication. These pupils also had an increased enjoyment of academic tasks, were perceived more positively among their teachers in all aspects of school and were more able to cope with stress, among other positive outcomes (DICE, 2010).

More recently the UK has seen a re-emergence of the arts for health and well-being agenda. The Royal Society for Public Health (RSPH) published findings from international arts-based projects, including those from the UK. The findings indicated a profound importance of the arts in preventing, managing and meeting the needs of people with a range of physical and mental health needs (RSPH, 2013). Specifically, the findings indicate arts projects were often more empowering and participatory in nature; these projects significantly reduced heart rate, cortisol levels, anxiety and depression among participants. Readers are signposted to Hammond (2013, 2015a, 2015b) to see examples of drama intervention specifically relevant to the educational psychologist.

Reflection point

Evidence such as that presented by DICE supports the legitimacy of educational psychologists using such approaches . What do you think are the barriers to using these methods and how might these be overcome: at the individual, school, service and local authority level?

CONCLUSION

This chapter has introduced social theatre in its many guises and applications. The relevance of the performing arts, with particular focus on drama, were discussed in relation to psychological theory and within some practical vignettes. Relevant political and social agendas arguing for the use of drama by educational psychologists were presented alongside recent examples of the available evidence base.

A range of arts, including performance art, with children and young people in a variety of settings is readily available, yet worryingly overlooked. Although there is recognition that a need to gather further research is important, the current evidence base remains too substantial to overlook (RSPH, 2013). With the increasing duty on educational psychologists to provide therapeutic support in schools to meet the mental health needs of children and young people outlined in the Improving Access to Psychological Therapies (IAPT) initiative, drama may offer another legitimate, evidence-based approach.

Training needs and competencies will be important considerations in rolling out such approaches. There is also a need to consider how using art approaches can be effectively evaluated by educational psychologists. Progress has been made in both areas and thus opportunities which further legitimise the potential use of dramatic forms are emerging and should be encouraged as genuinely child-centred approaches.

NOTE

1. Performing arts are highlighted in contrast to other art forms that are more dominant in the literature, such as storytelling and drawing. Performing arts specifically include drama, dance and music.

REFERENCES

Billington, T. (2002). Children, psychologists and knowledge: A discourse analytic narrative. *Educational & Child Psychology*, 19(3), 32–41.

Boal, A. (2003). *The rainbow of desire: The Boal method of theatre and therapy*. London: Routledge.

Brewer, S. (2012). School plays in secondary schools: an exploration of student and teacher perspectives. Unpublished thesis, University of Cardiff, UK. Online at http://ethos.bl.uk/OrderDetails.do?uin=uk.bl.ethos.567371 (accessed 25 November 2014).

Department for Education (DfE). (2015). *Special educational needs and disability code of practice for 0 to 25 years: Statutory guidance for organisations which work with and support children and young people who have special educational needs or disabilities*. London: Crown.

DICE Consortium. (2010). *The DICE has been cast: Research findings and recommenda-tions on educational theatre and drama*. Budapest: DICE Consortium. (See also www .dramanetwork.eu)

Griffiths, M., Berry, J., Holt, A., Naylor, J. & Weekes, P. (2006). Learning to be in public spaces: In from the margins with dancers, sculptors, painters and musicians. *British Journal of Educational Studies, 54*(3), 352–371.

Hammond, N. (2013). Introducing Forum Theatre to elicit and advocate children's views. *Educational Psychology in Practice, 29*(1), 1–18.

Hammond, N. (2015a). *Forum Theatre for Children: Enhancing social, emotional and creative development*. London: Trentham Books / Institute of Education Press.

Hammond, N. (2015b). Making a drama out of transition: Challenges and opportunities at times of change. *Research Papers in Education*. doi: 10.1080 / 02671522.2015.1029963

Leach, R. (2008). *Theatre studies: The basics*. Abingdon: Routledge.

Murphy, C. (2009). The link between artistic creativity and psychopathology: Salvador Dali. *Personality and Individual Differences, 46*, 765–774.

Murphy, C. (2011). An arts programme for excluded teenage females attending a PRU: An investigation of the experiences of pupils, staff and an educational psychologist researcher. Unpublished thesis, University of Sheffield, UK. Online at http:// etheses.whiterose. ac.uk/ 1601/ (accessed: 25 November 2014).

Nicholson, H. (2005). *Applied drama: The gift of theatre*. Basingstoke: Palgrave Macmillan.

Praglin, L. (2006). The nature of the 'in-between' in D.W. Winnicott's concept of transitional space and in Martin Buber's das Zwischenmenschliche. *Universitas Journal of Research, Scholarship and Creative Activity, 2*(2), 2–9. The University of Northern Iowa.

Royal Society for Public Health (RSPH). (2013). *Arts, health and wellbeing beyond the millen-nium: How far have we come and where do we want to go?* London: RSPH.

Slade, P. (2001). *Child play: Its importance for human development*. London: Jessica Kingsley.

22 'Being' Dyslexic in Higher Education: Reflections on Discourse and Identity

Harriet Cameron

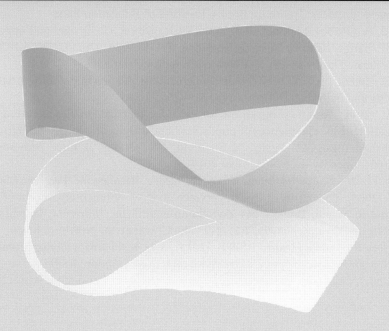

LEARNING OBJECTIVES

After reading this chapter you should be able to:

1. Better understand the different ways students can 'be' dyslexic in educational contexts.

2. Consider the power of discourse in shaping learning identity.

3. Reflect upon the question of choice in who we are, who we might become.

4. Think about how you use language to construct different kinds of learning and learner, and what implications these constructions can have for 'being' and 'doing'.

DYSLEXIA? WHAT IS IT, ANYWAY?

Most people who have been through Western education systems have heard of dyslexia. You might be dyslexic yourself, you might have someone close to you who has been given the label, you might know vaguely of people who are dyslexic who attend your classes, or it might be something you have no experience of at all. Whichever of these is the case, I would challenge you to be able to come up with a neat definition.

> **Reflection point**
>
> Take a moment to look up from this page and think about what you already 'know' about dyslexia and, perhaps more importantly, do you remember where this knowledge came from?

What you probably will have realised, and what I have also learnt, is that dyslexia is not a 'thing' you can describe in only one way. You can refer to the official definitions (I am not going to reproduce those here but, if you are interested, frequently cited definitions include those by the World Federation of Neurology, 1970; the International Dyslexia Association, 2002; and the British Psychological Society, 1999) but even the official definitions change, and no one seems to be able to agree on exactly how dyslexia should be described. Even the students whom I see who have a label of dyslexia rarely describe it in the same way and even the same student will describe it differently in different contexts and on different days. I am a specialist teacher for students at university who have been given labels like dyslexia and it is my job to work with them to help them get as much as possible out of their learning experiences and to join in at university on a more equal level with their peers who don't have the same specific difficulties with aspects of study.

WHY DOES IT MATTER?

How dyslexia is described both officially and by students in different contexts and at different times does matter; not because it is important to get it 'right', so to speak, as it is very unlikely there is a 'right' way 'out there', but because how dyslexia is defined has huge and immediate implications for people with the label (and for others, too, but I will return to that later).

When I first began my practice as a specialist tutor I had two very memorable introductory conversations with students who were part of my initial case-load. They were memorable because the students constructed dyslexia very differently from each other and because these constructions appeared to interact with their broader learning identities in striking ways.

The first of these students was a young man who arrived in my room wearing a T-shirt which read something like 'dyslexics of the world untie' (rather than 'unite'). A few minutes into our get-to-know-you interview it was clear that a construction of dyslexia as positive, as something to be proud of, was one he used fairly consistently in his life in and outside the university setting. He described himself as the creative one and the whacky one among his group of friends and he talked about how dyslexia was part of his character. The second student whom I introduced above was a young woman. She came into my room, sat down in the chair opposite mine, and spoke very quietly and reluctantly about her experiences of being assessed as dyslexic. She constructed dyslexia as a brain-based deficit, and at one point used the word 'disease' in part of the description. This young woman said she was ashamed to have this 'disease' which she felt meant she was broken, deficient and not as good as other people. She had not told her friends and family because she could not bear for them to know she was so afflicted. I do not remember this young woman once looking up from the table to meet my eyes. She did not come to see me again after that initial appointment.

These are two quite extreme examples but I have used them because they quite conveniently show the different ways of being that different constructions of dyslexia can offer or deny to people. The young man I describe went on to see me nearly every week for 3 years: he took every chance he could to get support from his peers and from me, he made use of his assistive software (e.g., speech-to-text programmes) and he approached his tutors without hesitation, for example, to ask for notes before the lectures. The young woman, whom I saw that one time only, said she could not tell her tutors and did not want to take her exams in a separate room as this would mean people would know she had something 'wrong' with her; hence, she could not make use of her extra time. I do not know if she changed her mind about using the available support, but I would not be surprised if she did not take up any of the adjustments she was entitled to.

My point here is that the ways students, and others around them, construct dyslexia arguably matters for their wider identities and informs what those students actually do; how they behave; their 'being' in the education context.

WHAT DIFFERENT WAYS OF 'BEING' DYSLEXIC ARE THERE?

Having worked over the years with hundreds of students who have been labelled 'dyslexic' at various points in their educational journeys, I have come across more different constructions of dyslexia than I could possibly include here; but I am going to talk about some of the more frequent constructions I do come across, and about those which are constructed in the literature around dyslexia. This is useful because it gives us a starting point from which to try to understand why students take on the particular learning identities they do (e.g., see Cameron & Billington, 2015a, 2015b).

Most of the research into dyslexia is still undertaken by people under the auspices of cognitive science or neuroscience, and they tend to construct dyslexia as a brain-based, or mind-based deficiency (cognitive psychology will normally talk about 'mind', and neuroscience will talk about 'brain processes'), though there is a lot of disagreement about what dyslexia is and whether or not it is different from more general reading difficulty (Elliott & Grigorenko, 2014). Researchers in these areas often assume that dyslexia, or specific learning disability is a fixed phenomenon; that it is innate; that it is a deviation from the norm; that it exists independently of time and culture; that it may be accurately assessed using psychometrics alone; and that the evidence for dyslexia, its characteristics, prevalence, relevance and remediability have been real-ised with motives only of improving lives or pursuing scientific understanding of the brain and mind. There is much work in this area, but leading authors include Rod Nicolson and Angela Fawcett (see their 2008 work for a neat summary of cognitive-level and brain-level explana-tions), Keith Stanovich (on controversy over diagnosis: 1991, 1996), Margaret Snowling (on phonological deficit: 1981); Wolf (on double deficit: 1999); John Stein (on magnocellular defi-cit: 2001); and Julian Elliott and Elena Grigorenko (on controversy over diagnosis: 2014).The ideas about dyslexia generated by these authors and disciplines dominate in the discussion of dyslexia within education, which is perhaps partly why so many students construct their learn-ing identities using constructions of deficit and speak using scientific terms when they describe their difficulties with learning. Kenneth Gergen talks about 'a technical vocabulary of deficit' that has entered the public domain (Gergen, 1991, pp. 14–15) and which, it appears, has been adopted as a way to talk about learning differences some people label dyslexia.

Both my students and students in the literature make use of metaphors which reflect the theories of cognitive psychology and neuroscience when conceptualising dyslexia or similar differences. My students often talk about 'input' and 'output', small 'memory drives' and 'glitches' in the brain while, in the literature, students have described their brains as 'mal-functioning' (Pelkey, 2001, p. 19); being 'jumbled' or 'stretched' (Reiff, Gerber & Ginsberg, 1993, p. 118); being 'back-to-front' or not being able to 'click open' (Osmond, 1993, pp. 27, 18); or they have referred to their brain's 'programming' (Reiff et al., 1993, p. 118), indicative of the idea of brain as a computer. In using metaphors like these, the scientific ideas may have been easier to make sense of, but they may likewise have become more easily twisted or oversimplified. The concepts of one's brain being 'jumbled', for example, or, indeed, 'back-to-front' do not support a positive view of one's intellectual capabilities, even if they are a quick and useful means of justifying one's need for support.

The dyslexia-as-specific-cognitive-deficit idea is not the only one available to dyslexic stu-dents. In fact, there is an array of slightly different conceptions to 'choose' from. One of the most confusing of these is the idea of dyslexia as a myth. Dyslexia as 'myth' includes refer-ences to the dyslexia label as an excuse, or cover for something else, such as parental anxiety about their child's apparent lack of achievement (Riddick, 1995); or a 'convenient fiction' for white, middle-class children who struggled academically (McDermott, Goldman & Varenne, 2006). It can also include the idea that the dyslexia label is intentionally perpetuated for institutional financial advantage (Soler, 2009). There is also a significant amount of research which frames dyslexia as a cognitive difference rather than deficiency (for a summary of this research, see Leong, 2002). And another group of conceptions moves still further away from the idea of dyslexia as deficiency, considering it rather as a gift or connected to specific abilities (Von Károlyi et al., 2003; Chakravarty, 2009).

WHY DO THESE DIFFERENT CONCEPTIONS OF DYSLEXIA MATTER?

Categories of person are not neutral, but powerful meaning-makers. When people are allo-cated to particular categories, argue Shakespear and Erickson (2001, p. 198). 'the possibilities of personhood change'. Following this idea, it is likely that adoption of some conceptions of dyslexia more than others may offer different possibilities of being for those individuals; and this is echoed by Burden (2005, pp. 196–197): 'those of us who possess characteristics considered to be socially undesirable will begin to perceive ourselves as undesirable or in some way wanting'. In this sense, then, even if the 'reality' of what the descriptions of dyslexia refer to may be questioned, the 'real' influence of these definitions on people's lives is less in doubt. In fact, the descriptions themselves arguably bring realities into being. Educators and educational psychologists can use this understanding to help students to recognise the multiple ways in which their learning performances have been constructed, and so to shift the focus away from individual responsibility for educational 'success' or 'failure'.

DISCOURSE, BEING AND CHOICE

In this section I am going to talk about the degree of choice we have in the discourses we draw upon and about the possibilities for resisting some discourses in favour of others. If we do not have a say in the discourses which define us, then some ways of being are arguably closed to us.

Parker (1989, p. 61) describes discourse as 'a system of statements which constructs an object' and Reid and Valle (2004, p. 466) as a 'system of rules that defines *what can be said*'. Burr describes wider discourse as a 'frame of reference'; 'a conceptual backcloth against which our utterances can be interpreted' (Burr, 2003, p. 66). These definitions suggest that discourse is something we use to make sense of our experiences, something that limits the positions we may occupy in the world, and something that creates objects. This idea of discourse is a key one in the discussion of how identities are constructed socially. In some sense, our words *do* things; the discourse is active in our interactions. If students take one of the more traditional/scientific perspectives on dyslexia, they may feel helpless to act against their 'fixed' 'condition'; whereas, if they understand dyslexia as a discursive construction, they may feel less bound by dominant conceptions attached to this label and freer to explore other meanings and identities. This brings me to the consideration of agency and a further reflection point.

> **Reflection point**
>
> Do people have choice in the discourses they draw upon? And if so, how much? And, specifically, how much say do you think dyslexic students have over the meaning they attach to their label?

'Do we use discourse or does it use us?' asks Burr (2003, p. 103). This is very difficult to answer with any certainty, yet it is such an important question. If we believe we have no choice in the discourses that define us, or the identities that become attached to us, then we lose the impetus to struggle against identities we perceive as oppressive because the fighting becomes pointless. Burr argues that we do, in fact, have some choice in the discourses we identify with, but that escaping from dominant discourses is often very difficult and is subject to heavy restriction. To begin with, any choice would be restricted to those discourses available in a given social context (McDermott et al., 2006). In other words, discourse 'defines what *can be said*' (Reid & Valle, 2004, p. 466), but within these parameters, we have 'the right of withdrawal, of throwing into relief one's participation by casting it in alternative frames' (Gergen, 1991, p. 196). Bruner (1990, p. 110) concurs with this position: he writes that, although we are 'creatures of history', 'the self, using its capacities for reflection and for envisioning alternatives, escapes or embraces, or reevaluates and reformulates what the culture has on offer'. However, some discourses, argue Anderson and Williams (2001), are so entrenched that they have become 'regimes of truth'; 'hegemonic discourses' that are very hard to challenge. We have to be active in resistance to these if choice is to be had. Bauman expresses this nicely: 'some [identities are] of one's own choice but others [are] inflated and launched by those around, and one needs to be constantly on the alert to defend the first against the second' (Bauman, 2004, p. 13). We may also find that we draw upon discourses to identify ourselves/position others unconsciously (Ivanic, 1998). People can 'become enmeshed in the subject positions implicit in their talk without necessarily having intended to position each other in particular ways' (Burr, 2003, p. 115). Educational psychologists and educators are likely to be in a position to help students build their own discursive tools to resist or embrace the different identities available. In other words, they have a responsibility not merely to observe, to deliver and describe test results or to suggest plans of action, but to critically interrogate their own practice and assumptions which will influence the student's possibilities for being and doing.

CHAPTER SUMMARY

In this chapter, I have drawn upon my own practice with dyslexic students in higher education to talk about how discourses can construct the learning identities students adopt. I have also talked a little about how the ways students and others position themselves in relation to these discourses can inform what students do as they move through the education system.

Reflection

As a specialist teacher, I have a responsibility to reflect on the language I use with students and with others, to take particular care with how the words I use can categorise and limit others' possibilities for being in educational contexts. This is an ongoing task for me, and one which I am sure will never be complete.

> Our ideological development is…an intense struggle within us for hegemony among various available verbal and ideological points of view, approaches, directions and values. The semantic structure of an internally persuasive discourse is *not finite*, it is *open*; in each of the new contexts that dialogise it, this discourse is able to reveal ever newer *ways to mean*.
> (Bakhtin, 1981, p. 79)

Reflective task

Take 10 minutes with a pen and paper and think about the people you work and study with, or those whom you teach or support. Consider, and note down, the degree to which you categorise individuals (even inadvertently). Do you ever describe people in these contexts as 'bright' or 'clever', for example? Do you know anyone in these contexts who has been given a label like 'dyslexia'? Have you ever categorised yourself using labels like 'stupid' or 'average', 'confident' or 'quiet', and so on? Think about the assumptions you have in connection to the labels you have used, and think also about the possible implications these labels might have for behaviour and identity.

- How did your teachers, parents/carers, friends contribute to your learning identities as you went through the school system?

- Have you ever resisted the labels given to you by others and, if so, how did you resist them?

- How do you construct or position others in your practice or study? What other ways could you construct them, and which discourses are you drawing on in order to do this?

REFERENCES

Anderson, P. & Williams, J. (2001). Identity and difference: Concepts and themes. In P. Anderson & J. Williams (Eds.), *Identity and difference in higher education: 'Outsiders within'* (ch. 1). Farnham: Ashgate

Bakhtin, M.M. (1981). *The dialogic imagination.* Trans. M. Holquist & C. Emeron, Ed. M. Holquist. Austin: University of Texas Press. In P. Morris (Ed.) (1994), *The Bakhtin reader: Selected writings of Bakhtin, Medvedev, Voloshinov.* London: Arnold.

Bauman, Z. (2004). *Identity: Conversations with Benedetto Vecchi.* Cambridge and Malden, MA: Polity Press.

British Psychological Society. (1999). *Dyslexia, literacy and psychological assessment.* Report of a working party of the Division of Educational and Child Psychology. Leicester: BPS.

Bruner, J. (1990). *Acts of meaning.* Cambridge, MA, and London: Harvard University Press.

Burden, R. (2005). The self-concept and its relationship to educational achievement. In J. Soler, F. Fletcher-Cambell, & G. Reid (Eds.) (2009), *Understanding difficulties in literacy development: Concepts and issues* (ch. 14). Thousand Oaks, CA: Sage.

Burr, V. (2003). *Social constructionism* (2nd edn). Hove and New York: Routledge.

Cameron, H. & Billington, T. (2015a). 'Just deal with it': Neoliberalism in dyslexic students' talk about dyslexia and learning at university. *Studies in Higher Education.* doi:10.1080/030 75079.2015.1092510

Cameron, H. & Billington, T. (2015b). The discursive construction of dyslexia by students in higher education as a moral and intellectual good. *Disability & Society* 30(8), 1225–1240.

Chakravarty, A. (2009). Artistic talent in dyslexia: A hypothesis. *Medical Hypotheses, 73,* 569–571.

Elliott, J.G. & Grigorenko, E.L. (2014). *The dyslexia debate.* New York: Cambridge University Press.

Gergen, K. (1991). *The saturated self: Dilemas of identity in contemporary life*. New York: Basic Books/HarperCollins.

International Dyslexia Association. (2002). Definition of dyslexia. Baltimore. Online at https://dyslexiaida.org/dyslexia-basics (accessed 4 August 2016).

Ivanic, R. (1998). *Writing and identity: The discoursal construction of identity in academic writing*. Amsterdam: John Benjamins.

Leong, C.K. (2002). Developmental dyslexia as developmental and linguistic variation: Editor's commentary. *Annals of Dyslexia*, 52, 1–16.

McDermott, R., Goldman, S. & Varenne, H. (2006). The cultural work of learning disabilities. In J. Soler, F. Fletcher-Cambell & G. Reid (Eds.) (2009), *Understanding difficulties in literacy development: Concepts and issues* (ch. 17). Thousand Oaks, CA: Sage.

Nicolson, R.I. & Fawcett, A.J. (2008). *Dyslexia, learning and the brain*. Cambridge, MA: MIT Press.

Osmond, J. (1993). *The reality of dyslexia*. London and New York: Cassel/Channel 4.

Parker, I. (1989). *The crisis in modern social psychology, and how to end it*. London: Routledge.

Pelkey, L. (2001). In the LD bubble. In P. Rodis, A. Garrod & M.L. Boscardin (Eds.), *Learning disabilities and life stories* (ch. 2). Boston: Allyn & Bacon.

Reid, K. & Valle, J.W. (2004). The discursive practice of learning disability: Implications for instruction and parent–school relations. *Journal of Learning Disabilities*, 37(6), 466–481.

Reiff, H.B., Gerber, P.J. & Ginsberg, R. (1993). Definitions of learning disabilities from adults with learning disabilities: The insiders' perspectives. *Learning Disability Quarterly*, 16(2), 114–125.

Riddick, B. (1995). Dyslexia: Dispelling the myths. *Disability & Society*, 10(4), 457–473.

Shakespear, T. & Erickson, M. (2001). Different strokes: Beyond biological determinism and social constructionism. In H. Rose & S. Rose (Eds.), *Alas poor Darwin: Arguments against evolutionary psychology* (pp. 190–205). London: Vintage.

Snowling, M. (1981). Phonemic deficits in developmental dyslexia. *Psychological Research*, 43, 219–234.

Soler, J. (2009). The historical construction of dyslexia: Implications for higher education. In J. Soler, F. Fletcher-Cambell & G. Reid (Eds.), *Understanding difficulties in literacy development: Concepts and issues* (ch. 3). Thousand Oaks, CA: Sage.

Stanovich, K. (1991). Discrepancy definitions of reading disability: Has intelligence led us astray? *Reading Research Quarterly*, 26(1), 7–29.

Stanovich, K. (1996). Toward a more inclusive definition of dyslexia. *Dyslexia*, 2, 154–166.

Stein, J. (2001). The magnocellular theory of developmental dyslexia. *Dyslexia*, 7, 12–36.

Von Károyli, C., Winner, E., Gray, W. & Sherman, G.F. (2003). Dyslexia linked to talent: Global visual spatial ability. *Brain and Language*, 85(3), 427–431.

Wolf, M. (1999). What time may tell: Towards a new conceptualization of developmental dyslexia. *Annals of Dyslexia*, 49, ProQuest Education Journals, 3–14.

World Federation of Neurology. (1968). *Report of research group on dyslexia and world illiteracy*. Dallas, TX: WFN.

23 A Future? Why Educational Psychologists Should Engage with a Critical Neuroscience

Tom Billington

LEARNING OBJECTIVES

After reading this chapter you should be able to:

1. Reflect on the transient nature of the contexts and conceptual bases for professional practice.

2. Critique emerging evidence from neuroscience relating to human behaviour, experience and how people learn.

3. Re-engage with William James's 'quest' for the 'conditions' in which we live our lives.

EPISTEMOLOGICAL CHOICES

Whither experience, emotions and feelings in educational psychology?

Psychology is the science of mental life, both of its phenomena and their *conditions*...the faculty does not exist absolutely, but works under *conditions*; and the quest of the conditions becomes the psychologist's most interesting task. (James, 1890, Vol. 1, pp. 1–3: emphasis added)

William James mapped out the field for a positivistic psychology while at the same time pointing educational psychology in the direction of what might become a more complete and genuinely scientific study of the human. Jamesian pragmatism recognised not only the importance of the 'conditions' (i.e., the context or circumstances in which people live) but also the futility of any science of the human which seeks to become what he refers to as a 'closed system' (James, 1890, Vol. 1, p. vii). Unfortunately, educational psychology in the UK was historically constructed in a manner which sought to restrict the scope of its inquiry (i.e., to psychopathology, constructed at the level of the individual).

From the time of its emergence as a discrete boundary of knowledge, educational psychology has required its practitioners to devise and support practices which are able to identify, separate and exclude individual young people from their communities (Billington, 2000; Billington & Williams, 2015). This premise suggests a very narrow field of inquiry, indeed one which would suggest that educational psychology has been constructed as a sociopolitical rather than a scientific endeavour. Arguably, educational psychology has been engaging not with processes, forms of knowing or scientific inquiry in respect of the human but with non-dynamic narratives of fragmented non-persons in which those who are scrutinised become positioned as 'other' than human. The histories of medicalisation and psychologisation are intertwined with the historical processes of racism, disablism, colonialism and sexism (Goodley, 2014; Goodley, Lawthom & Runswick-Cole, 2014) which have resulted in some people finding themselves as being considered as *less than* human, even non-human. It could be argued that various communities (e.g., indigenous people in the Global South, disabled people, women) have often been denied the status of being fully human and are still engaged with political fights for recognition under global discourses of human rights.

Educational psychology has arguably fanned the fires of exclusion by providing the rationale for epistemologies that can lead to a poverty of understanding in relation to young people who are frequently reduced to partial stories about 'difficulties', 'learning' or 'behaviour' which take little account of other aspects of their lives. These restricted accounts of the person have largely ignored the complex interconnectedness between aspects of functioning as understood by James (1890) or Dewey (1916, 1938). Even Hadow, the British academic who authored a landmark UK government document on psychological testing in education, understood the problems of assessing individual young people when subject to 'hasty and crude methods...the whole problem has proved far more intricate than was at the outset assumed' (Hadow, 1924, p. 60).

During the 20th century, theoretical paradigms such as 'cognition' and 'behaviour' tended to become 'closed systems' when performed in research or professional practice: for example, in psychologist training programmes, in agency or service criteria, education and health, and in subsequent assessment practices, analyses and reports. Those aspects of human functioning which might be described in terms of 'experience', 'emotions' or 'feelings' have either been overlooked or, even when acknowledged, incorporated within non-theorised, non-scientific, taken-for-granted accounts of the human which could too easily be overwhelmed by an *a priori* story relating to psychopathology. James himself suggested there might be non-scientific reasons for our reluctance to include 'experience' in psychological studies: 'The desire of men [*sic*] educated in laboratories not to have their physical reasonings mixed up with such incommensurable factors as feelings is certainly very strong' (Hadow, 1924, p. 134).

I argue here that attempts to construct a scientific study of the human which excludes complex theoretical understandings and narratives relating to the person, experience, emotions or feelings have resulted in major omissions in the research and practice of educational psychology.

During the past 20 years, however, neuroscientists have gradually been filling the void long apparent in educational psychology, realising only too well 'the scientific neglect of emotion in the 20th. century' (Damasio, 2000, p. 39). Damasio and neuroscientist colleagues have been taking positions hitherto often neglected by psychology in general, for example, elevating the importance of emotion and feelings, and asserting (in their more scientific research) that experience is not only inseparable from other forms of cognitive activity but intrinsic to thinking itself: 'input into the brain generates an experience and, next, by using the experience so generated to form concepts' (Zeki, 2009, p. 35).

The neuroscientist Joseph Le Doux (1999, p. 164) proposed a model for conceptualising the processes involved, arguing that our internal states are, in a primary sense, affected by external stimuli which trigger what he regards as emotional responses. For ease of argument Le Doux suggested that these emotional responses follow two different routes: one, the 'low road' to the amygdala, which is connected to the body's automatic responses; the other, the 'high road', which avoids the amygdala and passes towards the sensory cortex where, according to Le Doux, the initial stimulus connects to other cognitive (and yet again, inherently emotional) processes. To Le Doux, it is in this way that possibilities are created for the juxtaposition, interconnectedness and interpenetration of our thinking and feeling – in a reconfigured understanding of the cognitive.

While such theories are essentialist in their claims, the physiological landscape being represented is one of emotional and cognitive complexity and provides ample opportunities for resistance to the more simplistic knowledges which have frequently provided the foundation for our work as practitioner psychologists. For example, we have acceded to the use of a category such as 'emotional and behavioural difficulties' knowing that there are very different and, again, complex mechanisms and functions involved. However, in order to contain that complexity we have tended to work only with the behavioural aspects of functioning rather than the emotional. In brief, what Skinner was proposing was more immediately accessible than Freud, or perhaps just measurable.

However, the work of neuroscientists such as Le Doux suggests that as educational psychologists we have been remiss in disallowing emotion and feelings discursive space within our discipline. Challenges have emerged from within cognitive science to the notion of a cognitivism which eschews emotion, thus destabilising the rather mechanistic, deterministic models of mind which have pervaded many forms of research and practice in educational psychology during the past 100 years. Interestingly, some critical neuroscientific discourse seems more able to tolerate both the complex and the unknown in relation to the phenomena of persons, thus providing the basis for a more genuinely scientific exploration of the human.

That emotions and feelings are woven intrinsically into the experiential landscape as equal partners to (or indeed part of) cognition and other mental processes would until recent decades have been radical in the daily practice of many child or educational psychologists. Attention deficit hyperactivity disorder (ADHD), autism spectrum disorder, dyslexia, dyspraxia and a whole raft of 'difficulties' in learning and behaviour have traditionally been conceptualised as somehow separate from the young persons' emotional lives. However, critical neuroscience questions not only the scientific evidence for the psychological category but also the very existence of well-worn psychological paradigms of the cognitive, the behavioural and the emotional. To many neuroscientists, emotions are now considered integral to all human functioning which, of course, had been understood long ago by James and others (see Dewey, 1938). While neuroscience has been filling the epistemological vacuum, voices from within that discipline are cautious about the strictly neurological evidence of any psychological category:

> no markers in the brain have been found for any of the psychiatric diagnoses studied… categories may simply not exist as distinctive categories and the brain may well function in a manner that lacks any clear demarcations between the sub-systems that neuroscience has created. (Timimi, Gardner & McCabe, 2011, pp. 128, 135)

Those voices also urge caution in respect of headline media claims, warning that there is still some way to go before we fill the void between compelling coloured images of electrical activity in the brain and the actual feelings of the person which, of course, remain much less accessible to any form of psychological empiricism: 'there is an abyss between knowledge and experience which cannot be bridged scientifically' (Damasio, 2000, p. 308). Indeed, 'neuroscience lets us down. Somehow, bursts of electricity in the wetware of the brain don't seem adequate to the exquisitely structured mind that I, and you, have' (Tallis, 2008, p. 158). It is in the work of those neuroscientists whose critical acumen remain alert to the limitations of their science (i.e., often defined by the limits of their new technologies) that we find the seeds for more genuinely scientific analyses of the phenomena under scrutiny and from which educational psychology might benefit.

CRITICAL NEUROSCIENCE

Contemporary neuroscience has access to technologies of which previous generations of philosophers, scholars and scientists could scarcely dream, and it is these technologies which promise, finally, to reveal the mind.

Or perhaps not, since neuroscience has not actually located mind, only brains; indeed a crucial distinction is made, 'mind is a process not a thing' (Damasio, 2004, p. 183). Damasio usefully reflects on the nature of his own scientific investigations into the human brain, critiquing the origins of the scientific method and its omissions in relation to a scientific study of persons, and turning to a pre-Enlightenment philosopher:

> Spinoza's insight…that mind and body are parallel and mutually correlated processes, mimicking each other at every crossroad, as two faces of the same thing…his insight was revolutionary for its time but it had no impact on science. (Damasio, 2004, p. 217)

Damasio had as a scientist searched to discover truths about brains and yet retreated on occasion to find solace, inspiration or perhaps even knowledge, in the words of the 17th-century philosopher whose hypotheses, if acted upon, would have led to a very different kind of scientific study of the human. Damasio does not conclude that a scientific pursuit of the uniquely human is futile but realises that Spinoza and, centuries later, William James sought to avoid a science of the human constructed on a narrow basis of inquiry. I argue that as a consequence the practices of educational psychology have been constructed on a most incomplete approach to the study of the human, one which is oblivious to the assumptions it makes of a Cartesian dualism underpinning human functioning, namely, mind and body (Ryle, 1948).

The relationship between brains and bodies has become a central concern in the science of the human, discourses of 'embodiment' becoming increasingly well used in phenomenological philosophy (Rowlands, 2010) as well as critical neuroscience (Rose & Abi-Rached, 2013). The technology now exists, of course, to map the inner workings of both our brains and our bodies: computerised axial tomography (CAT scans), positron emission tomography (PET scans) and functional magnetic resonance imaging (fMRI). Neuroscience has thus been extending the scope of its activities beyond the brain to consideration of the whole body and indeed beyond, to the 'conditions' in which it functions, for 'the brain is not the sole producer of the mind but a relational organ that mediates the interaction between the organism and its complementary environment' (Fuchs, 2012, p. 341).

While psychology provided influential narratives in the 20th century concerning aspects of human functioning – for example, behaviourism, cognitivism – it is now neuroscience which is being used increasingly to inform understandings of the human in the 21st century. Glossy magazine images are frequently to be found claiming to reveal the infant brain, the adolescent brain and, even more problematically, the ADHD brain, the autistic brain or the brain of an abused or neglected infant. However, simplistic accounts which (perhaps intentionally?) feed the media frenzy and public fascination can ignore the ways in which scans can show, perhaps, not a snapshot of a category but:

1. 'how different people may use different regions of the brain to solve the same task, making the idea of localizing functions...very difficult...' (Timimi, Gardner & McCabe, 2011, p. 132) or else

2. '[a] brain that approaches a problem in a different way...' (Timimi, Gardner & McCabe, 2011, p. 133).

Indeed, these authors claim even that we never know whether 'neurological discrepancies are a cause or an effect of the disordered behaviour' (Timimi, Gardner & McCabe, 2011, p. 122).

The nature of headline claims made on behalf of neuroscience reinforce an overly zealous reductionism in attempts to seduce the reader to believe that the brain images are realist accounts of the organism. What we actually see in such images are, of course, invariably not real brains but, indeed, just images, representations which are the products not solely of a scientific inquiry but of a creative partnership in which algorithms of brain functioning are transformed into media artefacts or perhaps even works of art. Even before we begin to critique the nature of the science, therefore, we need to make a conscious effort to critique the actual technologies and techniques used to represent the inner workings of brain and body, for any representations are just that, mere 'images...[which are] consciously selected to enhance the textual argument' (Dumit, 2012, p. 219).

Dumit continues his analysis that the images of brains we see in popular culture are not actual brains, of course, but representations, texts which have been produced and which can be read in much the same way as this book and thus subject to different principles for reading and interpretation. The schism between the actual brains and the means by which those brains are represented provides a space which allows for ideas about the human to be inserted, once again ideas which will be shaped not just by any neutral science but by cultural, social, even political and economic discursive practices.

The allure of the 'normal' remains strong in this new science and the promise of more precise pathologisations or diagnoses will be difficult for disciplines such as educational psychology to resist, especially since we have embedded in our working practices strong links with various kinds of exclusion, social, psychological, cultural, political or economic. There are warnings, however, for 'The textual manipulation of imagi[ni]ng texts, if without challenge, can permit an otherwise untheorised "collapse from scan to diagnosis"' (Dumit, 2012, p. 221). Thus while the old psychopathologising tendency is waiting to reassert itself in the new technologies, reinforce the epistemological boundaries and restrict once again the narrative accounts of persons, there are many reasons for showing due caution and resisting any simplistic claims (see Broks, 2003; Rose, 2006; Gergen, 2009).

Such accounts are essential since 'neuroscience is increasingly being called upon to build prescriptions about how to live' (Choudhury & Slaby, 2012, p. 5) and, indeed, the technology is becoming available which would allow an even greater degree of individual scrutiny as part of the web of 'governmentality' (Rose, 2006). Perhaps more hopefully, however, the case for the complexity of the human brain is being made eloquently by many neuroscientists who issue an implicit challenge to those human sciences which fail to acknowledge that complexity, 'a comprehensive understanding of the nature of the human mind and behavior is impoverished without a theoretical and empirical approach that incorporates...multiple layers of analysis' (Chiao & Cheon, 2012, p. 290).

At this point in the evolution of the human sciences, it is interesting to note the similarities between current contexts and the circumstances at the beginning of the last century when James first mapped out a field of investigation into the human within the confines of psychology. Neuroscientists in the 21st century, armed with shiny new technologies, are now attempting to construct a new map of the person. If so, however, to what extent would any such bold new maps for investigating the human be able to escape those old well-established discourses of deficit and psychopathology which have stunted the scientific possibilities within psychology?

The tendency, once again, will be for a contemporary science to 'reveal' the disordered brain and to create, yet again, models of the person in the forms of categories and according to some notion of the ideal human. I argue that the conditions for such a process are not merely scientific but social, cultural, political and economic and both neuroscientists and psychologists, for example, will find themselves engaging in processes that create 'a baseline definition of "normal" [which] is both a physiological and a social judgment' (Dumit, 2012, p. 200). Such definitions lead to new models of personhood from which, if we are not careful, future generations of young people, as those before, will be at risk of becoming 'othered'; that is, as non-human. Any conjecture in respect of the 'normal', therefore, needs to be performed not only by neuroscientists but by social scientists and not least, I argue here, by those who will be at the receiving end of such theories. I thus concur with the view that critical neuroscience might usefully 'renew(s) the possibility for critical commentators to be engaged with, rather than estranged from, laboratory science' (Slaby & Choudhury, 2012, p. 42).

JAMES'S 'QUEST' FOR THE 'CONDITIONS'

The work of educational psychologists could be transformed during the next decades in terms of the potential technologies that could be made available and thus the mechanics of the work we actually perform. Test batteries relating to cognitive intelligence (crudely defined), whether considered curiously quaint or else cruel and harmful, present as anachronistic in the light of other potential forms of representation of the human – for example, those made available in digital worlds. Indeed, some of the mainstays of daily practice, such as intelligence tests, are beginning to have the 'feel' of artefacts which belong to a bygone age. Our tool use is changing and this might just be a moment when as educational psychologists we can explore new ways of working, engaging with people and resisting the urge always to construct and define the 'other' as damaged versions of the 'normal'. While new technologies might seek to create new forms of highly specialised forms of assessment, it would be a missed opportunity if all those efforts in production simply allowed the old psychological discourses of deficit to infect and restrict any new politically informed democratic potentials. Would we really want to embrace new technologies if all they achieved was to perform essentially the same activities as before, defining norms, consigning individual young people to awkward, ill-fitting transient categories as a precursor to lifelong social exclusion? Is that the kind of progress we envisage?

We need to renew our efforts to engage with James's 'quest' which would demand that we:

1. engage with new technology and its implications for theory construction;

2. ensure that we develop critiques which provide understandings of the 'politics implicit in scientific practices' (Slaby & Choudhury, 2012, p. 31); and

3. use such critiques to evolve new ways of engaging ethically with persons who are the recipients of our research and professional practice.

REFERENCES

Billington, T. (2000). *Separating, losing and excluding children: narratives of difference*. London: Routledge Falmer.

Billington, T. & Williams, A. (2015). Education and psychology: Change at last? In I. Parker (Ed.), *The Routledge handbook of critical psychology*. London: Routledge.

Broks, P. (2003) *Into the silent land: Travels in neuropsychology*. London: Atlantic Books.

Chiao, J.Y. & Cheon, B. (2012). Cultural neuroscience as critical neuroscience in practice. In S. Choudhury & J. Slaby (Eds.), *Critical neuroscience: A handbook of the social and cultural aspects of neuroscience*. Chichester: Wiley-Blackwell.

Choudhury, S. & Slaby, J. (Eds.) (2012). *Critical neuroscience: A handbook of the social and cultural aspects of neuroscience*. Chichester: Wiley-Blackwell.

Damasio, A. (2000). *The feeling of what happens: Body, emotion and the making of consciousness*. London: Vintage.

Damasio, A. (2004). *Looking for Spinoza*. London: Vintage.

Dewey, J. (1916). *Democracy and education: An introduction to the philosophy of education*. New York: The Macmillan Company.

Dewey, J. (1938). *Experience and education*. New York: Touchstone.

Dumit, J. (2012). Critically producing brain images of mind. In S. Choudhury & J. Slaby (Eds.), *Critical neuroscience: A handbook of the social and cultural aspects of neuroscience*. Chichester: Wiley-Blackwell.

Fuchs, T. (2012). Are mental illnesses diseases of the brain? In S. Choudhury & J. Slaby (Eds.), *Critical neuroscience: A handbook of the social and cultural aspects of neuroscience*. Chichester: Wiley-Blackwell.

Gergen, K.J. (2009). *Relational being*. New York: Oxford University Press.

Goodley, D. (2014). *Dis/ability studies: Theorising disablism and ableism*. London: Routledge.

Goodley, D., Lawthom, R. & Runswick-Cole, K. (2014). Posthuman disability studies. *Subjectivity*, 7(4), 342–361.

Hadow, W.H. (1924). *Report of the consultative committee on psychological tests of educable capacity*. London: HMSO.

James, W. (1890). *Principles of psychology*, Vols. 1 & 2. Mineola, NY: Dover Publications.

Le Doux, J. (1998). *The emotional brain*. London: Phoenix.

Rose, N. & Abi-Rached, J.M. (2013). *Neuro: The new brain sciences and the management of mind*. Princeton, NJ: Princeton University Press.

Rose, S. (2006). *The 21st century brain: Explaining, mending and manipulating the mind*. London: Vintage.

Rowlands, M. (2010). *The new science of mind: From extended mind to embodied phenomenology*. Cambridge, MA: MIT Press.

Ryle, G. (1949). *The concept of mind*. London: Penguin.

Slaby, J. & Choudhury, S. (2012). Proposal for a critical neuroscience. In S. Choudhury J. Slaby (Eds.), *Critical neuroscience: A handbook of the social and cultural aspects of neuroscience*. Chichester: Wiley-Blackwell.

Tallis, R. (2008). *The kingdom of infinite space: A fantastical journey around your head*. London: Atlantic Books.

Timimi, S., Gardner, N. & McCabe, B. (2011). *The myth of autism: Medicalizing men's and boys' social and emotional competence*. Basingstoke: Palgrave Macmillan

Zeki, S. (2009). *The splendours and miseries of the brain: Love, creativity and the quest for human happiness*. Chichester: Wiley-Blackwell

Further Reading and Resources

Chapter 1

Foucault, M. (1991 [1975]). *Discipline and punish: The birth of the prison*. London: Penguin.
Rose, N. (1999). *Governing the soul: The shaping of the private self*. London: Routledge & Kegan Paul.

Chapter 5

Dunning, G., James, C., & Jones, N. (2005). Splitting and projection at work in schools. *Journal of Educational Administration, 43*(3), 244–259.
Pellegrini, D.W. (2010). Splitting and projection: drawing on psychodynamics in educational psychology practice. *Educational Psychology in Practice, 26*(3), 251–260.
Williams, A. (2013). Critical reflective practice: Exploring a reflective group forum through the use of Bion's theory of group processes. *Reflective Practice: International and Multidisciplinary Perspectives, 14*(1), 75–87.

Chapter 6

Beauchamp, T. & Childress, J. (2013). *Principles of biomedical ethics* (7th edn). New York: Oxford University Press.
Hutchens, B.C. (2004). *Levinas: A guide for the perplexed*. New York: Continuum.
http://transformingdisabilitycultureandchildhood.wordpress.com/ – a new programme of research at the University of Sheffield that seeks to bring together critical disability studies, critical psychology and sociological theory.

Chapter 11

White Rose e-theses online, accessed at: http://etheses.whiterose.ac.uk/view/iau/Sheffield=2EEDU.html

Chapter 12

Critical psychology: Critical links – An article by Ian Parker giving a helpful cultural-historical account of the emergence of different 'critical' tendencies both within and outside the theoretical field defined as psychology: http://radicalpsychology.org/vol1-1/Parker.html
Ideology and ideological state apparatuses – This article is background reading for the concept of 'interpellation' introduced in this chapter. The concept was developed by Louis Althusser

and the reading via the link below is available on the Marxist internet archive: http://www.marxists.org/reference/archive/althusser/1970/ideology.htm

A (1970) starting point in the critical consideration of what psychology does – A link to the paper originally published in 1970 by David Ingleby in *Human Context* titled 'Ideology and the human sciences: some comments on the role of reification in psychology and psychiatry': http://human-nature.com/free-associations/ingleby.html

Chapter 13

Conrad, P. & Bergey, M.R. (2014). The impending globalization of ADHD: Notes on the expansion and growth of a medicalized disorder. *Social Science & Medicine, 122*, 31–43.

LeFrançois, B.A. & Coppock, V. (2014). Psychiatrised children and their rights: Starting the conversation. *Children and Society, 28*(Special issue), 165–171.

Mills, C. (2014). Psychotropic childhoods: Global mental health and pharmaceutical children. *Children and Society, 28*, 194–204.

Timimi, S. & Leo, J. (Eds.) (2009). *Rethinking ADHD: From brain to culture*. Basingstoke: Palgrave Macmillan.

See also Healthtalk.org to listen to audio and watch videos of parents discussing the impact of diagnosis and medication on their children's lives.

See Ken Robinson's talk 'Changing Paradigms' as part of the RSA Animate series at: www.thersa.org/events/rsaanimate

Chapter 19

Kennedy, H., Landor, M. & Todd, L. (Eds.) (2011). *Video-interaction guidance: A relationship-based intervention to promote attunement, empathy and well-being*. London: Jessica Kingsley.

For those interested in training in VIG, see the Association for Video Interaction Guidance on the UK website: http://www.videointeractionguidance.net/

Chapter 21

Anderson, P. & Williams, J. (2001). Identity and difference: Concepts and themes. In P. Anderson & J. Williams (Eds.), *Identity and difference in higher education: 'Outsiders within'* (ch. 1). Farnham: Ashgate.

Bruner, J. (1990). *Acts of meaning*. Cambridge, MA, and London: Harvard University Press.

Burr, V. (2003). *Social constructionism* (2nd edn). Hove and New York: Routledge.

Index